Hidden Truth

Forbidden Knowledge

It is time for you to know.

By Steven M. Greer, M.D.

Publisher's Cataloging-in-Publication
(Provided by Quality Books, Inc.)

Greer, Steven M.
Hidden truth, forbidden knowledge : it is time for you to know / Steven M. Greer.
p.   cm.
ISBN 0-9673238-2-7

1. Greer, Steven M.   2. Center for the Study of
Extraterrestrial Intelligence--Biography.   3. Human-alien encounters.
4. Unidentified flying objects--Sightings and encounters.
5. Civilization--Extraterrestrial influences.   I. Title.

BF2050.G74 2006
001.942   QBI06-600034

Cover Artwork
Ron Russell
PO Box 460760
Aurora, CO 80046

Cover design & graphics
Joel Howard
5111 Summerset Tr
Austin, TX 78749
joho@austin.rr.com

Printed in the United States of America

Address all inquiries to:
Crossing Point, Inc.
P.O. Box 265
Crozet, VA 22932

Produced by:
123PrintFinder, Inc.
27702 Crown Valley Pkwy. #148, Suite D-4
Ladera Ranch, CA 92694

*This book is dedicated to all of our children,
and to establishing a sustainable civilization on
Earth - living in Universal Peace.*

Other books by Dr. Greer:

"Extraterrestrial Contact: The Evidence and Implications"
"Disclosure: Military and Government Witnesses Reveal the Greatest
Secrets in Modern History"

To obtain Dr. Greer's books or for more information about the
Disclosure Project:
www.disclosureproject.org

Disclosure Project
P.O. Box 265
Crozet, VA 22920

For more information about the Center for the Study of Extraterrestrial
Intelligence:
www.cseti.org

CSETI
P.O. Box 265
Crozet, VA 22920

Table of Contents

Acknowledgements 8
Foreword 9
Introduction 12
Author's Notes 15
1 - Improbable Messenger 16
2 - Coming Full Circle 23
3 - Out of the Shadows 35
4 - Marriage Made in Heaven 42
5 - Forgiveness and Faith 45
6 - Ineffable Oneness 49
7 - Universal Peace 56
8 - Total Transformation 61
9 - Information in Unconventional Ways 65
10 - Tone of Creation 73
11 - The Offer 82
12 - Gobsmacked! 86
13 - Truth Stranger than Fiction 92
14 - Disinformation 100
15 - The Crossing Point of Light 108
16 - Circles of Power 114
17 - Legacies Lost 122
18 - Astral Body Extractions 131
19 - "We are always with you." 136
20 - A Different Day 147
21 - Electromagnetic Transfer 156
22 - A Billion Scintillating Lights 161
23 - Infinity 167
24 - Stagecraft 177
25 - Out of the Loop 181
26 - The New Era 188
27 - Truly Quantum, Cosmic Moment 193
28 - Unraveling the Matrix 197
29 - Witness Testimony 205
30- Monster of Unchecked Power 221
31- Separation of Church and State - A Myth 228
32 - Behind the Scenes 233
33 - A New World - If you can take it 242
34 - Solving our Own Dysfunction 249

35- A Guided Meditation: The Structure of the Universe 257
36 - Boundless Mind. 265
37 - The Drop and the Ocean are One 269
38 - Celestial Perception 277
39 - Gradations of Energy. 282
40 - Inter-stellar Community 289
41 - Phase Transition 297
42 - Universal Spirituality. 305
43 - Accessing Consciousness. 312
44 - A Celestial Quality. 315
45 - The Generation of Transformation. 319
46 - The Group Meditation: Contacting ET
        Beings and a Meditation and Prayer For Earth. 321

Acknowledgements

My heartfelt thanks to the following people who directly helped with "Hidden Truth - Forbidden Knowledge"
and to the many, many others - too numerous to count - who have supported my work over the years.

Norm Fletcher who took his time at the book dictation to take care of all the taping;
Joan Korenbilt and Vicki Longhofer for their help with the editing;
Brian O'Leary for the foreword;
Ron Russell for his artwork for the cover;
Joel Howard for his graphic skills;
Jan Bravo for her devoted support in every way
and my wife, Emily for her support and love and her help in her position as - as one of the witnesses called her - "Chief of Staff".

Foreword

"UFO research is leading us kicking and screaming into the science of the twenty-first century."

J. Allen Hynek

The human experiment on planet Earth is on the verge of self-destruction. Looking at the threats of nuclear war, the chemical and biological ecocide, global climate change, proliferating weapons on Earth and in space, the greed of corporations, and the gross cronyism and mismanagement of the U.S. government, the bloated military budgets and aggression, the distractions of our cultural conditioning, the spread of fear and ignorance, the suppression of life-saving technologies, the disparity of wealth and poverty among us, it is amazing we are still here. Barely.

Do we have any hope? My answer is, we can only try. And if we do try, where can we find the answers? Enter Dr. Steven Greer.

Almost twenty years ago I first met Steve Greer at a lecture I gave at the Unity Church in Arden, North Carolina. Having left my career as a mainstream space scientist at Princeton University and Science Applications International Corporation, I was then beginning to liberate myself from the confines and expectations of Western science. I was also intensely studying the UFO/ET phenomenon rejected by most of my fellow scientists. Now I felt free to explore and express our transcendent reality.

So was Steve. A brilliant young ER physician with UFO/ET experience, Dr. Greer and I talked into the night when we first met. We began to make connections we were both just beginning to understand: that ET visitations were not only real, they could assist us in overcoming the human-caused global crisis. Since then, Steve has provided amazing leadership in penetrating the mysteries not only of the phenomenon itself, but the shadowy corners of U.S. government and corporate cover-up of it. As a result, Dr. Greer has proven himself time and time again as a fearless and energetic warrior on the leading edge of planetary change.

First he founded the Center for the Study of Extraterrestrial Intelligence (CSETI), in which he introduced the concept of ambassadorship between humans and off-planet cultures—but this time not merely science fiction. Holding all-night expeditions in UFO hot spots around the world, his groups would vector in craft through the use of lights, sounds and visualization which he coined as Close Encounters of a Fifth Kind, aka. CE-5. The workshops continue to be offered to interested students.

Then he embarked on the difficult task of locating and receiving video/DVD testimonies of over one hundred U.S. government UFO/ET witnesses under The Disclosure Project, culminating in a major press conference in Washington, D.C., in May 2001. These revelations underscore a long, sordid history of governmental and media secrecy and the acquisition of technologies such as microelectronics, anti-gravity propulsion and zero-point, or "free" energy, from our visitors. This massive cover-up has been going on for almost six decades, since the UFO crash near Roswell, New Mexico in July 1947, an event which was certainly not caused by balloons, as alleged by the U.S. Air Force. Such myths are only accepted by the ignorant or the powerful and their subjects.

Dr. Greer's pioneering work on disclosure inevitably led to further understanding the depth and credibility of ET contact accounts as well as the cover-up itself, for example, the "above top secret" research going on near the infamous Groom Lake, Nevada and elsewhere.

Steve Greer is a spiritual warrior of high calling, juxtaposed against those forces identifying themselves as the "United States". The latter are criminals who must be brought to justice, for so many reasons evident to ever more of us, as we watch the fall of the American empire. Dr. Greer, more than anyone, has produced the clearest evidence of a UFO/ET cover-up and now it is up to the rest of us to embrace it. "Hidden Truth – Forbidden Knowledge" gives us the most up-to-date account of the vast accumulation of that evidence from an autobiographical perspective. It's a story about disclosure of the greatest mysteries of our time from a courageous soul unbeholden to the tyrannies that grip us in the most powerful nation on Earth.

Just as importantly, it provides us with a narrative of the benign nature of these off-planet cultures, that we are being visited by those who are empathetic about the human condition, while at the same time not directly interfering (the so-called Prime Directive made famous by Star Trek). It is sobering to think that, only since the United States pioneered the nuclear age in 1945, causing the most frightening devastation of Hiroshima and Nagasaki, the modern sightings, contacts and technology transfers have been taking place. The long-range atomic bombers were stationed in Roswell, the bomb was created in Los Alamos, the first one exploded in Alamagordo, and missiles to deliver future bombs were tested in White Sands—all in New Mexico, a nexus of the military-industrial complex. Was it just coincidence that the 1947 Roswell UFO crash also happened there? Doubtful: the horrors of nuclear technology would make any compassionate ET race want to rush to that area, as they have ever since to military and nuclear installations elsewhere. Perhaps they are helping to prevent the horrors they too don't wish to see unleashed by irresponsible humans.

We Earthlings need all the help we can get, so why not embrace the phenomenon for what it is, to marvel at the wonder, leaving behind our cultural biases? Only through expanding our knowledge and taking political action can we make the needed shifts, and that is what Dr. Greer is so good at doing.

In many ways, the UFO phenomenon tells us more about ourselves than about our mysterious visitors, and the mirror they hold in front of us is frightening—yet hopeful, if we listen to Dr. Greer's words. For example, his founding of Space Energy Access Systems (SEAS) is providing support to inventors with revolutionary new energy technologies that could give the world clean, cheap and decentralized energy, thus ending the oil, coal, and nuclear Age and the virtual end of human-caused pollution and climate change. We at the New Energy Movement are working closely with SEAS Power and other organizations to advocate the importance of R&D of new energy technologies, currently suppressed by powerful vested interests.

On the evening of my first meeting with Dr. Greer, the Unity minister Chad O'Shea presented me with a bumper sticker, "The truth shall set you free but first if will piss you off." If we allow ourselves to vent about, not to deny, our dire circumstances, and then move onto solutions, we might have a chance as a civilization.

This courageous work is not for the meek. Many cutting-edge scientists have been threatened, murdered, and otherwise suppressed by cascades of disinformation and personal attacks. Dr. Greer has endured all this, to our benefit.

This book could be the most important you will read. It is not only full of transcendent truths, it is a call to action to shift the paradigm from terrestrial tyranny to peaceful, sustainable and just cosmic community.

Apollo Astronaut, Dr. Brian O'Leary, 14 Sept. 05

INTRODUCTION:

HIDDEN TRUTH – FORBIDDEN KNOWLEDGE

In April of 2004, about 25 people gathered at our country home in Albemarle County, Virginia, not far from Thomas Jefferson's Monticello. The purpose was for me to provide an oral history, over the course of a week, of the events of my life.

This book is the result of that gathering.

To be honest, this book is released with more than a little trepidation. It reveals personal experiences and events that frankly seem incredible. Even reading through the transcript of the tapes was at times a tearful and emotionally difficult experience. And I know that much of it can be used to attack me personally.

But it is time for you to know: Why did an emergency physician who had been chairman of a busy ER leave his career to get out to the world the information that we are not alone? What had I personally experienced –from childhood onwards – that gave me the knowledge of cosmic cultures, cosmic consciousness and a glimpse of the wondrous future that awaits humanity? What are the new energy and propulsion technologies that can give us a new world, free of pollution, poverty and conflict? What is the nexus where Mind, Space, Time and Matter all come together- and how might this be used technologically by an advanced civilization? What does the blue-print of the next 500,000 years of human civilization on earth look like – and how can we transition to that time? What did I find- and experience – as I met with heads of state, CIA officials, billionaires and covert operatives who in turns are desperate to maintain the secrecy and yet pray for relief from the black box they have nailed shut around them?   Who has been keeping this Hidden Truth and Forbidden Knowledge secret – and most importantly, why?

This book addresses all this – and more. It is my own Disclosure. Having founded and led The Disclosure Project, I feel it is time that the millions of people who follow our work know the truth about how I got here – and what I have found.

I do not expect the general reader to accept all of this -or perhaps any of it. I expect nothing in fact. It is the truth as I have found it and this is my heartfelt effort to share that truth. I hope you find some meaning in this sharing from my heart and mind.

A meeting I had with a senior General at the Pentagon a few years ago illustrates the gravity of the situation. I had been asked by this General, who at the time was head of a major intelligence operation in the Pentagon, to brief him and some of his staff on the UFO issue. As our military advisor and I waited in the General's reception room, we noticed a female officer looking up from her papers at us, curiously. Finally she asked if I was Dr. Greer, and I said yes. She then proceeded to explain that they were very excited about the briefing and that she and her colleagues had drawn straws to see who could be in attendance! Apparently, only one officer from her office could be present.

We were escorted into the General's conference room and some time into the briefing this General said, "Well, I have no doubt that what you are sharing is true, but I have made inquiries through channels in my Agency and nobody can tell me anything! In fact, all I have gotten is *this*!" He then went over to a book shelf and took a small ET doll down – and held it up for all to see. He said, "This is all I have gotten – ridicule- for inquiring about this through channels…"

I then explained that the CIA Director and other high officials had similar experiences when they made inquiries into the subject.

This senior General then told me a disturbing and exquisitely personal story: When he was young, his father had discovered a corrupt enterprise and conspiracy in the government that was deeply disturbing – but nobody would listen to him. It was a matter of enormous importance – but even the General admitted he just thought his father was a kook. Eventually, his father committed suicide (or was murdered and made to look like a suicide) over the matter. Then the General said, "It wasn't until I got into *this* position at the Pentagon that I realized the old man was right!"

Until the General was confronted with the truth as a high official in the Pentagon, he never believed his own father. So how can I expect you to believe me? All I can do is share with you the truth as I know it and the rest is up to you.

A few comments on the book: It is not a written book, but merely an edited transcript of over 45 hours of audio tape that were created in April of 2004 during my oral presentations at our farm. I ask that the reader forgive any errors or editing oversights. This book should be viewed as an oral history, transcribed and edited into a narrative. I had no notes or text as I made these oral presentations.

Between 1991 and 1995, I kept a diary (via transcribed audio tape) that was over 2000 pages just up to that time. Clearly this book, which encompasses experiences that span half a century, can only reflect the major highlights and lessons gleaned over that time. It is by no means meant to be all-inclusive or recall all the information conveyed to me by thousands of conversations and meetings with covert contacts within the Shadow Government.

Many of the names of these covert operatives are changed or abbreviated. However, the original tapes and transcripts, which are in multiple secure locations, contain all of the names, corporations and entities involved with these illegal clandestine operations and will be released, if needed, at a later time.

Also, this book is not a recapitulation or even summary of the extensive documentation which exists in my two prior books. The reader should refer to the extensive case-files and ET contact experiences of the Center for the Study of Extraterrestrial Intelligence (CSETI) contained in the book "Extraterrestrial Contact- The Evidence and Implications". Moreover, a nearly 600 page book of government documents and transcripts of over 60 top- secret witness testimonies to official government projects and events is available in "Disclosure". These books may be obtained at www.DisclosureProject.org.

It is time for one chapter in human history to close and another to open. Do we have the courage to embrace this new world, the hallmarks of which are universal peace, enlightenment, and a genuinely high technology civilization on earth that is sustainable for thousands of years? The retrograde forces that are attempting to hijack humanity to a time of war in space, global destruction, environmental ruin and cultural insanity must be supplanted, through the courageous acts of others, with an entirely new way of being.

It is time for you to know – and for all of us to act. For it is only through the collective actions of those who yearn for the good future that awaits humanity that we can leap across the abyss of impending destruction and secure a world ready to take her place among the cultures of the cosmos, enlightened and at peace.

Steven M. Greer MD
Albemarle County, Virginia
1 February 2006

Author's Note

This story is told in three parts. The first of these illuminates the events that set the stage for all to follow; it covers my childhood through early adult life, up to 1990. The second traces the years from 1990 to the present day. During this time, we formed the Center for the Study of Extraterrestrial Intelligence, the Disclosure Project, and Space Energy Access Systems. The third part moves into the future, gazing into a time when the fulfillment of the promise of humanity will be realized – a time that will endure for 500,000 years.

In order to first give you a frame of reference, I'll share some important statistics. In 1980, the world community eradicated smallpox off the face of the earth. The World Health Organization predicts that by the end of 2006, we will reach the last remote villages of Africa and Asia and we will wipe out Polio. These are accomplishments that should bring much gratification to us all as citizens of this world. Yet, it is with restrained joy that I celebrate these feats. Why? Because, sadly, by the time you read the first chapter of this book (approximately 15 minutes), the following will happen: 250 children will die of starvation; 15 people will die of AIDS; 31 will die of Malaria and 50 will die of TB.

You might ask how this possibly relates to ETs or CSETI or the Disclosure Project. It is all connected to control, power, religious ideology, and greed. We know that the technologies have existed (for many years) to alleviate Small-Pox and Polio much earlier, plus the diseases I mentioned above, as well as other ills that plague the world community. We know that technologies have been around that can supply the world with an abundance of energy without using up our valuable natural resources. Unfortunately, the people who have access to these technologies have not shared them with us.

I mention this not to depress you, but because it is a reality. Yet it is a reality that can be changed. As you read HIDDEN TRUTH – FORBIDDEN KNOWLEDGE, you will see that changes have already begun in some of the very people who are involved with these technologies; changes that can and *WILL* make this a peaceful world.

1

Improbable Messenger

"We'll get the little Holloman room for this event...It's all you'll need."

"Oh, no - we need the ballroom."

"But, that room is never used – except for very large and important events."

"This *will* be a very large and important event!"

"You've got to be out of your mind."

"No, we need the entire ballroom!"

"Well, the last time they filled the ballroom was when President Reagan was there!"

"Just get it! Do it."

"Okay - you won't listen to me... but I'll get it."

The room in question is The National Press Club ballroom in Washington, D.C. The verbal wrangling between myself – Dr. Steven Greer – and a press agent, proved worthwhile on May 9, 2001. She kept her word, and my instinct proved to be on target! We watched the ballroom fill to capacity: nearly two dozen television cameras and a battery of journalists assembled to hear and record statements offered by twenty-one witnesses from military, intelligence, government, corporate and scientific organizations.

The witnesses had stepped forward to relate their personal experiences with extraterrestrial vehicles (ETVs; aka UFOs) and extraterrestrial life forms. More than two hours of public testimony ensued, verifying the reality of ETV/UFO contact and a largely unknown outcome: the interaction with extraterrestrial intelligence has produced advanced energy and propulsion technologies. This information has been kept secret from the masses for years.

The event marked the launch of the Disclosure Project; an outgrowth of years of effort by the Center for the Study of Extraterrestrial Intelligence (CSETI). It was also a milestone in my personal journey, having moved from a career as an emergency room doctor living in Asheville, N.C into a new role - the unlikely courier of a message that is insisting to be heard. It was one more step along the sometimes rocky path I'd stumbled upon as a nine-year old playing on the streets of Charlotte, North Carolina.

A sunny afternoon in 1965 saw me out roaming with the usual group of neighborhood urchins. We were typical Southern kids, wandering about in search of all manner of adventure - something to build, or see, or take home. Little were we prepared for what suddenly appeared in the southwest sky: a silver, oval-shaped, gleaming craft - obviously not an airplane or helicopter. It was seamless, totally silent - and unlike anything we'd ever seen. After hovering for a short time, it instantly vanished.

We felt this was something truly unusual. My family, predictably, passed off the incident as a childish musing. But my cohorts and I knew we'd seen something way beyond the ordinary. It was my first encounter with an "ETV," the term used by the National Security Agency for extraterrestrial vehicles, also commonly known as UFOs.

Since that day, my sense of connection to that spacecraft has endured. Events over the next few weeks strengthened the tie: I experienced a series of lucid dreams and night encounters with beings who were not from the Earth. Because I was simply a young boy I was able to take it "all in stride" - it seemed a natural result of the incident with my three friends. I believe the ETs were focused on instilling in me an awareness and acceptance of things beyond the world I could see. My innocence allowed me to view this without prejudice, although I didn't speak publicly about it (due to the potential ridicule) until a few years ago.

But this early connection was life-altering. It was clearly the dawning of a larger search for truth that grew stronger as I matured.

My interest and curiosity about these matters intensified, although I didn't have another direct ET encounter for years. Until around the age of twelve, I would collect relevant articles from such magazines as "True", "Argosy" and "Life" as well as books about UFO encounters, and accumulated a large stash in my closet! The idea of knowledge of people from other planets enthralled me, and fed into the sense of wonder and joy I felt when looking at the night sky. Fear never entered my mind - it seemed as comfortable as home. So my approach to the idea of extraterrestrials was that their existence is understood, or a "given," and that these beings are aware of our evolution on earth. This sense of familiarity with the great expanse of creation has always induced a sense of joy and peace, even as a preschooler. When out in nature, I gained this sense of something awake and divine beyond everyday existence. I believe there was always something, like a hand on my shoulder, helping and guiding me toward a perception of awakeness, a mysterious conscious presence that would open to me when I looked at the sky or played outdoors. There is a Persian expression: "the best way to love God is to love His creation." I was blessed with this reality in a very innocent, elemental way.

It was an unconventional view of life, perhaps the natural outcome of an equally unconventional childhood.I grew up in a deliciously eccentric Southern family. Mother was like Scarlett O'Hara blended with Bette Davis in "Hush, Hush, Sweet Charlotte", mixed with a touch of Joan Crawford's "Mommy Dearest"! Father was half Native American, his mother a Cherokee.

But I was raised in a family that was extremely troubled. Children from such difficult backgrounds generally follow one of two life paths: they either succumb to self-destructive habits and addictions, sometimes to the point of suicide, or find sufficient inner strength to build a meaningful and productive life. I took the latter course, through the grace of God and the intervention of the seen and unseen world.

In reality, I have perhaps never known of a more traumatic, dysfunctional family situation than ours. Most people are unaware of this background; they see me as a successful physician and public figure(albeit somewhat eccentric at times!) and assume a conventional, normal upbringing.

As a young adult, I once attended the movie "Mommy Dearest" with my twin sister. Afterward, we looked at each other and said, "My God, that would've been the best day of our childhood!" People are horrified to hear this. Because of parental alcoholism, and home conditions that often attend it, we children also lived with elements of abandonment, neglect and abuse. I remember, as a little pre-schooler, eating cigarette ashes, sand, and dirt when nothing else was around. As a medical doctor, I now realize this was at least providing some of the mineral supplements my body needed: one of those instinctual cravings demanded by the body to enable survival. I was frequently very sick, especially every winter, with terrible pneumonias and bronchitis. My lungs still have scar tissue from those bouts.

However, blessings often become apparent through hardship. The challenges made me one tough bird! Any bitterness I might have harbored from childhood has dissipated through the realization that this made me strong – a survivor. By the time I reached high school, I vowed to take hold of my life and turn it around, and did.

Through some of those years I was actually self-supporting, with my own apartment. I held down a job in a local restaurant, working each night until 1:00 A.M., then rose at 6 each day to bicycle across the city to school. I managed to maintain an A grade average, becoming an Honor Society student involved in numerous school activities.

My budding sense of responsibility extended to my three sisters. I often unintentionally referred to them as "my daughters", so strong was my protective, caring instinct for them. Having parents who were anti-role models, I learned how *not* to do things. The challenges brought the realization that we all create our own future, and transcending the limitations of birth, poverty, abuse, or any other hardship is possible through the exertion of human will.

I was far too busy during high school to become enthralled with the stuff of pop culture that absorbed many teenagers from the late '60s through early '70s. I simply didn't have access to the luxuries most middle class kids took for granted, and basic survival was a constant preoccupation. Carousing with drugs and alcohol was out of the question!

Instead, I began to read the Vedas (the ancient, sacred literature of India) and study Sanskrit. On my own I learned about meditation and the concept of transcendence, which fit quite comfortably into my psyche. I'd been raised outside the confines of formal religion. My parents did not involve me in church as a child (in fact, they were emphatically atheist). The lack of attachment to an institutional doctrine left me open to ideas that might have been outside the comfort zone of someone growing up in a conventional religious tradition. The result is that I moved naturally into the realm of meditative experiences and higher consciousness, without tutoring from outside parties. I taught myself prayer and meditation, from reading as well as direct experience. These pursuits, coupled with my school involvement in environmental and peace issues, created a new layer of experience and growth in consciousness for me. It was at this point the experience I now call "non-locality of consciousness" made itself known. When I could find free time, I loved to bicycle out into the countryside seeking this connection.

I'd lie in a field, and practice those techniques that had emerged from inside me. I'd find myself traveling to observe other parts of Charlotte, or to see other areas of the Earth, or going out into space and seeing it clearly. This became routine. At the age of 15, a beautiful, unstoppable force was opening up inside of me, independent of any sort of tradition. It manifested completely from within.

And then, in the spring of 1973, I injured my left thigh. I had made plans to bicycle from Charlotte to the barrier islands on the North Carolina coast, a 200 mile trip. I neglected the injury and went ahead with my plans, traveling the entire distance to the coast in one day, then returning to my small efficiency apartment, in Charlotte. A horrible infection developed in my leg, and spread through my body.

I was so sick! Because of a too demanding work and school schedule I was run down even before this happened. I was also poor, so seeing a doctor was out of the question. As a physician, now I know what happened to me: I became septic, which means my bloodstream was infected, accompanied by a very high fever. There was also skeletal muscle break down, overloading my kidneys. All these are potentially fatal symptoms, and I was spiraling to that point: a 17 year-old alone without a phone, trying to nurse myself back to health, not fully understanding the severity of my condition. It brought me to a near-death experience, finding myself suddenly released from my body.

I was carried out into the depths of space, where I already felt at home. Then I experienced what I now understand to be God consciousness, where my individuality became faint as it merged with the effulgent, unbounded, pure, infinite Mind. There was no duality. It lasted for what seemed to be an eternity because a normal sense of time disappears in that state of being. I could see all of creation, the vastness of the cosmos, and it was beautiful beyond words. There was nothing frightening about it - only infinite awareness, joy, and the perception of an endless perfect creation.

Eventually, two brilliant, scintillating lights approached out of the stars. I now understand them to be Avatars: Manifestations of God. They were not anthropomorphic or anthropocentric, but appeared as brilliant points of light - pure, conscious energy. These were the twin Avatars for our era.

As the Avatars approached me, I entered a state of oneness with them. It was incredibly beautiful. Then there was a conveyance of *knowledge* in a pre-verbal form; before and beyond words. It's as if when you say "apple," within the word is the actual image of the apple, which could be astral (a light form). And within *that* conscious image is the pure idea form of the apple itself - its essence. That is how information was being transmitted to me.

I have no sense of how long this union with God lasted. I was affected by the beauty of it all, yet very overwhelmed at the same time.

Eventually, the episode moved into more of a linear style of communication. One of the Avatars said, "You may come with Us or return to Earth." I had the presence of mind to ask, "Well, what is Your will?" And the Being replied, "Well, it's Our desire that you go back to Earth to do other things." With that, I became depressed, having no interest at that point in coming back to Earth. I would have been very happy to remain in that state of awareness, in that place of the placeless. But I somehow knew the highest response of human will is acceptance of the Divine will, and said, "Okay, then."

And with that, I acknowledged their reality and the very exalted celestial beings that exist and the existence of the Godhead and the oneness of creation and divinity. And that's what I experienced: complete, perfect oneness of unbounded Mind and creation as one. Then I sort of lost consciousness, and fell back into my body, just sort of whoosh.

I was back in my body, but must have been out long enough to lose conscious connection with all of my neural centers, although my sensory input was working. I remember clearly, as if it's today, seeing the maple tree outside the little apartment, moving in the wind against a street light. But I couldn't move! I thought, "Oh, great. Here I am, back in this messed-up body, paralyzed." I truly thought that I had been so damaged from this severe infection that I'd been paralyzed from a stroke.

(As it turned out, that was a temporary phenomenon. Today, it is understood that in prolonged near-death experiences it takes some time to be reconnected to the physical body.)

I then felt a being in the room sent there to test my will to live. It was somewhat frightening, but perhaps a necessary experience that forced me to use my willpower to remain here. There was this force that seemed to be *pulling* me back out. So I would go back out of my body and then return. I had to exercise volition to remain in the physical body and keep my astral body of light and conscious body integrated with it. And after about half a dozen tries, I nailed it and remained here. I then became fully awake and regained my motor skills.

As they say in Britain, I was quite 'gob-smacked'! This experience altered my life like nothing before, changing everything I had been taught - that there was no Divine Being or conscious existence after the death of the body. I now know from direct experience this is false. God does exist, as do His Messengers. For me, nothing would ever be the same. I'd learned that death is not to be feared, that, in fact, there is no death – only a transformation from one state into another.

As I got up and re-integrated with the world, I remained in this state of incredible bliss, a rarefied state of higher consciousness where the unbounded quality of cosmic awareness, was still awake in me. Enclosed in a room, I could be infinitely aware at the same time. The mystics call this cosmic consciousness – a state I continued to experience some time thereafter.

Interestingly, my diseased leg spontaneously healed. I didn't see a doctor or receive antibiotic medication during the entire episode.

2

Coming Full Circle

I marked my 18th birthday by learning a structured form of meditation called Transcendental Meditation or TM. I was hungry for anything that would give me an ability to experience higher conscious awareness at will. It appeared that the TM course would be the avenue to take.

I quickly realized that without its ceremonial trappings, TM is a simple process. It consists of sitting with a thought mantra or sound in order to transcend conscious, linear thought and move into unbounded awareness.

Sitting next to my teacher, we began the technique. What followed seemed bizarre to him, but felt normal to me. I entered complete transcendental consciousness - full *samadhi*. So I was there once more - in the state of cosmic awareness. It was very beautiful, and the technique worked for me so easily because the channel was already open, due to my near-death episode the previous March.

The teacher looked at me afterward and said, "You went there, didn't you?" I said, "Yes." He said, "On the first time?" And I said, "Well, I'm not so sure it's the first time, but the first time with you!"

I began thereafter to practice the ability to experience cosmic consciousness at will. This opened up an even more extraordinary view of the world and of myself. I could now re-connect to the very pure state of Earth, nature, and divinity that exist untainted by human corruption. I was rediscovering the purity and innocence of that awareness I had as a young boy, but *understanding* it more fully.

I left the following summer to attend Appalachian State University in Boone, N.C. I selected ASU based purely on its wilderness location in my beloved Blue Ridge Mountains, for which I have a deep affinity. I believe this feeling comes from a genetic connection based on my Cherokee heritage.

I wanted to spend every moment possible out in those mountains, in every kind of weather, being totally connected like a spirit walker in nature. I was eager to practice my newly acquired meditation skills and to continue having the experience of connecting with Divinity. Thus, at the threshold of my adulthood, I'd gone from growing up in a home with no prayer - not even knowing about it or about the experience of com-

munion with God to experiencing cosmic consciousness. I'd found all
of this on my own.

The absence of religious upbringing was actually a blessing in dis-
guise. I think there's an inverse relationship between religiosity and spirituality, with only a few rare exceptions. Having been spared the religiosity, I could simply search for the truth, without the baggage of embel-
lished doctrines.

What happened that fall was an extraordinary amplification of that
near-death occurrence about six months earlier. I was on   Rich's
Mountain, about 5,000 feet above the town of Boone. At the top, there
was a fire tower at the end of a gravel road that was closed at its base.

One crystal clear afternoon, I decided to go to see the sunset from
atop this mountain. I reached the top in time to sit in meditation at sunset.

Before starting, I glanced towards the southwest and saw an extraterrestrial vehicle. It was some distance away, but was just like the one I had
seen as a nine year old. For some reason, my reaction at that moment
was, "It's them again" - and I didn't really think much more about it - I
simply accepted the fact that they were here. Then the ship winked out,
just like the one I'd seen years before.

I then began meditating and had a beautiful, deep experience in
unbounded Mind. Afterward, I opened my eyes and it was pitch dark,
with the stars all visible. Imagine being at that altitude in the crystal clear
dry air, viewing the Milky Way and countless stars! Standing there, suddenly a thought not my own came to mind: "Behold what a beautiful
universe God has made."

With that, I went into the exact state of consciousness I had when I
died, that God consciousness where I was fully awake, at one with the
entire creation, and yet present standing on the mountain. It was magnificent.

When I began the walk down, I noticed a glow off the edge of the
mountain and sensed someone was there. Suddenly, on my right, an
extraterrestrial biological life form appeared and touched my shoulder so
firmly that it was like a strong finger touching me. I looked down and
saw the imprint on my jacket: every hair on my head stood on end!

Somewhat childishly, my first thought was, "What does this creature
want with me?" I got down close to the ground (I hate to admit this!)in
a fetal position, looking up – and he was looking back. Its gender was
male. He was quite peaceful and non-threatening, with beautiful, deer-
like eyes.

Then I suddenly found myself transported onto the craft. We were just out in space, sitting. I recall that the craft became completely translucent. It felt like I was floating in space with nothing around, as if the whole craft was made of fiber optics, and its shell could disappear. Space was visible all around us.

So I stayed there with these ETs, who were three or four feet tall, all with those appealing eyes. It appeared that we were there for one purpose; meditating together. They were interested in me because they wanted contact with a human being experiencing cosmic consciousness as we do, participating with them. At this point I taught them what that state is like for us. We shared it together - an incredible encounter, entirely different from stories usually circulated about extraterrestrial contact.

It was a very non-local experience, with time, space, and relativity in a realm unlike what's normal for us. In that state of consciousness seconds, hours, or years no longer matter, because time and space have been transcended. This infinite eternity is the true nature of the mind, the awake self within all of us.

While with these beings, we co-created a code for humans communicating with them. This was actually the birth of the CE-5 - Close Encounters of the Fifth Kind – initiative. We utilized not only sounds and light but also non-local consciousness and directed, coherent thought to communicate with extraterrestrial beings and their electronic devices. This was October of 1973, during the time of the Yom Kippur war.

It was clear to me that the ETs wanted humans to move beyond mutually assured destruction and into a peaceful civilization that could co-exist with space in harmony. Earth needed to find people to be ambassadors for this objective. And so, I offered to do this, and to help teach the same to our fellow humans. Nothing more, just that.

Then very suddenly I returned to a "regular" state of awareness and found myself back on the gravel road near the fire tower, a little further down the path from my previous spot, but still at the top of the ridge. I thought, "Oh, my God, how wonderful." The experience of oneness with them had a key message: the conscious mind we are awake with at this moment is the same as that of the Divine Being, *and of all beings*.

Erwin Schrodinger was absolutely correct when he said the total number of minds in the universe is one. There is one conscious mind, and we are It. So, there are only one people in the universe, and we are they. No 'alien' or human; just an unbroken, perfect, seamless conscious life in the universe, and we are all a part of it.

I'm reminded of a saying from the Sufi tradition: "Thinkest thyself a puny form when within thee the universe is folded?" It's a rhetorical question. We're *not* just this puny form. The entirety of the universe *is* folded within us. And that's really what I experienced with the ETs.

They know that the only chance for peace on Earth -- never mind the cosmos -- is for humans to understand there's no real difference amongst us. It doesn't matter how we look- consider the variety in physical appearances that exists on Earth alone! What really matters is that within us lives the same singular light of consciousness, infinite, eternal and always present, whether we're open to it or not at any given moment in time. It is the basis of our relationship with each other and with the universe. This is enduring and eternal -- and that is what we experienced in its absolute, purest form. It was beyond beautiful. And there was absolutely nothing frightening about it.

It didn't matter that I was only 18. They didn't care about such things as age, race, family of origin, or wealth. They cared about the fact that I was pure-hearted enough to see the truth clearly and unattached to the materiality of this world. I could discern the universal aspect of teachings in various cultures that humans have learned through the ages, because truth is one and the same in any language. What we created together that day proved that humans can be, each of us, connected to each other and to the unbounded awareness of the universe, but also to these other civilizations, if we simply understand the fact that we're awake. If you are awake, reading this or hearing this right now, the awake-ness whereby you're hearing it is a singularity. And it isn't divided. We divide it into our own egos and intellect, but in reality, the light of awareness is the same in every being, in every star. And the entire cosmos is suffused in this same light of Being. There is this great Sun of awareness reflecting and refracting in everyone, yet still singular. So, if you return to that and if you experience it, none of these life forms seem far away or unusual-or alien - because they really are not.

So, it was on this occasion the CSETI concept of one universe, one people was conceived. There is really one people in the universe, and we are they. There is a single conscious being shining in all of us. It can never be divided, no matter how much we try. We may want to divide it, but it's always one. It's always a singularity, always perfect. The extraterrestrial beings that are here understand this, because they cannot travel through interstellar space without understanding non-locality. And understanding non-locality, necessitates a high level of knowledge and enlightenment.

In a real sense, then, the heart of compassion and the foundation of peace is found in the reality that we are all one. Without that experience, intellectualism is all that's left – and it never lasts. So, I came to realize at a rather young age that the world's problems are essentially spiritual, therefore the solutions must be spiritual as well. And so it has turned out to be.

I found myself back on the mountain under the beautiful, starry sky, only to experience another strange phenomenon. I was perhaps 100 yards further down the gravel road. As I started down the mountain, I found that with each step, I was in a state of near- weightlessness, as if walking on the moon!

My steps were actually leaps of 20 to 30 feet at once! It was more like floating than walking. There was a strange, magnetic, anti-gravitational effect around me, making me lighter. It wasn't a product of my imagination; my physical body *was* light.

I was just happy as a lark! Here I was, fresh from this experience on an ETV, and now bounding down the mountain, traveling in "boing, boing, boing" leaps across impossible distances with each step. It was incredibly blissful. As I got closer to town, the phenomenon faded, and my weight returned to normal.

Upon reaching the little town of Boone, it looked so deserted I thought there had been a nuclear war! I thought it was about 9 or 10 o'clock at night – everything should have been open. Remember, it's a little college town up in the North Carolina mountains. I thought to myself, "What in the world is going on? I wonder if the Yom Kippur War got out of control and there was a thermonuclear war and I'm the last to know?" A check of the time told me, it was nearly 1:00 A.M! My cosmic experience had lasted three or four hours!

After this amazing evening, I decided to practice all I had learned, taught and shared with the extraterrestrials. Every night before going to sleep, I would lie down and put myself in a meditative state. I would enter unbounded Awareness, then expand the sense of conscious mind around me, filling the room, knowing that it was omni-present. On the wings of that omnipresent sense of Awareness, I would expand upwards into space, seeing the stars and space, filled with the sense that it was awake. And I was one with that awake-ness, which placed me out there, in space.

Then I would send a thought like a beacon to the extraterrestrial beings, to announce my presence. In a somewhat childlike way, I'd say, "I don't know if you remember me, but my name is Steve. And here I am - let me show you where I am." So, I would do the protocol we developed for the CE-5 initiative:

In this higher state of consciousness I would turn it around, and instead of seeing outward into the vastness of space, look back - and show the ETs my location on earth.

I would show them the Milky Way Galaxy and then zoom in from there to our Solar System, with the sun and the Earth. Then I would zoom to the Earth and North America, further in to the eastern United States and the Appalachian Mountains. Then I would zoom in to show them my location in Boone, North Carolina; then to my exact spot in that building. And with that, I would fall asleep.

For months my experiences were really quite extraordinary. From October '73 onwards, there began an unprecedented wave of UFO sightings in those mountains. I did this as a way of beta-testing the system, to see if what we had co-created and agreed upon on the ship would actually work. Well, it did. There were newspaper reports of forest rangers seeing these huge ships hovering over the mountains, down in Shining Rock Wilderness to the south, and over in the Linville Gorge area. . . here, there, and everywhere!

I continued to do this until one day, in the local paper, a story appeared about a guy driving nearby on a road outside Morganton, North Carolina. As ETVs travel, it was only seconds away from me. This boy, who looked a lot like me, was driving on that road, and the car suddenly stopped. There was a ship hovering by the road, with an ET at the boy's window! The driver was completely freaked out.

I saw this as an indirect way for the ETs to say, "You know, we're getting this." So I thought to myself, "Well I'm playing around with fire, here. I think, until I figure out what I'm supposed to do with this, this is enough."

I didn't tell anyone about this episode for a very long time. However, people need to understand why I gave up an established medical career – and the quarter-million dollars per year that came with it - to make known what I know to be true. Certainly not because it's "only a theory"!

While still in this state, asleep, I continued to have some kind of ongoing dialogue with these extraterrestrial beings. My roommate told me quite some time later, that for a number of months he would awaken late at night, and would hear me speaking quietly in my sleep.

He said, "You were speaking, but with a language not of this world." And I thought, "Oh, my God. Somehow, I was in a state of consciousness where I could connect to the language used by the ETs. And he was hearing that very clearly. He said, "Absolutely, it was not an Earth language."

After this, I pretty much decided that, until I had a specific reason to utilize these protocols I experienced with the ETs, it would be wiser to be just quietly aware of the ability, but keep it to myself.

In 1974, I left the traditional college at Boone to enter teacher training at Maharishi International University in Iowa. My experiences during the training there were really quite extraordinary, in part because I remained independent in terms of the institutional, dogmatic aspects of the group. However, there was an enormous amount of profound knowledge being discussed.

I immersed myself in the study of the Vedas and the Sanskrit language. I was enormously impressed with the amount of knowledge in the Vedas – how the experience of consciousness and universal awareness was articulated. This experience enabled me to have a time and place to be completely dedicated to the development of higher states of consciousness.

One of the most profound things I absorbed was the unfolding of the cosmology. This came not so much from didactic learning as from direct experience, which included the astral or causal thought realms and the realms of light.

Once one understands the structure of creation and begins to experience it in detail, it becomes very understandable how people can have dreams of the future, alter their physical body to levitate, or to de-materialize and re-appear in another place. All the things you've heard about in what are considered mythological stories or so-called miracles become more comprehensible. They are also completely attainable by every single conscious human being. All beings will one day be capable of experiencing these things. The ability is our birthright- not just humans, but every conscious being in the universe. We are all children of God and all of these gifts and states exist within each of us.

That year, I began to have experiences that brought the infinite Being into this world. I could see a rock and know that it also contains pure awareness. Within the rock is the energy and the frequency of a light form, an astral form that gives it structure and its crystalline matrix form. And within that is the idea of it, and within the idea is the primal thought that created all things. And within that is pure, quiet conscious mind. In fact, the totality of everything is nothing but pure conscious awareness, phasing, resonating and playing in different forms and in different ways.

Much of the knowledge that goes with this has to be realized from experience. The good news is that everyone, at some time in their life, has experienced that type of integration and oneness. They just have to remember it. My intention is to try to describe it in a way that will help you remember. If I could accomplish this from my personal background - having grown up with a total absence of exposure to the world of spirituality, then anyone can!

As all of this began to unfold, I dedicated myself for a number of years to teaching meditation and higher states of consciousness. During those years, I took an advanced course in the Catskills, in New York. On that retreat, I fasted and spent several hours a day in meditation, in a really beautiful, quiet state.

I began to awaken to an ability I'd had since childhood -- but then only beginning to emerge -- of being able to see things within consciousness that were not visible to the naked eye. Walking down a corridor, I would try to see what was around the corner. Almost every time, I would see what was there or who was coming. And I wasn't trying to guess until I got it right. It was like staying in a steady state of consciousness and actually *seeing* it.

Then I would attempt to see things happening at a distant point on Earth or at a distant point in time -- the next day or the next week. I practiced this a great deal. It became routine for me to be able to go to sleep and see a distant place or event, and know what was going to happen the next day.

Now, this is no mystery, if you understand the omnipresent nature of consciousness. Because it is omnipresent, it is beyond the restrictions of time or space, which means that you can break those bonds through entering this state of awareness. And when you do, you will find yourself able to see things one isn't "supposed to be" able to see. Space and time are obliterated, and you are free to *really* see.

One day during this retreat I wondered about some of the so-called siddhis (or spiritual powers) described in the Vedas.

I thought it would be interesting to test the limits of this for the physical body. I began to think about the abilities we have- if we are all consciousness and our bodies are actually filled with the light of awareness. What might we really achieve? Well, one day I was in an enormously happy, joyful, peaceful state. I was out walking on a magnificent, clear spring day. Being so affected by Earth and nature, the moment was right for what followed.

As I was walking in the field behind the manor where we were staying, I spontaneously -- without effort or forethought -- levitated. It was reminiscent of that prolonged experience of bounding down the mountainside after my ET encounter in October of '73. This time I just lifted vertically, maybe two or three feet above the ground.

Instead of walking to my destination, I glided there in an upright, vertical levitation experience. And then at the moment my intellect kicked in and I exclaimed, "My God, look what's happening. How can I be doing this?", I settled down to Earth. It was halted by my own intellect and ego!

One of the many lessons I learned from this is that there's a certain grace, along with faith, needed for such extraordinary experiences. I don't mean religious faith per se, but the *certainty of,* or *knowing* the capacity latent within. It is beyond self, ego, and intellect. If we can give ourselves freely to it, incredible things can be accomplished. And if it fails to flow, it's because we are stopping it. Ultimately, it is recognizing and embracing the power of God within each of us.

After this experience, it became increasingly clear that we have within us any capability, and that anyone can acquire and develop them. We're coming into an era where such things will become routine and accepted as "the norm."

There is sometimes a tendency by people involved in various spiritual and religious groups to put people who have this level of experience or knowledge on a pedestal, as if it's unattainably unique. It's *not*, and that's very important to understand. It is, in fact, a disservice to the nature and potential of humanity to idolize something that should be understood as the birthright of everyone.

In 1975, I went with some friends to Isola, France, up in the Maritime Alps, to become instructors of meditation. While on this particular retreat, I had a number of experiences with higher states of consciousness, what might be called unity consciousness and God consciousness.

One day, remembering what had happened two years earlier in the North Carolina mountains, I wondered if that same extraordinary experience could be repeated. So in the hotel room, I went through the protocol we'd created in 1973 on that spacecraft.

I then went into the state of unbounded consciousness, and then expanded awareness off the mountain, around the Alps, into space, and out into our Solar System. Seeing the vastness of space, I said to these craft and the ETs on board, "My name is Steve. I don't know if you remember me, but we met a couple years ago, and now here I am up in the French Maritime Alps, in Isola."

And so I showed them the beautiful spiral galaxy, the Milky Way, our star system with the sun and its planets, and the Earth. And then I zoomed in to Europe, to the Maritime Alps of France. I showed them our location in the hotel complex and said, "If you can come visit, please do." This occurred in an unbroken flow of consciousness for about 20 minutes

Later, after lunch, some friends and I decided to go for a walk in the mountains near the hotel. It was about 1:00 in the afternoon. I looked up in the crystal clear, Alpine sky to see a beautiful, huge tetrahedral-shaped ship, shining in the sun. It was clear and fully materialized, and drawing down towards us, silently.

A good friend in the group who knew of my experiences with extra-terrestrial vehicles gasped, "My God, Steve, did you call them here?" And she just came unglued. "Oh, my God, I can't believe it." And I replied, "Yeah, I did. I did this protocol that I told you about." She asked, "My God, why didn't you warn me?!"

At the point this anxiety was shown by some of the group, the ETV stopped approaching us, hovered, and then backed off silently. Then this huge craft just completely "de-materialized," disappeared out of our space-time. I turned to her and smiled, "Well, I guess the protocol does work." And she says, "My God, next time, let me know. Warn me before you're going to do it!" But I was laughing hysterically!

This taught me that, in fact, we could contact the ETs and this could be experienced by others. It was the first time since I was nine years old that I had actually seen one of these ET craft in the company of other people. In this case, it was a true CE-5, where a human invited the craft and they came, witnessed by others. Clearly, the protocols worked. I began to feel that maybe this should be taught to people at some point, because everyone should learn that this is possible.

But as time passed, I began to question it again. When something this extraordinary happens, doubts always creep in! After a while, I was living back in the mountains of North Carolina, outside of Blowing Rock, with a friend who had been on the training course. We had become teachers of meditation together.

One day in late fall 1977 I decided to test the protocol again. That night I sat up in bed and meditated. I went into the expanded state of consciousness, felt it expanding into space, saw the fullness and infinity of space being filled with the light of awareness, and in that light I saw these extraterrestrial people and said, again, "My name is Steve."

But, thinking so much time had passed that maybe they didn't remember, I said, "Well, my name is Steve Greer and I was born in Charlotte, North Carolina on June 28, 1955." I then gave them an entire brief biography! I showed them Charlotte, and how to get to my location. From space, they could go to Charlotte, then up to the North Carolina mountains, about 100 miles away. After following this technique in a stream of consciousness, I fell asleep.

Suddenly, I awakened in the wee hours of the morning between 1 and 4 a.m. And here was this beautiful blue-white craft outside the window and about 30 feet above the house. And the consciousness of the occupant was being projected right into the room I was in! It was very palpable.

We were out in the middle of nowhere, totally surrounded by mountains and meadows and silence. And here was this ship silently hovering right outside my window! Suddenly my housemate woke up in his bedroom; jumped up, rushed into my room and exclaimed, "Do you see that?" I said, "Yes," kind of sheepishly, like, "Uh-oh." And he says, "My God, there's a space ship right outside our window." I said, "Yeah, I know. I kind of invited them."

He became really unhinged and said, "Damn it, don't ever do that without telling me! You scared the hell out of me!" He could feel, also, that there was an intelligent being, de-materialized, but like a projection of awareness, from the ship inside the room.

We went into the living room, and the ship followed us around to that side of the house, to the big picture window overlooking Grandfather Mountain. By then, I think they sensed my friend's fear, and with that, the ship backed off, went out over the valley, and swoosh, streaked away - off into space over Grandfather mountain.

The very next day, we heard on radio and in news reports that two space ships were found on the radar at Douglas Airport in Charlotte, North Carolina. They were pursued by a police helicopter called Snoopy. I was stunned to hear that the area of the city where the sightings were centered was where I was born and grew up - the spot I'd shown them in my vectoring through consciousness.

One of the craft apparently got very close to the police helicopter, and also to an Eastern Airlines jet. This was all recorded by the air traffic control tower, and it confirmed the CE-5.

Years later, a man who had acquired the FAA audio tape of that event shared the tape with me. (We have it in the CSETI archives.) In the transcript, one of the craft just vanished, and the other one was seen and tracked going off towards the northwest: the mountains where I was located. And, in fact, it then appeared outside my window.

So, that was an interesting early CE-5 that not only had another witness - my hapless housemate - but also was tracked on radar, observed by commercial airline pilots, and chased by a police helicopter.

Frankly, I was stunned and a bit unnerved by the precision of the event. I thought, "Wow. This is serious! I really shouldn't do this anymore until I formalize a program for it." And, in fact, I didn't do it again- from 1977 to 1990- when I formed the Center for the Study of Extraterrestrial Intelligence, or CSETI.

3

Out Of The Shadows

Those youthful experiences made me understand something important about the nature of advanced ET civilizations: they have selected non-hostility as a natural evolutionary step. In other words, their high level of consciousness is incompatible with divisiveness or conflict. Otherwise, with the incredible technology at their command, they would have long since destroyed one another.

Without the realization of oneness, differences are perceived as a cause for alarm, fear, hostility and violence. The history of human experience over the millennia is proof…

One has only to look at the state of humanity today. Globally, hostility and mistrust abound among divergent religions, ethnic groups, and nations, bringing war and untold suffering in its wake. The consciousness of difference and division must be rejected, or there can be no peace.

Humanity now stands at a crossroad; we will either continue to destroy the Earth and its inhabitants through ignorance, warfare and conflict, or we'll reach a state of spiritual enlightenment and social maturity from which we acknowledge our inherent oneness. If not, then powerful technologies will remain in the hands of people who are submerged in ignorance, superstition, and conflict.

But, those conditions cannot exist alongside the state of oneness that is the true wellspring of compassion. As the Buddha said, you can not do violence to another when you realize oneness

There are those who might go through what I've described in my ET encounters, and react in stark terror, even with the same stimuli: a ship by the window; a sighting on the mountain. But my near-death experience allowed me to approach these things without fear. There is no death; why be afraid?

It is critical to understand that an enormous and sophisticated disinformation campaign exists around the whole extraterrestrial question- at least 90 percent of the information and images portrayed to the public are selected to evoke fear – followed by hatred of all things alien. Movies, TV shows, and books about the subject prove this point: if one is to believe that rubbish, you would think that every other person in America is being snatched from their homes at midnight and tortured! It simply isn't true. But fear and horror sells, and the usual suspects benefit from a terrified, misinformed populace.

We know that clandestine paramilitary operations exist, controlled by a shadowy group staging simulated UFO/ETV events. This is not speculation: we have interviewed many independent corroborating military people who have participated on the teams that have deliberately "abducted" people to create the illusion of real extraterrestrial encounters.

In the 'UFO industry' there is the multi-million-dollar abduction subculture, funded by powerful, wealthy interests (including certain European royal families along with industrial scions in the United States). Stories publicized are very deliberately selected. If someone comes to one of the abduction support groups and researchers with the account I've shared, they will be shown the door. They only want to select the terrifying stories – those from people who have had simulated encounters, foisted on them by a military effort that is trying to create psychological propaganda. This will support future Star Wars expenditures down the road by sowing the seeds of division between humans and extraterrestrial people.

It is part of a well thought-out plan to divide one group against another. And in order to do this, a threat must be demonstrated, and the supposed "enemy" demonized. So most of the UFO/ET information put out is designed by counter-intelligence, PSYOPS and disinformation people for a specific, intended effect.

The first is simply to discredit the subject, because most of their stories don't hold up under scrutiny. The second, in my opinion, is to create a foundation of fear upon which to build the edifice of Star Wars. And no less a figure than Werner von Braun told a member of our team, Carol Rosin, that, in fact, this was exactly what was going on: that weapons will be based in space – hence, the need to create a psychological nexus where people will fear all things alien. Then, down the road (when the folks enjoying the multi-trillion-dollar bonanza of current industrial and military operations decide the deception has gone on long enough), they can declare the world needs to unite around 'kicking alien butt' (as quoted from the movie, "Independence Day").

Keep in mind that the Cold War and all the things going on today will pale in comparison to the financial benefit to be gained by stampeding the masses into a false idea of a threat from outer space that must be resisted. Instead of extracting unlimited dollars for the military operations from the United States and the West, the imagined 'threat' will produce enough xenophobia to insure a "blank check", or steady flow of government dollars, in the name of preserving safety and world peace. Sound familiar?

This assessment comes from having interviewed numerous military people inside the organizations dealing with this. I've been told point blank that this has been an ongoing agenda since at least the 1950's. These operations have used something called "alien reproduction vehicles," manufactured by a consortium of companies that include Lockheed Martin, Northrup, SAIC, E Systems, EG&G and Mitre Corporation (among others). These are man-made anti-gravity devices that we've been using since at least the '50s, along with other powerful electronic weapons systems and "programmed life forms" or PLFs. These are biological, artificial life forms being produced to look a lot like these so-called "greys" -- that are not from outer space. They're manufactured in a few facilities, one of them located in the four corners area near Dulce, New Mexico.

This is a concerted effort to create a false "alien threat." If someone comes forward with a dissimilar story, they're blacklisted from lectures and subsequently unable to get their story out to the public or the media in book form or through any other significant channel. But those who create terrifying messages - akin to the movie "Independence Day", or certain abduction books, – receive high dollar advances along with big publishing deals and film contracts. This is assuredly by design.

The power elite want those alarming stories seeded into the mass consciousness, and for the truth to be buried. I have met with people who are funding abduction cults in the United States and Europe. Aside from having interviewed military people who've perpetrated these pseudo-abductions, I've personally been told by no less a figure than the reigning member of a European royal family that he helps fund these efforts. He reasons that the frightening stories need to be out there, to make the world aware that these "evil aliens" exist and must be fought.

He went so far as to say that, in fact, every major Earthly problem since Adam and Eve is attributable to the machinations of these demonic extraterrestrials. He genuinely believes this! And he is also the chief funder of Opus Dei, which is the sensitive right-wing group at the Vatican with an internal secret cell operating these programs. Additionally, I was told that his reason for terminating support for a prominent author in this field (who will remain unnamed here), is that his stories weren't sufficiently alarming. He was portraying interaction between humans and ETs too positively – the sponsor only wanted the most terrifying tales put out to the public!

A prominent leader of one of these abduction groups told me point blank that if someone attends their meetings whose experiences don't fit the mode of military abductions (which are harrowing), they'll kick them out. So, it's a self-selecting, fraudulent process.

This well-oiled machine marches out false, contrived "alien encounters". These are then funneled to specific researchers, who then get channeled into specific movie, documentary, and/or book deals. And it's all lucrative. It is being done specifically to generate propaganda designed to marshal the masses against this supposed threat from outer space, thereby perpetuating and augmenting the hoax already thriving.

Within the Shadow Government is a hard-core group of eschatologists: people obsessed with the end of the world who would like to see it go out in one big eco-alien cataclysm, to hasten the return of Christ! This is their agenda: They maintain that the world has to be in the most dire of conditions for the Second Coming to occur, and they hope to make circumstances ripe for that goal. It is just plain madness. With this degree of hyper-religiosity, fanaticism, and cultish secrecy combined with enormous power, the results are predictably outrageous.

A few years ago I attended a meeting in New York with Mrs. Boutros-Ghali, the wife of the Secretary General, and some of the "New York 100" crowd. A woman approached me to say, "Well, I'll have you know I've read 26 books about UFOs and abductions,". I said, "Well, with all due respect, that means that you've incorporated into your awareness 26 times more disinformation and rubbish than someone who's only read one book." I'm not quite sure I endeared myself to her, but it is the truth.

I have shared my insight with some very senior military personnel as well as people like Mrs. Boutros-Ghali and others. Their first response isn't that it can't be true, but they're just horrified that it may be.

Often people ask whether the road that the human race is on is atypical or typical of what other planets have gone through. I think there's a whole range of capabilities and experiences that happen with different people. I understand that there are some extraterrestrial civilizations that have never had conflict and warfare. And there are others that have, perhaps, passed this way, learned the lessons, and evolved to a peaceful world.

The more a civilization moves away from spirituality, the more violent it becomes. Here, I mean genuine spirituality rather than religiosity. What now passes for "religion," for the most part, is a man-made contrivance - a corruption of it's original intent.

If a civilization separates from its intrinsic spirituality while at the same time developing enormous means of intellect and technology, conflict is inevitable. Earth, is now trying to sort out that dynamic. And we haven't done a terribly good job of it so far.

It is fair to say that ETs would be aware of the risks and the pitfalls of this tumultuous transition we're in today - which I liken to humanity as an organism going from childhood to maturity - and we're in this prolonged adolescent phase. We are chaotic and rebellious and trying to find our footing, but we are not yet mature. And unfortunately, some of us are like adolescent boys who've gotten hold of some hand grenades and are pulling the pins out.

That being the case, if you look at humanity and the state of the world today dispassionately, and look through the eyes of an extraterrestrial civilization, you know that there is cause for concern. For this reason, actions taken by ETs that have contained some of our efforts and clipped our wings as we've tried to weaponize space, are understandable (We know this has happened from testimony by numerous corroborative Disclosure Project witnesses).

Those actions *could* be considered an act of hostility... However I view it instead as an enlightened act of compassion. They know that we could be a threat not only to ourselves but also to other worlds. Alas, our technology has marched ahead of our spiritual and social evolution, making us, frankly, a dangerous people.

The time we live in is very pregnant, but growing short. We haven't really changed directions enough to avoid some very serious consequences that are a natural outgrowth of our retrograde behavior. If you combine extraordinary technologies with a predisposition to vilify anything we don't understand or control, a very dangerous situation results.

So, these extraterrestrial civilizations are monitoring Earth very closely. I have no doubt that this is why many of our military witnesses have recounted these extraterrestrial vehicles monitoring inter-continental ballistic missile silos, weapons storage facilities, weapon plants, space launches and ICBM launches. They want to be very clear that these weapons must not be used and that they're watching our behavior. If we were to get completely out of control, there would be an intervention to stop a worst-case scenario from unfolding.

We're reaching the point where the Earth will have to end the burden we've placed on her, if we don't lift the burden ourselves. We have another couple of generations to get it right; I would be surprised if we could go 50 more years on the path we're on right now.

I was approached by a number of the people who run the super-secret projects related to UFOs and advanced energy systems in 1991. They had read one of my early papers about the concept of oneness and our civilization and the experience of cosmic awareness and cosmic people. They emphasized the importance of sharing this information with their group. These were people who called me from the CIA, Lockheed, McDonnell Douglas, and similar operations. Everything I've written was primarily intended for this group.

The masses of people simply want to live their lives peacefully. They don't care about ripping each others throats out. There is only a very small minority of humans who are psychotically violent and controlling. The fires of hatred and conflict, that keep getting ignited, have been lit deliberately because it's benefiting this violent group.

People within the general population have a strong need to know about this information. They have a need to know, a right to know and a responsibility to act, because they can restrain the worst abuses of a covert group like this if they exert their will. But the entrenchment and the ferocity of some elements within this dangerous group are such that a spiritual perspective needs to be elucidated.

This is why, when I sit down and write something, until now, it has been written with the primary audience being those people who most need to hear it. Most people on Earth would love to simply live together peacefully, enjoy their diversity in cultures, have these technologies, and evolve and go on and raise their children and send them to college and have a nice life.

It's not like there's 99 percent of the world's population who's in favor of going hell bent over Niagara Falls without a barrel. There are a relatively small number of people who have a perspective that is retrograde. They are looking in their rear view mirror and mistaking it for the future. So our task has been to turn their heads and look forward.

It is important that we view these very powerful industrial, military and religious interests as educable.

We have frittered away the last 50 years while the Earth was speaking to us, the people of the Earth were cautioning us, the mountains were weeping, the polar ice caps were melting and the ETs have been warning us. And we've been heedless for 50 years. We need to listen and we need to act - now.

The people running these covert projects are conscious beings who are educable and can learn and can grow and can get this information and change their paradigm before it's too late. In our own meditation and prayers we should ask for transformation and enlightenment for these people, rather than creating enmity and tension.

4

Marriage Made in Heaven

I went to live in Israel in January of 1978, initially just to visit for about ten days. I ended up staying for three years, working at the world headquarters of the Baha'i religion on Mount Carmel in Haifa. It was a wonderful and interesting experience being at some very sacred places. In all my travels throughout that area, I could feel the presence of the spiritual teachers that have come to this small area. And at the same time, I sensed that every rock is soaked in the blood of conflict.

It is a very strange juxtaposition of extremes -- the manifestation of these very exalted prophets such as Christ or Moses or Abraham or Mohammed or Baha'u'llah or the Bab. At the same time there's this incredibly primitive enmity and fanaticism. But then, the prophets always come at the darkest time and to the darkest place.

For many years I've been able to go to sleep at night and see something that will happen the next day or the next month or at some point in the future. This started happening more and more intensely, the more I experienced these higher states of consciousness. In the winter of 1978, I was living in an apartment on Mount Carmel, overlooking the Mediterranean. One night, I had a dream: I was suddenly in a space that was defined but didn't have walls, and it was very light. Near where I was living were the remains of a nobleman who had been head of the Baha'i Faith named Abdu'l-Baha. He was known as a very gentle, wise, sweet, loving figure who was greatly enlightened – in the perfect state of man. He appeared to me in this dream and introduced me to a woman and said, "This is who we wish for you to marry." He then told me many details about her and said, "She'll come from far away and visit here and then leave, but you'll be married here in Israel. She'll be older than you, but that won't be a problem." And then this woman and I were introduced, and I could see exactly who it was and how she was dressed.

This happened every night for four or five nights in a row. Now, here I am, 22 years old, and no more interested in being married than the man in the moon! But one thing about spiritual guidance: it doesn't do you any good if you don't take it. So, I said, "Well, I guess I should be looking to find this person."

A month or two later, I was in the gardens where Abdu'l-Baha is buried, on Mount Carmel at his shrine. In through the gate walked Emily. I was delighted to see that she was the person from my dream. But you don't go up to a complete stranger and say, "Hello, I've had a dream with you and we're supposed to be married!" We met and talked for maybe an hour and a half; it was like we'd always known each other. But I still didn't mention my dream.

She was there for a convention, and the very last day she was there, I saw her again, briefly. They were about ready to close the gates to these beautiful gardens and to the shrines, and Emily was going to go there and say some prayers. I said, "You'd better hurry, because they're closing soon." So, she went and that was the last time I saw her on that trip.

Later, I went to the shrine and prayed and said to God, "If this is really who You wish for me to marry, she's going to have to approach me, with me never telling her the dream or trying to contact her again."

Well, Emily was going to meet her mother in London for a vacation. When she got there, she had a strange compulsion to try to write me, but she didn't even know my last name! She only knew my name is Steve. Someone that she was traveling with happened to know my last name, and so she was able to get the letter to me, through the headquarters of the Baha'i religion there in Israel.

Emily wrote me a letter saying how much she enjoyed meeting me, etc. That was what I'd been waiting for. I wrote a first letter to her that was just normal and friendly. In the second letter, I recounted the whole story of how we had been introduced and what Abdu'l-Baha said in the dream. She wrote me back and said, "Well, if this is the divine will, this is what we'll do."

We corresponded for a whole year. In June of 1979, Emily packed up all her things. We met in the Seattle airport and went to Alaska for a ten-day courtship and then decided, yes, we would be married. And in August of 1979, we were married on Mt. Carmel in Israel! This year (2006) is our 27th anniversary. So some marriages really are made in heaven!"

I tell people this story because many people are given guidance that they don't take, because it doesn't appear to make sense. But if it is right, it doesn't have to make intellectual sense all the time. We've had splendid times, a wonderful marriage and four beautiful children. We've done all these things that you're going to read about, and I love her now more than ever!

Emily picked out a beautiful silk sari with gold thread to wear at our wedding. She didn't know that was exactly what I saw when I was introduced to her in the lucid dream state by Abdu'l-Baha. When I saw it, I said, "This is exactly it."

Our first daughter was born on Mount Carmel in Israel, and we brought her home on our one-year anniversary, so we named her Carmel.

After our first child was born, we came back to the United States, and I went into medical school. I went into emergency medicine because I found it not only very challenging, but it's where I could apply the science and the technology of modern medicine in its highest form. During that time, I was involved in running programs dealing with meditation and holistic health. We formed the Shambhala Institute and offered programs on holistic health and healing.

For many years, I raised our four children with Emily, was chairman of emergency medicine and worked in an emergency department, and was founder of CSETI and the Disclosure Project. Life was quite a three-ring circus!

5

Forgiveness and Faith

One of the great lessons I learned as a teenager was forgiveness. I think it's so important that if people contemplate the sort of situation the world is in on a macro-scale, that it really comes down to a very personal matter: The microcosm of our own lives is recapitulated through society, and we're all operating as a universal resonator. I found the divine and sacred exists and it is real and it is made manifest through lovingness and forgiveness.

So the very first thing that I did was to forgive my parents for actions during our childhood. You don't forget it, but you can forgive. And this frees up an enormous amount of inner peace and energy because you have let go of the negative. The act of forgiveness and the act of love is really one of the highest expressions of spiritual realization.

And so what I found is forgiveness and love require a genuine selflessness - one where you go beyond yourself. As I looked around the world as a teenager, I saw that most of the problems in the world were because of selfishness. There's a wonderful saying attributed to Abdu'l-Baha that says, "Where there is love, nothing is too much trouble and there is always time." I really believe that. This is part of what we're on planet Earth to learn.

I had to create my own spirituality from nothing. This is the blank slate phenomenon: With my near-death experience, I didn't go to the pearly gates where there was this angry old man with a beard, throwing down bolts of lightning at people and judging you and throwing you by your lying sinful forelock into hell.

As I mentioned, one of the first challenges I had was to forgive the people closest to me. People have to learn to forgive. This is why, even though I'll speak with great force about the need to change the path we're on, it's not that I'm wanting to do this by taking a pound of flesh in a vengeful way from those who have gotten us into this mess. It's that they should be educated and, if necessary, restrained.

But even those actions are done out of love and out of a sense of what needs to happen. And it must be done with forgiveness. I continue to practice that now. Being here on this planet, to me, is not about trying to pretend like you're perfect. There's a saying that's attributed to a

German writer: "those who would pretend to be angels are destined to behave as beasts."

The scariest cultists ever are the ones who set themselves on a dais. It's better to be who you are and be real and be human even while you begin to bring into this world those attributes that are spiritual and divine. But you don't have to be perfect to do that.

There is no one perfect on Planet Earth, unless that being is an Avatar- that is one of the high prophets or a Manifestation of the Godhead. And there are none of them living on the Earth today and haven't been for over 100 years, and there won't be for another 1,000 years.

The major prophets or the Manifestations of God are very rare. And they're actually a different species. They have a station that is beyond that of the capacity of even a fully enlightened human. In other words, you could evolve to the highest level of capacity as a human and never reach that station. It is another lineage, another level. And that's how important those figures are and how powerful, but also how unique. And that's why I say it's one of the worst things ever for someone to claim to be that when they're not. The most we can do is to reflect the light from that Godhead.

We are all relatively imperfect, and we're here to manifest degrees of perfection. And beyond that, nothing else should be claimed. And those who claim beyond that are frauds. Period. I don't care who they are. Only by being who we are and knowing where we are, can we evolve.

The South is so crazy - love every minute of it and it suits me just fine! When I was growing up back in the late '50s and '60s, it was really the Old South, still. There were wonderful black women that I knew, and they would come up to me and say, "Oh, you're an old soul." They'd look at me and they'd say things about my future. These were very unpretentious, salt of the Earth, wonderful beings.

You meet people like that all over the world, and you won't meet many of them in temples or in cathedrals or in ashrams, but you will meet them in other places. As a child, I had things affirmed to me from some of these wise and sagacious people. This happened from the time I was four or five years of age on. I was not drawn towards the trappings and formality of spirituality that gets subsumed into the world of priests and the hierarchy or gurus or ashrams, but was more attracted to that genuine spirituality you find in honest, direct, clear, simple spirituality. Because that's where I stayed, it enabled me to open up my heart and do things such as acts of forgiveness and acts of love that really were outside of what my upbringing should have allowed.

The message here is: you can transcend your own limitations, if you let yourself go there. You must exercise your free will to create your own reality. As I look back on it, that was the big lesson of the first 20 years of my life. The specific experiences that I had were in a sense wonderful, and I was blessed to have them even though they happened in the crucible of much difficulty and suffering. It's easy to talk about it, but going through it was not easy. Life on earth is not necessarily easy. There are perfections and imperfections here, and our task is to manifest as many of these good qualities and attributes and perfections as we can.

I had to re-create my life- physically. I had been so sick growing up. I had to re-form my body, re-form my mind, re-form my spirit, re-form my heart. It was like a Shamanic process. And the way that happened was not only through the exercise of will but also through an ability to transcend my own limitations.

You can call this faith- not the faith that most religious people think such as certain beliefs and dogmas. To me true faith is a knowingness and a certainty of things not yet seen and not yet fully known. And yet in your heart and spirit a certainty exists that it can *be*. I found the ability to actualize and manifest through faith and through vision and saw things happen that were miraculous.

I remember, for example, being in college after I had learned meditation techniques, and I started experimenting with the power of prayer. I lived in a dorm and there were these guys who were getting drunk all the time and really on a dangerous path. Every year there were a few of these college kids who ended up drinking and getting killed, driving between Boone and Blowing Rock on a treacherous two-lane road.

One afternoon I was sitting in the dorm room meditating. I heard these guys come in, completely drunk and rowdy. So I went into a state of divine awareness, and without any irritation or negativity on my part at all -- I wasn't judging -- I just went in that state and I saw them. In my mind, I could see them coming down the hall. And I put this divine light around them, and I asked for their forgiveness. Then I asked that they wake up to what they were doing and that they stop harming themselves in this way. About five minutes later, there was a knock on the door. And there they were, looking completely sober, asking for forgiveness- *through* me to something greater. It was a transformative event for them, and I never saw them drunk again!

That same year, I found that the same thing happens with animals-that there was this ability to connect with what people in the East would call the devas and the nature energies. I would sit out under the trees in a huge ancient forest behind my dorm and meditate.

One day, while sitting against a huge old Hemlock tree and meditating, I felt I was being watched. I slowly opened my eyes and to my delight, there was a semi-circle of animals around me. There were a couple of birds, a squirrel, a chipmunk and a raccoon, just in a semi-circle. I know this sounds like something out of Siddhartha, but it really happened. These animals were peacefully staring at me and appeared to be in a state of great calm and bliss.

We have within us a wonderful divine spirit -but we have to know it, practice it, and affirm it in our lives so that these things are possible. This is what, to me, faith is: You act as if it is so, and it is so. And when you act as if it is so, it will be. Ultimately, it is an exercise of surrender, of giving up self to the great Spirit.

6

Ineffable Oneness

In the Sufi tradition there is the story of the master who is trying to teach a student how to levitate across the water. The student is at the edge of the body of water, intellectualizing and thinking, "Well, I'm heavier than water; I'm going to sink and I'm going to drown." The master turns to the student and says, "Leave thyself behind, and then walk upon the water."

This is the grace - I call it operative grace- that you have to find to achieve these things spiritually. You have to practice it and let it unfold.

You have to *know* in your heart that it is possible -- not just believe in something in the ordinary sense of belief. You have to say, "It will be," and you then do it. But it is being done not because of your ego; it's being done from the greater Mind that stands within you.

Realizing this is a paradox: On the one hand, our individualities are the vehicles through which the unboundedness can manifest and express. Once you understand that, you understand the concept of being a clear vehicle for spirit. So, on the one hand, there has to be individuality to be able to have it happen. On the other hand, you have to be freed up enough from self to let the larger divine Being shine through and let these things happen. And then it will happen.

I survived my own adolescence by finding this pretty much on my own, with some help from the unseen realms. But if I hadn't found it, I am quite sure I would have been dead by age 20. Most people who would have come out of the kind of situation I was in as an adolescent boy would have ended up a drug addict or a criminal. I attribute this transformation to the guidance, protection and inspiration from the Great Spirit, the Divine Being -- and somehow I was willing to be open to that. When I opened to It, It all rushed in. It was all there for me. And It is always there for each of us.

I tell people, "As soon as you're ready to open to That, it's there." And it's there for any purpose. I don't care if you're in the emergency department, trying to save a life, or you're an airline pilot, or a carpenter. The unbounded Divine Mind is always folded within us. It's a matter of knowing this, being open to it and letting it operate. So, you have to get out of your own way and let It happen.

When I was living in Israel, my father, who was a chain smoker and an alcoholic, became deathly ill. I now realize that he also had very serious Post Traumatic Stress Disorder from World War II, from doing hand-to-hand combat with the Japanese in the Pacific islands. One day, I heard from family that he had an inoperable golf ball sized tumor in his right lung. Back then -- this would have been around 1978; it was not thought that the available chemotherapy would work, but they would try it anyway. And so I was called back to the States to make burial arrangements: the doctors said he had about six weeks to live. When I saw Dad I asked him, "Do you want to die from this?" He said, "No, I'm not ready." So, I taught him meditation and I taught him prayer. Now, you have to understand what a hard-boiled atheist, and bitter man he was, and of that generation, born in 1916. But still he said, " I'll do this." So, I gave him some books to read and then I personally taught him meditation, visualization and how to heal with mind from within.

You have to first center and go into a deep, quiet state of consciousness that goes beyond self, where the real power is, which is divinity. It's that which transcends ego. And then from that state, do the visualization. So, you bring in what I call the God factor or the divine spirit factor.

So I taught my father to do this. I said, "Just do it. This is a matter of saving your life. Whether you believe it or not, act as if you do." So, he did.

I then went back to Israel, and I would go to the beautiful Baha'i shrine on Mount Carmel. Every day at lunch, I'd go there and I would do the same visualization as I taught my Dad. Then I would pray for his healing.

Well, a few weeks later, he went back to his doctor. (We did pick out the cemetery plot, but I knew he'd be okay.) The doctor took some x-rays and found, suddenly, that the huge tumor was gone. And the doctor went, "My God!"- it was one of these "miraculous," spontaneous healings. But we knew exactly what happened.

My father ended up living several more years and dying of congestive heart failure and emphysema from smoking, because his lungs were just blown. But before he died, a memory came back to me of sitting with him in the back yard of our house in Charlotte when I was young, maybe 12 years old. He said, "You know, I really don't want to live much longer, just long enough that you kids are all grown and out of the house." (He was pretty inebriated when he told me this.)

Now, when he had his lung cancer, my little sister was still living at home. And the year after she left, he died. I told my sister, "You know, we do create our own reality." He scripted that. The cancer that should have killed him didn't, but he totally gave up on his life and died as soon as all the children were grown and gone. He did exactly what he said he was going to do, even though I am sure he did not consciously remember saying it.

So, we're much more powerful than we think we are, no matter who we are. And we do create the life that we have.

During this same period of time, I learned that I could be in a state where I could visit people at remote distances. Now, a lot of people say, "Oh, that means you were astrally traveling." I did astral travel as a teenager, but this was different!

What I learned to do was to realize that you don't have to separate the astral body from the physical body, but simply realize that the entirety of creation is folded within each individual. We are truly a quantum hologram of the whole creation. When it is said, "Thinkest thyself a puny form when within thee the universe is folded?" a rhetorical question is being asked which illuminates a profound truth: All is folded within the awake mind within.

A relatively primitive way of visiting others through spirit is to actually have an astral projection, where the physical body and the astral body separate and you fly off. But a more developed, simpler and safer way of doing it is to realize that all this is folded within you.

By going into a state of consciousness that is non-local, that is the transcendent state of awake-ness, every point in space and time can be accessed. And when you experience that, then, using your will subtly, you can open up and see a loved one in another place. And this is what I would do with my loved ones.

Just before I went to Israel, I had this shown to me. I had a great aunt who was very sick who had lung cancer, and was dying. She was one of the few members of our family who really did care for us, so I always felt very close to her. And I remember her as being always very sweet and very kind, Aunt Irene.

The day that she passed away, I awakened in my bedroom and she was there. And I saw her as, probably, a 40-year-old woman, instead of a 70-some-year-old woman who'd been very sick with cancer. She was radiant and beautiful. I don't remember anything being said; it was just a beautiful, loving presence and at once a goodbye and a lasting connection. The next day, my twin sister called me and I told her the experience. She said, "Well, I'm calling you because she passed away." I asked,

"What time?" And this experience was *exactly* at the time of her passing.

So, we're always connected through the Oneness of the great Spirit with each other. It's a beautiful thing to realize, because once we do, we realize that time and space are not barriers at all.

I remember one time camping with a friend in the petrified forest in Arizona. My wife Emily was back at our home in North Carolina.

Suddenly, I sensed that she wanted to be able to know that she could communicate with me, but I was in the wilderness. So as I laid down to go to sleep under a full moon ,I meditated and went into a state of unity consciousness.

I expanded into that peaceful state of awareness and saw Emily in our bedroom. Now, Emily is someone who rarely remembers her dreams. I knew she was sleeping, so I went into the bedroom and connected with her soul. I showed her exactly where I was and what I was doing. I sent the message that anytime she really needs me, I'd be there – that we're always together - that we are one in Spirit.

A few days later, when I came out of the wilderness, I called her. She said, "You wouldn't believe this lucid dream I had! You were in this place… " and she proceeded to described exactly where we were camping! "And you told me this:.." and repeated the message I had given her. It was a beautiful realization and it was reassuring for her and for me. It showed us what we can do and that we're never alone; we're never apart; there is never separation.

When we chose to unlock the box of separation, we have the key. The key is this awake mind within us and the will to use it. You must have a living faith. Yogananda (a famous Vedic teacher) once said that spiritual lassitude and the lack of spiritual adventuresome-ness is why people never grow.

Once you have these experiences begin to unfold and you say it is possible, your certainty that it can happen increases; then you do it more often and it becomes more and more and more powerful. A positive feedback loop is created.

It's like a snowball going downhill. It picks up its own momentum- but you've got to leap over the edge!

One year for our anniversary, Emily and I went to Costa Rica and stayed someplace on the Pacific Coast. One night, after we'd fallen asleep, an amazing thing happened to us.

Emily woke up in the middle of the night and as she looked over towards me she saw a silvery grey form lift up out of my body and fly out the hotel window and leave. And she thought, "Oh, my God. Here I am, stuck in Costa Rica, and we have four kids back home, and Steve just died!"

I was having what I had always called one of my flying lucid dreams, which I've had all my life. I was flying over the jungle and the edge of the ocean. Even though it was the middle of the night; I was seeing with celestial vision, so I could see the gorgeous quality of the water and the jungle, as if it was day time; but everything had its own light from within it, as opposed to light coming from the sun. I saw the most beautiful, alive colors and light. It was one of the most beautiful things I've ever seen. I was flying along in a state of complete freedom and happiness.

All of a sudden, that ended, and I found myself back in the room, thinking I was just waking up from a dream. And I felt Emily looking at me. I looked over, and her eyes were like saucers! She exclaimed, "Thank God, you're back!" And I said, "Back? Where have I been?"

She said, "Well, you left." I said, "I've done no such thing. I've been here the whole time." And she said, "No, I saw you leave your body!" And then she described to me what she had seen. That's when I realized that many of these lucid brilliant dreams are soul travel experiences. Now, Emily normally doesn't have these metaphysical experiences -- she is your quintessential Earth mother and loves every minute of it! But she actually saw my soul fly away, because I think she was in a relaxed state of mind, where her filters were down. And the filters being turned off allowed her to actually see my spirit, lift up out of the physical body and fly away. She saw me as I left to enjoy the deep, spiritual beauty of earth.

I first found divinity through the doorway of the creation that the Divine Being has put here. The highest expression of it, of course, is the Earth around us and the sky around us. It is very Native American: Being part Cherokee and Catawba, I have a deep love for the Earth.

This has a lot to do with the work I'm doing now. My love and passion for nature and Spirit is what moves me. I'm motivated by the future I see of Earth and her children. I see it and know it is possible.

It has been said that the best way to love God is to love his creation. I view it this way: There's the divine, Infinite Mind that's the inner being of God, of the Supreme Being. But the entire creation is equally infinite, and that's the outer robe, or raiment, of God. The creation is the outer expression of the same thing, and it's all one, perfectly one.

Even as a child, when I'd look up at the stars and see the sky, I didn't see empty space. I saw joy and felt an awake presence. I felt the divine being, expressed through nature and through the creation. As a scientist, I view it that way. This view is not incompatible with the study of the biochemistry of flowers - seeing how incredibly wondrous and extraordinary it's all put together, whether it's genetics, whether it's physics, whether it's electromagnetism, whether it's quantum physics, whether it's string theory, whether it's biochemistry, molecular, anatomy, physiology -- it's all an expression of an incredible conscious living Being. All of this is the outer body of God, phasing, resonating, moving as matter or space or time or energy.

Thus, every created thing is a doorway to the Creator. Walt Whitman certainly knew this, and Thoreau and Emerson. Nature is a great teacher. We have come out of the womb of Mother Earth, which is an outer expression of the infinite Godhead. Infinity is within us and within all things, but not divided – eternally in Its perfect wholeness. Everything is within and perfectly connected to each other. It's the perfect quantum hologram.

The question is: Is there a meta-theme that encapsulates all these experiences? The big theme and the transcendent theme is an ineffable oneness. Oneness.

If you have the ability to experience this state of consciousness, where you transcend space and time and materialism, you can encounter someone from another culture on Earth or another person from another planet or another realm, and rather than seeing them as "other," you see them as "same." This is very important, because the consciousness of 'otherness' is rooted in ignorance. Otherness is ignorance, whereas oneness is enlightenment.

If you can look at all beings and see that they're awake and conscious, just as we are, you can experience your oneness with them. This is true no matter how different their intellect, body, emotional timbre, or fund of knowledge may be. All these things that we usually focus on are really ephemeral. If we look at the fact that they're awake and experience that state of awareness where we see the transcendental value of the unbounded Mind, then we won't see them as "alien" or "other." And this is true whether you're talking about someone from Zimbabwe or Saudi Arabia or Alpha Centauri. It really doesn't matter - because it's another sentient, conscious being who has folded within his reality the awake-ness that is this universal aspect of our own selves.

If you can experience this state of Oneness, first of all, you can communicate, which is very important. Secondly, you will not feel that there is anything to be afraid of. Thirdly, you will see nothing to have a conflict over, because the things that are different really aren't essential and aren't important.

I think you could put the founders of every religion on Earth together and they'd have a grand old time with, probably, no differences amongst them. It's the divisions that men create, out of egotism, materialism, chauvinism, ignorance ,hatred and stupidity, that cause the problems. The experience of Oneness is the indispensable experience so needed at this time...

So, the meta-theme that I have taken away from my own experience of these states of awareness is that of oneness. It is the meta-theme of the next half a million years: growing levels of oneness. And out of that grows perfect harmony, peace and enlightenment.

You see this all around us. The world is becoming more integrated and more related. One of the great challenges of the extraterrestrial question is - what level of oneness must be attained for humanity to be universal – to be able to relate peacefully to conscious but non-human life?

We live in a cosmic moment, where humans are starting to go into space, and we're beginning to wake up to the fact that we're being visited by extraterrestrial civilizations, and simply realizing the oneness of humanity isn't enough. We're going to have to transcend even that and go to a level where we understand the universal aspect of the mind; the fact that conscious mind, awake-ness itself, is a universal singularity and that the awake-ness within the being of a life form from another planet is identical to the awake-ness within us - even if our intellects are different and our bodies are different and our fund of knowledge is different. All those things really are not essential.

This, then, speaks to the need for a universal spirituality. We live in a time not just of the need for the establishment of world peace but of universal peace. A time where such a peace can only be actualized fully through the acknowledgment of the universal nature of spirit and the universal nature of conscious mind. Otherwise, we will say, "Well, humanity is all one, and humans can have peace, but then there are all these others out there" – and what shall we do with *them*?

The truth is that these life forms are conscious and awake through the same inner awake-ness that shines within each of us. There is absolutely no difference.

Knowledge of This eliminates all fear -- if you can be in that state of awareness, you are in the state that is eternal and immortal, because it is outside the limits of time. And it's infinite, because it's not restricted by space. So, that state of consciousness is the safest path to being able to establish world peace and universal peace. This is why the fundamental challenge in the world today is spiritual.

7

Universal Peace

We are in a cosmic moment. Humans today- albeit in classified programs - have the means to travel among the stars. So, we must evolve from a human oriented spirituality to a genuine universal spirituality. And if that doesn't occur, we will not be able to evolve to the next level of human destiny.

Some say, "Well, this is a tall order. We're still here beating *each other* up - and now we're going to have to deal with relating to life forms from elsewhere." But look at it this way: when we acknowledge that we're not alone in the universe, it will make humans -- all humans -- seem like very close relatives. Now, in order to deal with the challenge of understanding other civilizations, we will have to transcend the anthropocentric view of spirituality and evolve a universal spirituality. This is actually an extremely positive development. These challenges will propel humanity into truly developing a larger, genuine spirituality that has been missing for so long through our misguided belief system of separation.

The truth is that there is no separation. I've spoken to many Native American peoples who relate that one of the extraordinary things in the early days of native peoples encountering Europeans was the extent to which we lived in the sense of things being separate. The Native Americans considered this thinking quite strange. As for the aboriginals in Australia who still practice 'dream time' and are aware: they know that there is no separation. There's a sense of integration with the stars, with the infinity of things, with other peoples, worlds, and with each other. The extent to which we live in a separate way, we suffer. And the extent to which we live in a sense of oneness within ourselves and with all that there is, we are freed from suffering.

So, that's the essential theme that I see that keeps repeating. It is the experience of a universal oneness rooted in the experience of non-local, cosmic mind. World peace isn't going to be enough: it is time for universal peace. It's that or nothing. There can be no human future without universal peace.

That's the time we live in, and that's the challenge of the coming era. We must know ourselves as universal, awake beings, and on that foundation universal peace can be established. It may first be just studied intellectually, but ultimately it must be experiential.

We live in a time where universal education and the universal ability to read should open up the whole array of knowledge to every denizen on the planet. And those who would care to be gatekeepers or bottle-necks - and keep a choke-hold on the flow of knowledge - simply need to step down and stand aside.

Let's be honest. There was a time when one out of 1,000 people on Earth knew how to read. And the clerics were scribes, and they would read and repeat to the masses what were in spiritual teachings.

But this is not needed in a time of universal education, where the majority of people can read. So, go read, and then gather together in your own spiritual community and share. But you don't need to anoint some-one to be a guru or priest. To do so is actually deleterious to your spiri-tual development. It does not matter if it's some New Age guru or peo-ple running around in robes saying that they're your entry point to the forgiveness of God. To me, it's all a harmful holdover from a time now gone.

I'm not saying that everyone who shares and teaches such things are frauds. I'm saying that people who set themselves up as final arbiters, special priests if you will, of spiritual knowledge are missguided. That time is over. We are at least 100 to 150 years into a time when no one on Earth has needed a priest, a rabbi, a mullah, or a guru, *except* as a facilita-tor to teach.

Ultimately people will wake up to the truth, but the fact is that the spiritual infantilization of the masses is something which is a very entrenched institution. What I mean by spiritual infantilization is the sit-uation where the power and access to enlightenment or spiritual knowl-edge goes through these filters, or control points. And everyone else is acting like children, rather passively receiving it. That is a type of learned behavior - and you have to un-learn that behavior. This is spiritual co-dependency.

Granted, there's a role for people who want to share and teach spiri-tual information and pass it from one generation to another. But, I'm talking about hierarchy and the power grab and the control drama and the mind set of spiritual dependency. Unfortunately, this spiritual code-pendency is very, very powerful in terms of getting into people's minds where they feel like they can't learn and experience truth on their own without having someone there directing every step.

One of the positive things about the early years of my life was learn-ing that an individual can learn these truths and experience enlightenment with little formal education and no specific person directing it.

The close-minded orthodoxy of religion is equaled or exceeded by the close-minded orthodoxy of scientists who, in our society, have become the new high priests. Remember: Scientists are humans first and scientists later. So, they have all the failings and all the foibles of humans. Just because a Harvard professor has a PhD, it doesn't mean s/he doesn't have the same pitfalls that a priest would have in terms of self-aggrandizement and egotism. They, too, can become fanatical and dogmatic in the belief system in which they've been indoctrinated, in lieu of searching for the truth.

Most of the problems that we face in our world today, whether they be spiritual and religious or scientific, political and economic, are all because people are holding onto some perspective that has nothing to do with the truth but has to do with their own belief system and addiction to something that's outdated, and they can't let go of it. This is certainly true of scientists. There are countless examples of how the mainstream scientific community has rejected enormous breakthroughs because it didn't fit into their belief system.

This is why I say to people, "One should have very few beliefs, but an abundance of faith." You can have infinite faith- but the specific *beliefs* you hold need to be minimal. Otherwise, people get trapped in brainwashed dogma, whether it be scientific or religious. They then become chauvinistic and egotistically attached to it. And as soon as that happens one has stopped searching for the truth.

We need a genuinely humble, universal spirituality. We must want to find the truth. And if the next door that opens cancels some of our previously held convictions and beliefs, then so be it. This is one of the reasons why, whether you're a physician or a scientist or someone doing spiritual work or an economist, the mind-set of being attached to an idea — as opposed to being clearly focused on wanting to know the truth -- is a hindrance to finding truth.

On a personal note, I'm very grateful that, prior to going into medicine, I had studied meditation, health and diet so that I came into medicine with a broader paradigm. I could take what was good in the medical and scientific area, without getting brainwashed by it.

This meta-system trapping happens in every profession and in every field. It happens because people confuse the current state of knowledge with the ultimate state of knowledge. And the ultimate state of knowledge, no one has but the Divine Being. But because they know what they know, they think they know everything. And the truth is, most of what there is to know isn't known by anyone, ever.

And so I think the only way to avoid the pitfalls of the high priests of scientific circles or of religious circles is to have enough genuine devotion to finding the truth and a willingness to reform what your assessment is. Thus, there are very few things that become fixed and absolute. And everything else is relative. But that's the nature of the world we're in. It's a relative world. And there are very few things that need to be fixed and absolute.

If you study the central teachings of every spiritual tradition on Earth, they all agree: the existence of God; the qualities of forgiveness and love; and these larger spiritual themes. They're all universal. Where they differ is in one social teaching or another, or one cultural bias or another -- which are really ephemeral and changing with each spiritual tradition and aren't that important, anyway.

You know, you may be very orthodox in some areas, and that's fine if it works for you. But don't think that that is the end and the beginning of all knowledge for spiritual traditions. It isn't. There are very few things that need to be in the category of ongoing, certain truths. And most everything else should be in a state of evaluation and evolution.

But we're not trained to do that. Our educational system, whether it's religious or scientific, is designed to create rigidity and, in that way, engenders fanaticism. It then becomes a fiefdom that those benefiting from the structure of belief want to protect at all costs. And certainly this is true in science, where there are people who, no matter how much evidence you put in front of them, would say, "This can't be true."

Our science advisor for the Project, Dr. Loder, has a colleague at the University of New Hampshire who said he wouldn't care if you gave him one of these new energy machines and he tested it and proved it worked: he still wouldn't believe it because it's not possible!

So, these become fanatical belief systems that are just as tragic as the fanatical belief systems that certain religious extremists are attached to. And all of it ends up hurting society.

One of the things I want to share is what happened at MIU where I was learning to become a meditation instructor. There, I was experimenting with the applications of higher states of consciousness. One night, late, I was sitting, meditating, and I saw a young woman in my class in my mind's eye, and invited her to come over to my room. We were going to talk about spiritual matters and then meditate together.

All of a sudden I saw her, in my mind's eye. I was in a deep quiet meditation, and I saw her leave her dorm, come out, walk around the campus, come up the steps, and then, bang, bang, knocked on my door. And it so startled me, because it was almost like a dream, except I was actually seeing it in living color. I opened the door and I said, "Oh, it *is* you." She said, "Oh, were you expecting me?" I said, "Well, I saw you coming." And it was just crystal clear.

During those years between ages 16 and 20, I started experiencing these sorts of things on a daily basis, if not many times a day- and at times continuously. And I have used this ability to create CSETI and the Disclosure Project and to identify a lot of the intelligence sources and the witnesses we have. Some of them find me, but I find them, also, or draw them in. We'll talk about this later. It gets into high strangeness.

Remember, the universe is folded within us, and we have enormous powers, every human being -- not just me, and not just you; everyone; they're the same -- and that when needed, we can call upon this Higher Power to do what is needed to achieve something wonderful.

Now, if you're willing to make the ultimate sacrifice and you also have this knowledge, then you cross over into what's called a spirit warrior: someone who's willing to do what's needed, no matter what the risks are. You exist beyond fear.

I believe that these early years prepared me to do what I then later had to do and was part of my purpose in being here. I always felt that when I had the near-death experience and was told, "You may come with us or return back to your body on Earth" and was told that Spirit wanted me back on earth, that I had this work to do. I could have chosen to have not come back here and gone on and stayed in that state of awareness with those very high celestial beings. I chose to submit to their will- not that I was happy with it. I told you initially it was rather depressing- having had the childhood I had, and being very sick -- I wasn't really interested in coming back here. But I acceded to it.

Transformation doesn't come into being except through the agency of the free will of humans. And that means us. Now, obviously, between 1980 and 1990 I was aware of these things- but having recently been married and having four children in eight years (between 1980 and 1988) and becoming a medical doctor and residency and starting my medical practice, I had a full plate. Yet, I didn't forget these lessons. I knew that it was the time to establish the family and career and the ability to further do this work.

8

Total Transformation

We cannot just stand back passively and let rogue kleptocrats run roughshod over the entire Earth and cannibalize the Earth, killing millions of people. In a discussion I had with a Special Ops person from Fort Huachuca, Army intelligence headquarters in Arizona, I asked, "At what point would it have been appropriate to restrain, by any means necessary, Hitler and his inner circle?" My opinion: "At the earliest possible moment."

There are rabid dogs amongst us. And some of them may never be amenable to either reason or spiritual enlightenment. Do we then say, "Oh, then we can't do anything"? The right of self-defense is a universal one.

This is where I am, clearly, not a pacifist. I believe in peace, and I believe in using higher spiritual abilities, but ultimately, there is a place for intervening and protecting innocent people when there is someone who is truly mad and on the loose. In a sense, we live in a society that has a large component of collective insanity. It's a society gone mad. And there are some things that need to happen that require discipline and decisive action.

But you don't cross over into vengeance or anger. It has to be done for the right reasons, just like when you discipline a child, you're not doing it out of vengeance and anger, but you're doing it for their edification and their enlightenment and for their future.

In raising our children, we have had high expectations and firm discipline. We were not permissive. At times, our children thought we were too strict, but as they have grown older they are so grateful for having been raised with values, discipline and love. I share this about my own family philosophy to say that, in society, it's the same way. One can be very loving but also see where there's a place to intervene and be disciplined and not to indulge misbehavior or to look the other way when there are rabid dogs ripping apart a peaceful flock of sheep.

This requires wisdom. We live in a world where people polarize around either an impractical New Age spirituality and pacifism or a traditional "us versus them, let's kill everyone we don't understand" mindset. Neither is going to get this right. We have to be cognizant of the time we live in. And the time we live in is not the time of the perfect world- yet.

There was a 400,000-year cycle that literally started with "Adam," who was the first Avatar of that cycle. That cycle ended in the mid- to late 1800s.

What opened at that point is a 500,000-year cycle, the hallmark of which is universal peace, the oneness of human and universal life, and the eventual establishment of a genuine enlightened civilization on Earth. This will be a time of an unbroken period of peace that, at first, will be a political peace, a time of no more large wars and conflicts on earth. But that will then give birth to a period of a great peace – the peace of enlightenment where the entire Earth and everyone on it will grow in spiritual oneness. Earth will become one of the extraordinary centers of enlightenment, and known as such throughout the cosmos.

So, as bad as things seem now, that's not where it's going to stay! And it isn't going to be like this much longer. This shift to a new time, a new era, has been going on for about 150 years. But out of 500,000 years, we are just at the early crack of dawn. And as one cycle closes and the other opens, a time of maximum chaos is created. This is why we are in the most chaotic period in known recorded history. But soon that will give way to another reality on Earth.

The knowledge and spiritual capacity for world peace was available through the people who lived on Earth 100 years ago. The means of communication were there and the "Divine Will" and "Divine Plan" were there. Humans elected not to act. It wasn't done, because we failed to do it.

So, this is our choice. And now we're living through the ramifications of it. It's our choice right now, this moment. We're all making choices, collectively and individually. And the aggregate of the operation of that free will has given us the world we see today.

The events that happened back in the mid- to late 1800s are that a universal Avatar, as I understand it, appeared and then disappeared during that time. That is, the over-soul Avatar for the next half a million years appeared, created spiritually a new world, and then vanished. The information, knowledge and, within the finest realm of creation, the means for this new time, were all created. It's all here now: Look and you will see it! We as humans have to see it, realize it and manifest it. We're the ones, now, who have to carry the rest of the water. The oceans are there, but the water has to still be delivered to where it's needed, and we're the ones who have to carry that water.

It's a wonderful time, actually. And I'm quite certain that most people have no idea of the time in which we live. What they're waiting to happen has happened already. In the Bible it refers to "a thief in the night," - that this new world would be created spiritually, and this knowledge would appear -- and it would be like a thief - nobody would know until He was gone. Well, that's very true.

So, I'm saying a lot of those events are 100 to 150 years in our rearview mirror. And most religious, political and other leaders are looking backwards. They're waiting for something to happen that happened already. So, the Earth and everyone on it, in a sense, is in a state of retardation, because it's been hijacked, mostly out of ignorance. And so the only way to fix ignorance is to share knowledge.

As I said earlier, one of the problems is that nice people have a serious flaw: They're nice. And because nice people are nice, the rabid wolves and the mad dogs can rip them apart. So, we live in a time where a certain amount of clear-eyed spirituality and genuine knowledge has to be joined with some real courage.

We live, unfortunately, in a time where spirituality has been equated with passivity. This is a very dangerous thing, because it's a propaganda or indoctrination that's designed to create people who are spiritually oriented and very nice, but very passive and ineffectual. And in that passivity, the rabid dogs can have full sway.

People like Gandhi or Martin Luther King, Jr.: These were people who were flawed human beings just like we all are, but they were spiritually oriented, and had the courage of their convictions- and they *acted*. They were threatened and took risks and ultimately were killed.

I am asked in almost every lecture I give, "Aren't you afraid?" I answer: "Well, look. You have to understand that as an emergency doctor, I've taken care of I don't know how many people killed over a 50-cent beer. "

Two high school boys came in Code Blue, dead on arrival, that we tried to save. This happened because one of them had patted the other one's girlfriend on the fanny and they pulled out knives and sliced each other's guts and hearts open. I've seen people die over such ephemera and over such trivial things that if you understand what these issues are about and you're not willing to step up to the plate and take a bullet, you're a coward.

I've said flat out to some of these folks who are involved in these projects, "You want to whack me? Go ahead."

I'm on borrowed time anyway. I figure that everything past the age of 17, when I was clinically dead, is a gift.

The world needs people who understand what the task is and are willing to go the distance.   The time we're living in right now is a real test for people to get that balance -- it's a yin and yang, male-female attribute sort of thing. We must combine the spiritual and loving with the active, assertive and disciplined. Change requires that we bring those qualities together. It's like two wings of a bird. And it's often said that in humanity, the male and female, are two wings of a bird. And so long as one is impaired, the bird will never fly straight and will never stay aloft.

This is not only in terms of men and women, and basic equality, but it is also about the attributes that we have to evince and demonstrate in our life to manifest that kind of harmony.

We live in a world where women generally are taught not to be assertive and active, and men are not taught to be spiritual and loving. This is a perversion of human nature. It has nothing to do with male or female. There may be dominance in these areas in one sex or the other, but the task is to bring them into harmony. The duality of 'this or that' we have to transcend. We have to bring both of these qualities and attributes to bear in our lives.

Unless we do, we're not going to be successful in establishing the kind of civilization on this planet that will be enduring. Had we done so for 100 years , I have no doubt in my mind that we would have already had a permanently established peaceful world civilization here. I'm certain by the mid-1900s we would have had electro-gravitic transportation between cities; we would have had free energy and non-polluting energy forms running the Earth; we would have had all these things. People laugh and say, "Oh, it's like the Jetsons." Well, in fact, some of these cartoons and science fiction stories that were created were based on very well-known facts and prototypes of technologies that were up and flying around back in the '50s and '60s.

We have not collectively or individually exercised our powers through the operation of free will and the knowledge that goes with it that can create this new world. As soon as we do, we'll have it. And until we do, it won't happen.

This is why I encourage people to not look at this as some visionary, futuristic effort, but in reality, as doing a bit of a catch-up. We can talk about the real future, because the establishment of a peaceful civilization using non-harmful technologies to run our civilization is something that really could have been achieved decades ago.   It's a total transformation of the way humans will live on Earth and explore the cosmos.

9

Information in Unconventional Ways

The love of higher states of awareness and the study and application of such knowledge continued even in my medical career. I've spoken to a number of physicians and others who are in high stress jobs. Believe me, a busy ER is a stressful place to be. Everything in our lives can be applied if we're open to keeping ourselves integrated to that experience, including these experiences with consciousness and higher states of awareness.

One morning, I was back in the call room at the hospital at about three o'clock a.m.. I was lying there, just sort of relaxing. There was no one in the ER at that particular moment after hours of non-stop patients. As I was lying there, in my mind's eye I saw very clearly a woman coming in with congestive heart failure, and she was dying. I saw it so clearly that I got up and put on my scrub top and shoes and went out to the ER.

The nurses said, "What are you doing here?" I said, "I'm expecting a congestive heart failure patient - an elderly woman - to come in." They said, "Well, there's been no call." And about two seconds later, the radio call came in from the paramedics: "We're on our way in with a woman with congestive heart failure, respiratory distress...."

This type of intuitive experience would happen frequently in the ER, but it wasn't appropriate to talk about, because our society wants to keep spirituality and this kind of experience separate from our careers, our families and, our politics and from everything.

Another time, a 26-year-old male came in during flu season who thought he was sick with the flu. The nurse triaged him and put him in a medical room. We were very busy - we had 14 trauma and exam rooms, and one doctor! I went in and saw this man. He had fever, chills, nausea, body aches and headache and all the symptoms that you would see with the flu. Normally, most doctors would examine him, do a couple tests and give him a prescription for Amantadine for the flu, and off they'd go.

I looked at this man and enigmatically sensed that he had a brain tumor. Now, there were no symptoms of a brain tumor. He did not have any neurological findings such as paralysis, numbness, seizure, etc. But

I had the power of my convictions. So I turned to the nurse and I said, "I want a stat CT of the head." Well she looked at me like I was crazy and said, " Dr. Greer, he's only got the flu!" And I said, "Just do it."

Thank God I didn't have to go through an HMO or some insensitive bean counter, because if I had, this man would be dead today! (Memo to the politicians and money whores ruining our medical systems: Medicine is an art, as well as a science.)

So, from this intuitive knowledge, I ordered a CAT scan. He really did not, objectively, meet any criteria for ordering one. But I said, "Whoever's on the table, yank them off. Get them out of the scanner; I want this one in, stat." So, he goes in, and the radiologist calls back, stat, and says, "Dr. Greer, this man has a massive astrocytoma" --a big brain tumor -- that was herniating the brain stem!

Now, here's what was happening: All of his symptoms were because the brain stem was being pushed through the opening at the base of the skull, the foramen magnum, and it was putting pressure on the area that controls temperature regulation, nausea, etc. So, he was having all these symptoms of fever and chills and nausea, but it was all due to this tumor and its strange presentation. The shape of this tumor was such that it wasn't affecting any specific sensory or motor function. It was a very atypical situation.

It was serious enough that, with this kind of pressure being built up in the brain, it eventually would have herniated the brain stem, cut off the respiratory and heart center, and he would have suddenly died. I immediately referred him to neuro-surgery for stat decompression. We had to helicopter him, actually, to another facility.

"Dr. Greer, why did you think this patient had a brain tumor? I would have never suspected it with his presentation! I would have never even gotten the CAT scan," the neurosurgeon told me. "Oh, I just had a hunch...," I said. The truth is that it was a type of sensing -- the pop culture would say "remote viewing."

It was an intuitive knowing, because the symptom complex, if anything, would have led me into a facile diagnosis of the flu, and I would have "treated and streeted", as we say. But if I had not followed my inner knowing, in less than 12 hours he would have been dead. As it turned out, he had neurosurgery and it was successful.

We really can bring this kind of capacity and knowledge into our careers, even though we're not "supposed to"-- and particularly those of us who are hard science people. In science and medicine, this sort of thing is very frowned upon. And yet, I have found that there are a number of physicians who have had similar experiences that they won't talk about openly for fear of ridicule.

Another time there were two Code Blues going on at once. Well, I'm one doctor and I've got two people who literally have had their heart stopped. The one we had been working on first had been in arrest a long time. Then another one came in. The first patient was in a type of rhythm that is fatal if you don't get them out of that rhythm. We'd used everything that could be used: cardioversion, all the medicines, everything. I won't go into the gory, technical details. The fact is, it wasn't working. Finally, we were going to have to call the code – end it - but I just sensed that this person could get back into a normal rhythm. So I put my awareness on the heart, visualized the conduction system of the heart, and called on this higher power- the power of God- and mentally visualized and willed his heart going back into a normal beat. And it did, at that instant! Now, it may have been a coincidence. Some of the skeptics would say, "Well, these other things kicked in." But I don't think so. It was *very* specific. But it was out of necessity – do or die, literally. So when you *have* to do it, and you call on the divine power in the universe- and it is *urgent*, *heart-felt* and done with a *pure heart* - almost anything is possible! When you have to do it, then suddenly you find this ability, by turning within to the power of God, to do it.

A number of things like that happened over the course of my medical career and actually continue to happen. A few years ago I was driving outside Helena, Montana. It was before we moved here to Virginia, and I wanted to move my family from North Carolina to someplace, and I wasn't sure where. So I was driving around Montana, exploring the area. All of a sudden I found myself driving along in broad daylight and I saw what I call an image override. It's like you have two screens, like a screen within a screen on TV.

As I was driving down the road, in my mind I saw an intersection in broad daylight with a terrible traffic accident, where I knew there'd be fatalities. It wasn't vague. I said to myself, "This is going to happen- -- I'm going to come across this soon." So, I started looking around the car for what I might have in the way of any medical items - even a straw if I had to make an airway or anything.

About an hour later, I was at an intersection on the east side of Glacier National Park, in the middle of nowhere. It was one of these dangerous highway intersections where it was a stop on a busy highway, and someone just didn't stop. A Suburban went through the intersection and T-boned a Ford Taurus rental vehicle that had a German couple in it. When I got there, the elderly couple in the Taurus were dead at the scene- both of them. And the other people in the Suburban were very seriously injured and pinned under the dashboard. So, I focused on helping the survivors in the Suburban. Finally a rural paramedic crew came along, and we all worked to stabilize them.

Then as I was doing this, I looked up and I saw the mountain that I had seen in my dream a week before I traveled to Montana. One evening I had a dream where there was a mountain that reminded me of the shape of the Mount of Temptation in Israel, outside Jericho. I clearly saw a scintillating light, like a spirit, over this mountain. The dream experience was very spiritual, but there was no other message or image, and I thought, "How strange."

After helping the survivors, I connected with God and said a prayer to send the deceased man and woman to the highest level spiritually and to connect with God. As I did that I looked up and saw a beautiful white light appear above the mountain at the exact moment that I was connecting their souls to God. And then it was clear to me that this was why I went to Montana – to be there at that moment in time, but beyond time, because it was also eternal. I was there for that purpose, and to also help these two other people, who did survive.

We got a chopper in there, but they could only take one patient, and I had to decide which one was going by chopper; the one who had to go by ground could have died. I prayed I made the right choice.

You have to be willing to follow your guidance and the intuition you get- and you have to be willing to act. I've done that throughout my medical career, no matter what the situation. And I recommend that people accept that responsibility. It is accepting your power and then accepting the responsibility that goes with that power.

I've spoken, since then, to a number of people who've been fighter pilots or who have been commercial airline pilots in a critical situation where they've had similar pre-cognitive experiences that helped them avoid disaster. Many people have these experiences in their lives. And the more critical or stressful the work is, the more likely this type of ability might be called upon. But I think it can be brought into almost everything you do.

This can be a way of life, and not something that you do just on the side occasionally. The understanding of spirituality and divinity need not be reserved for an hour or two on Sunday or an occasional event here and there. It can be an inner awakening that is with us all the time – and called up and applied all the time.

There may be a ritual or a service that does something for you, but the reality is that the conscious connection to the unbounded Divine state is something that can be cultured and *lived* and brought into everything that we're doing at all times. That's a discipline and way of living where we are always connected to Spirit and living in that state.

Once the nephew of one of our nurses was brought into the ER because he had been hit head-on by a pick-up truck while riding a motorcycle. It was a stormy, horrible day. He was very critical, and basically had the same injury that killed Princess Di, which was a ruptured thoracic aorta -- often not survivable.

I began working on him with the great nurses we had and somehow I sensed that he had a ruptured aorta. We took a chest X-ray. The X-ray was rather ambiguous, but I felt that it confirmed my sensing this injury.

Well, the general surgeon on call came in and said, "Oh, he wouldn't be alive and look like this if he had a ruptured aorta!" I said, "Man, he's got a ruptured aorta." The surgeon asked, "How do you know that?" I said, "I'm just certain that he does." So, I wrestled with this surgeon, fighting with him not to ignore it or treat him in a way that could suddenly kill him.

I got him to a thoracic surgeon and CT Scan of the chest, and it was then confirmed. But if we had not treated him very carefully in terms of hydration, blood pressure, everything else, we could have blown open the thoracic aorta completely and he would have died.

Over and over and over again, these events happened in the ER. I would love to give a course integrating medical science with intuitive knowledge. Yes, our gadgets and our technologies and sciences are wonderful, but there is also a role for the art of knowing and intuition. It is a balance and we need to regain it in every aspect of our lives.

Someday we will have a civilization where people working in critical areas, no matter how material the science may seem, will also accept that there is a role to play for higher states of consciousness.

When in the thick of something that serious, I find myself operating in a way where I am connecting to multiple levels at once. It's very intellectual, and there's a lot of specific scientific knowledge to call on. There are many physical, material things to do and a lot of management decisions to be made.

Part of it is the compassion, but there is also a fierce, unrelenting determination to help that person. The nurses would tell me that if anything happened to one of their loved ones, they'd want me to be the doc on call. It didn't necessarily come across as compassion, but that's where

I was operating from. Good God, emergency situations are intense – we are not sitting around swinging crystals and counting prayer beads!

If a doctor got in there and didn't know what he was doing, in my quest to protect life I would physically remove him and say, "Out. You're killing this person. I'm taking over." So part of me is very alpha male.

I was awake on these other levels as well. See, I wasn't shut off. If I got an intuitive image or some sort of a clear view of something, even though it was coming out of a non-"scientific" intuition, I would not rule it out. I would be open to the possibility that I needed to pursue it.

It gave me an edge in situations where I really shouldn't have "known" to get the CAT scan for the brain tumor. I should not have known to treat that person like he had a ruptured aorta, because it was not typical or clear enough. I would catch things earlier, or find hidden problems because I was connected to this non-local, expanded and intuitive Spirit that is within all of us and within all things. It is a very interesting dynamic and very nuanced.

Before I started CSETI, I was in my bedroom one afternoon, sitting on the side of my bed. Suddenly, I got what I call an override, an image. Again, it's like a screen within a screen. You don't lose consciousness or your view of the 'real world', but you also see very clearly, in full color, another scene or place.

In an instantaneous packet of information, I saw Air Force One either landing or taking off from Colombia, South America. It was hit by a shoulder-held, surface-to-air missile that was fired by rogue elements within the Colombian defense forces that were on the payroll of the drug cartels. They were going to kill the first President Bush when he was visiting there. I saw the facility, the landing strip. I saw the grass around the field. I saw the woods on the edge of it and precisely where the missile came out. It was catastrophic — the President was killed. "God," I asked, "What in the world am I suppose to do with this information?"

I prayed for guidance. The dream lay heavily on my mind.

Weeks later, Emily and I went to Washington for a medical meeting. That night, I had a dream. In this dream, I was with Barbara Bush, and she was all dressed in black and getting out of a black limousine, and we were at the funeral of the President, George Bush. I thought, "Oh, my God. He really is dead." An enormous heaviness came upon me; "This should have been prevented."

I awoke in a cold sweat and turned to Emily, telling her my nightmare.

Emily is my closest friend, companion and soul-mate, and I tell her everything! I asked, "What am I going to do? Call the White House and Secret Service and tell them about this?"

"Well, why not?" she asked. We continued to discuss it all day and that next evening, we got out the phone book and looked up the number for the White House. Below was a number for the Secret Service. We were amazed it was actually in the phone book!

I called the number and I said, "My name is Dr. Steven Greer, and I'm an emergency doctor." I apologize, "I know this is going to sound completely crazy, but I had a very clear image of an assassination attempt on the President. And it's serious." The first person I talked to said, "Hold on, sir. I'll forward your call." And there was a long silence, I knew they were putting me into some super-computer database. Then, the chief of the protective detail for the President, at the White House with the Secret Service picked up the line.

I started to apologize again and he said, "Sir, we take this sort of information very seriously." I assured him, "You know, I've never done anything like this. I don't cry wolf. I met my wife in a lucid dream; I have this ability to see things in the future that come to pass. This happens spontaneously when it needs to." He was very serious and attentive and said, "Just tell me everything." So I explained, "In my dream, the President is going down to Colombia; either on take-off or landing, Air Force One is hit." I described everything -- that it's an inside job and it is Colombian defense people who betray the security detail and are acting on behalf of these people who run the drug cartels.

The Secret Service agent said, "What do we need to do to avoid this?" I said, "Well, if you can't get the President to cancel the trip, you need to, at the last minute, change where Air Force One lands. You need to be sure that everyone within striking distance of a shoulder-held missile is connected to your people and not Colombian. And you need to sweep the area that far out. He said, "We'll do it."

Weeks later, in "Newsweek" I read an article that said that, in fact, a contract for $5 million had been put out on the life of President Bush and that arms merchants in the Middle East, including Israel, had sold the drug cartels in Colombia shoulder-held missiles! This article, which came out AFTER my vision, stated that advisors to the President were asking him to cancel this trip.

It turns out, of course, he did take the trip and he wasn't killed. I was told years later by a very high intelligence official -- and also a Secret Service Agent -- that what I had said, was taken to heart, and they did make security changes. I doubt President Bush ever knew anything about it.

That's when I learned that, in fact, there were some very smart and good people in the intelligence community and in the Secret Service who understand the power of consciousness. They clearly respect this type of ability.

I tell people: Don't be afraid of your convictions—trust them. Sometimes you have to go out on a limb. I certainly took a flyer when I made a cold call to the White House Secret Service and told them this story. But I also think this episode built credibility in these covert circles, because they knew that what I was saying was accurate information.

After calling the Secret Service, that night I had another very lucid dream. Except this time I was with Barbara Bush and we were all dressed in white, and riding white horses, and everything was light and very happy. It was clear to me then that the President would be safe.

I think many people receive important information in unconventional ways, but it's just not talked about. We need to make it okay to talk about these things. We need to make it okay to bring this sort of discussion in without the fear of ridicule or the opprobrium of our peers. We can do that by the dynamic force of our example- by walking the talk.

10

Tone of Creation

In 1990, after being, in medical training and practice for a while, I had a series of events happen that suddenly brought me back to the experiences of the late 1970s. This is the story of how CSETI got started. On the full moons of January, February, and March of 1990, I had some really extraordinary experiences, that awakened in me the contact of many years before.....

The first one happened when I was in our bedroom of our home in Biltmore Forest. I was walking around in the bedroom getting undressed. All of a sudden, very clearly, a thought was projected or came to me that said, "Pick up that which you have dropped." It wasn't in a pejorative or accusatory way at all. It was a reminder to just pick up that which I had not been doing for a while. It was *time*.

It was very specific - almost like a code phrase that opened up an entire universe of knowledge. It's hard to explain in words. But I knew what it meant. I knew exactly what it meant. So I immediately connected to universal consciousness, to the whole concept of universal peace and to the extraterrestrial presence. And I thought, "Well, I guess its time..." And I started wondering what I was supposed to do with this sort of instruction?

Initially, I simply considered it. I began looking into ET related issues again. Then one day someone told me about a group that was meeting in Asheville that did a lot of meditation and they wanted me to come to the meeting. So, I went, and there was a woman there, who never had met me and knew nothing about my experiences.

After about 30 of us sat down, she looked me right in the eyes and said: "You're connected to extraterrestrial beings from other worlds." And I'm looking for the door! Here I am, an emergency doctor living in this city! She stated, "You need to pick up that again." She used almost the same phrase. That was on the full moon of February of 1990.

On the full moon of March 1990 -- I meditated in my bedroom. That next day I had to get up early to go to the hospital, but I decided to do something I had not done since 1977: The CE-5 protocol. I did the protocol and invited these extra terrestrial beings to visit me. After reminding them who I was, I showed them exactly where I was located in Asheville, NC. I showed them the house and the large front yard and its exact setting. It was a three-story Tudor house, about eight thousand square feet, and set among huge beautiful trees. I showed the ETs all the details and then I went to sleep.

I woke up with a beautiful craft semi-materialized out in the front yard of the house, in the wee hours of the morning, and found myself consciously floated on board. We were all in a quasi-materialized astral state, and as we floated out and went out into space I could look back and see the beautiful earth receding away, floating in infinity.

Then we went by what I am assuming was the moon. There wasn't a sign there that said, "This is the moon, Welcome to the moon, population 39," but it looked like the moon to me. And there were enormous ships that were hovering over the moon. They were oval with struts that came up from a large craft with two other similar shaped oval discs above and towards the rear of the main ship. They were just floating silently along where the terminator section of the moon is, between the light and dark side of the moon. An incredible amount of energy, like magenta colored plasma discharges, were going between the surface of the moon and the underbelly of these ships. They were enormous and as we passed by I was told by these ETs that these craft were there making preparations for the coming decade or so. This happened in 1990, so it is clear that they were making preparations for major events for around the time we are in right now.

We went further out into our solar system, and the experience transformed so that the material aspect of the ship disappeared - it was just like in 1973 when I was 18 when everything became translucent, and I was out in space without a craft around me- and yet somehow it was still there. It was very multi-dimensional, but at this point transcendence beyond linear time/space became the dominant perception. It's like the most perfect fiber optics: Imagine the walls of your room completely disappearing, even though they are there and you are still protected in a controlled environment. At that point, I went into a state of meditative awareness and transcended into unity consciousness; I was infinitely awake and the entire cosmos was awake and perfectly synchronized as one.

As I entered that state I began to gaze around the solar system and saw that every planet was surrounded by space which was filled with infinite energy and light. The empty space was actually teeming with light and energy. I could directly see the baseline energy of the universe - the field of energy and light from which the entire material cosmos emerges from Infinite Mind – from the Godhead. Instead of the darkness between stars and planets, there was an enormous light and energy with solid planets moving as islands of energy in this field of energy and power. Then, As I gazed at each planet, I directly perceived that each one was awake and conscious and had a *specific tone* and *personality*. Each created sphere had a very specific tone -and if I were more musically inclined I could recreate it. They were all pure tones and very specific. As I looked at Mercury I saw he was rather androgynous but more male; Venus was definitely female. Jupiter was just fantastic. And Mars is definitely male. The Earth: Definitely female.

As I gazed at Earth, there was a very beautiful tone emanating from her. Remember, each planet had its own tone of creation -- no two tones were alike. Some much higher and some very deep and baritone, but all were beautiful tones. As I gazed at the Earth, I connected with her as an awake conscious being and she communicated to me this infinite and crushing -- I use the word crushing because I couldn't tell the story for years without weeping – love. And there was a sense of melancholy also, for what was happening to her and the damage being done to her and the suffering of humanity upon her. It was profound and beyond words. It was one of the most emotional and moving experiences of my life.

Earth was very clearly saying how great her love was for her children and that her purpose was to be the womb for creating life that could become enlightened and grow towards Divinity. But she was also suffering tremendously from the recklessness and selfishness of her children. So there was this enormous melancholy - a sadness beyond my ability to convey in words. And yet, towards the end of our communion, she made it very clear that this suffering would not continue for much longer. Earth made it clear that this burden would be lifted *suddenly*.

By now, I was in such a state of deep love and emotion that my heart chakra opened fully and an enormous love and celestial perception dawned. This celestial perception of the cosmos caused me to see the light of creation and all things suffused in love – the pure love of God. And as I went into that state, I heard all the distant worlds, every star and planet and the entire creation, singing as one - like a trillion tones blended into the one pure tone of the creation.

At that point, I transcended into a state that I cannot describe. It was a state where I heard a singular tone that was the perfectly harmonized tone of the entire creation humming, singing. It was the primal tone emanating from the earliest manifestation of relativity out of the infinite mind of God that maintains creation. It was the most beautiful experience of my life.

As I transcended into that - I became one with that state and stayed within that state of Being. I don't know how long I was in that condition. But know that this is what is all around us. The music of the spheres is a reality - and within the tone, one can transcend to the infinity of the cosmic Being

This primal tone wasn't "Om", per se. I believe that is a human attempt to *reproduce* this ancient experience that is the perception of the sound of the primal thought emanating from the Infinite Being that creates the entire creation. It was on the level of the near death experience in terms of the transformative effect it had on me. After I stayed in that state of complete unity consciousness and God consciousness, my individuality dissolved. All that existed was infinite Being - and even the creation and Creator were one, the same, infinite awake-ness. I stayed in that state with it vibrating through me - just permeating me – for what seemed like eternity. Because I was beyond space and time, it is meaningless to talk about it in terms of how "long" it was. But after, I found myself relatively conscious again. Suddenly I was back in my bedroom and became aware of the glowing outside the window where the craft was. I layed there peacefully and went to sleep.

The next day I learned that one of our children had a lucid dream with little ET children, who were teaching her games ET children played on their planet! This daughter did not understand the games, so she began to give the ET children rides on the back of her banana seat bicycle, up and down our driveway! This child had never heard me talk about ETs or any of these experiences! It confirmed what happened to me as real. And it became very clear to me that I was supposed to pick this whole issue up again just as I had heard two months earlier in January, 1990.

At that point, I began wondering: What am I going to do? How am I going to do this?

I decided that I would just start looking into the subject again and find out what was out there. I found out there was an organization that was having a meeting in Florida where there had been many UFO sightings, the so-called Gulf Breeze Sightings near Pensacola. This meeting was in July of 1990. I had the concept of what I wanted to do and that was create in the world interplanetary ambassadors that would be doing what is now called the CE-5 Initiative, the Close Encounters of the Fifth Kind Initiative. I went to this meeting, and started sharing these ideas and concepts, and the right people suddenly just surfaced and came into my life mysteriously who said, No, don't do it through any existing entity, create your own reality.

Then a man who had been involved in national security issues connected to this subject for years and who was a lawyer came up to me and told me what I needed to do: "Form an organization; hermetically seal it so it can't be penetrated -- in other words, no open board and no open membership; avoid, if you can, being obscure; and as quickly as you can, given what you are going to be doing and what your role is – get out in the public. You must let millions of people know what you are doing - otherwise you won't survive. If you are obscure, you are dead." He gave me the best advice ever.

I knew that much of the information at this conference was false, that it was disinformation. I immediately recognized that.

Then, in August of 1990, I was in the upstairs den adjacent to the master bedroom, sleeping because Emily was up and down with the youngest baby and I had a 24 -hour shift at the ER the next day. Around 2 am I awakened – and was calmly super-aware, very awake. In the corner of the room was a cluster of scintillating lights that was hovering near the ceiling. I acknowledged it, and immediately sat up and picked up the pad of paper beside the bed. I then wrote out the entire plan and concept for everything we have been doing for the last 15 years. This included the CE-5 Initiative protocols, the plans, everything. It was as if this scintillating light had awakened all the organization and plan within me and they were just pouring through me. This lasted for an hour or so, and then I went back to sleep and got up around 6 am to work in the emergency department for 24 hours. It was then that I formed CSETI, The Center for the Study of Extraterrestrial Intelligence, came up with that name, the concepts, the CE-5 Initiative, the need for disclosure, and the entire interplanetary ambassador program. All of it just unfolded in that one night. So things can come in packets of knowledge, all at once, mysteriously.

Of course, I didn't know anybody and nobody knew me. I mean, I was just a country doctor in North Carolina with four kids and a golden retriever and a couple of cars in Biltmore Forest, just living my life. But these experiences made it clear: I must start working on this. But how do you take that vision and actualize it? We had to bootstrap the whole thing.

Over the next couple of years, when I would articulate something that I needed to do or somebody I needed to meet, through mysterious means that person would be introduced to me, within hours, frequently. I will never forget the time that I said, "We really need to get this information to the Secretary General of the United Nations…" and within about an hour or two someone called who I had never heard of and said, "You don't know who I am but I am very good friends with Boutros-Ghali and Mrs. Boutros-Ghali, Leah Ghali, wants to have you come to a meeting…". That is how all this happened, in a very inscrutable way. It was all guided, supported - from behind the veil, a hand was moving.

Our ability to get the truth to the right people all came about because the doors opened mysteriously. And this is how I knew that what I was doing was the right action.

By 1991, I had decided that I needed to begin to train people in the experience of the Close Encounters of the Fifth Kind Initiative, the CE-5 Initiative. A CE-5 is when humans deliberately welcome and make contact with extraterrestrial people by using a set of protocols to vector them into an area to interact with them. That was the first project of CSETI.

Within a very short time I also wrote all the assessments of the situation. Those white papers were created very quickly. They immediately got picked up by people at the CIA and distributed throughout the aerospace industry. I had a top covert aerospace person call and say, "This is the most accurate assessment of the UFO and extraterrestrial issue we have ever read." It is the original paper and is in the first book, "Extraterrestrial Contact: The Evidence and Implications".

This aerospace scientist then asked me, "How do you know these things?" I said, well, that is a long discussion- so we had a long discussion!

In the winter of 1991, we decided to go to Belgium, where we had heard there were an enormous number of encounters with massive triangular shaped craft. As you know, in '89, '90, '91, outside of Brussels, thousands of people had seen huge triangular UFOs and they had been filmed, photographed and tracked on radar.

Well, at that time I really didn't train people for this. In my innocence, I thought that everyone could just sit down the first time and enter cosmic consciousness, bilocate into space, vector them in and be ready when a ship showed up! I soon learned that much preparation was needed!

In the early days that is what we did. We just took a group of people over and we did it. The 1st group was me, my wife Emily and two others. We went out and we had the most extraordinary experiences. You can read about them in, "Extraterrestrial Contact: The Evidence and Implications". We ended up meeting some of the top people in Belgium who were working with the Belgium Air Force on this. We then went out to the areas where these huge craft had been seen.

One area was near Eupan, which is in eastern Belgium, near the German border. While at a farm, suddenly a string of lights appeared. It was in an area where one of the gendarme had seen a massive craft. But all we saw were what looked like a string of lights in a field. Of course, everyone said, "Those are just some lights on the farm." I knew they didn't look like normal lights. We sat there and we watched an object sitting in the field and suddenly the lights vanished! The next day we went back and discovered that there were no street lights, no wires, nothing in that whole area where the lights had been! It had been a craft sitting there.

On another night we were near Henri-Chappelle, at the military cemetery on a ridge. It was a terrible night: raining; sleet mixed with rain. We stayed in the cars and did the CE-5 meditation and vectoring. All of a sudden we heard a deep rumbling vibration. Imagine something that felt like the size of the Empire State Building, rumbling, humming like a transformer. It had a deep vibration. And suddenly, as we looked up in the cloud -- the cloud cover was only a couple of hundred feet above the ridge or less- something that looked like a full moon dipped down, and moved underneath the clouds. Emily saw it first, actually. It was a corner of one of these massive ships. Then it slipped back up. It just stayed there right on top of us, resonating, humming with a deep vibration. As this was occurring, I saw in my minds'-eye the occupants of the ship. The energy vibration that we were feeling was because they were completely checking us out and connecting with the vehicle and with us as a group and individually. It was very close; close enough that you could feel it.

In the course of this trip to Belgium, I learned that many of the people that had reported seeing these objects had had their stories sanitized by the mainstream UFO research groups. For example, I went back and met with some of the police who were in a small village where a massive ship the size of three football fields was hovering over a steeple. Part of their story was 'sanitized out' of the report so that they, "wouldn't lose credibility" The way it disappeared was not that it glided off and then zoomed out into space like a movie from Hollywood. This huge triangular ship, 800 feet long on each side, hovering above the town square, suddenly collapsed into a pulsing red ball of light the size of a basketball. It moved a little bit and then vanished straight out into space, in the blink of an eye!

Now, the reason I relate this is that many people will see an orb and they will think it is just an orb. But it could be an enormous half mile long craft that has changed energy forms, some would say dimensional shift, and appear as a ball of light. So having that experience taught me two things.

First of all, the extraterrestrial capabilities are extremely advanced. But also, what is in the UFO literature has been largely sanitized so the most salient aspects of the technology have been taken out- sometimes so that people won't be discredited because it *is* so unusual. But then, if it *isn't* very unusual, most of the time this means it is an "alien-reproduction vehicle," that is being manufactured by Lockheed and Northrup!

People often ask, "How do you know the difference between a man-made UFO and an extraterrestrial vehicle?" It's very obvious if you are ever close up to one, because the entire *quality* of it is different. The ones that are extraterrestrial are extremely advanced, in the sense that they are "awake." The actual craft itself has artificial intelligence and is conscious. The beings on board are connected into it and can connect to you consciously. And the kind of light it gives off is like nothing you have ever seen on Earth: It is extraordinary. It looks like it is not of this world- and has an energy and intelligence associated with it that is very advanced.

By 1991, I began to branch out and I appeared at a few conferences to present these concepts. My point was: These ET craft are here and they are under intelligent control, and these life forms are able to interact with us. If they know that there is a group of humans willing to do this for peaceful purposes rather than for military purposes, they will respond, if possible.

One of my great concerns is that the relationship between humans and extraterrestrials has been hijacked by a military-oriented group that are mismanaging the relationship. They are not conscious about what they were dealing with. There is nothing written anywhere that says we have to cede that relationship to a group of people who have arrogated it to themselves- and who are ruining the embryonic relationship between ET worlds and humanity. The relationship between humans and extraterrestrials, has been totally neglected because there is no formal program that is open and honest dealing with it in the State Department or the United Nations or from any other peaceful group. So, it became clear to me that we should reach out to the ETs; if we don't, a vacuum will continue to exist into which others intent on doing harm will step.

Those approaching this issue from a purely military perspective or technological perspective can only do harm. To correct this dangerous situation is the purpose of CSETI and the CE-5 Initiative. We must create a peaceful rapprochement between humans and extraterrestrial beings and create a relationship that would redound to the benefit of all concerned - rather than to only a clandestine operation that would benefit a handful of people trying to commandeer the technology for their own selfish purposes.

By 1992, we had found enough people interested in this that we started doing some larger expeditions. In March of 1992, I went to the Pensacola area and taught about 50 participants this protocol.

The very first night I decided we should go to the state park beach. We were out there just a few minutes, and at around 8:30 p.m. an ET craft appeared. Initially there were two ET craft, and then there were four of these UFOs, shaped like globes with an amber-red light in the center of the bottom of the craft. They appeared to simply manifest in the sky near us. We started making a big triangular shape in the sky with very powerful search lights. Suddenly, three of these UFOs made a perfect equilateral triangle in response.

Then I would signal to them twice and they would signal back twice. I would signal once and they would signal once. But what was actually going on was that there was a conscious ET presence that was on the site. There was a non-visible and electronically projected consciousness of the occupants of these vehicles on site. A few other people sensed this and jumped in their vehicles and roared away! They were thinking, "Oh my God this is actually for real!" There were four separate cameras that filmed this, and there were also two former Air Force pilots who saw it, one of whom was connected to a UFO organization as the Eastern Director of Research. That organization would not let him write up this event and put it in their journal. It was sanitized out. This mass witnessed Close Encounter of the Fifth Kind was filmed and witnessed by everyone. The next day it was reported in the local paper with photographs of the UFOs. But then the UFO subculture itself (which traditionally has been controlled by the counter-intelligence 'spook department') sanitized all of the reporting out of the literature. This was a real eye opener to me about what was going on in the so-called UFO community....

But we also learned that humans could come together, decide to contact ETs, and have an event take place - all in the framework of peace and cosmic awareness.

11

The Offer

Once word of this CE-5 in Florida got out, it was a feeding frenzy. A few weeks later I was invited to a conference, in Atlanta, that had a whole group of spooks (covert intelligence operatives) present. They had heard what had happened and wanted to learn the details. It was a quasi-public conference that was run by a group as a front operation to gather intelligence for the covert programs dealing with UFOs. (This is not unusual.)

I arrived in time for the main banquet of the conference on Saturday night. They had put a place for me between the former head of Army Intelligence, General T.E. and Dr. Death, Col.MK who was head of the psychotronic and so-called non-lethal weapons systems programs. There were also NSA people and other intelligence operatives there. I knew something was fishy - there was also present a slippery shadowy-ops psychiatrist who was a side-kick of the general. And I'm thinking, "Oh, brother, here we go into the snake pit." But I had nothing to hide. I am not doing this as a secret operation. I was certainly savvy enough to know who they were and why they were there and why I was there. At this point it was very clear. There were also present some people who were friends of the British royal family.

The banquet speaker was General T.E., and after his talk he asked me, "Could we get together with you for a little while after this?" I said, "Sure." So they took me to a hotel room and it turned out it was packed with people who were connected to covert programs and black operations, corporate, military and intelligence- this hybrid MJ12 successor entity. And quickly this little gathering became a barrage of questions - all directed at me. Again, I had nothing to hide, so I openly shared. It takes two to play a spook game and I felt I didn't need to. But they began to ask all kinds of questions.

At one point I remember someone saying "Just who the hell do you think you are, going out there, basically bypassing the national military command to do this?" They knew that we had discovered the Rosetta stone of extraterrestrial contact. So I said, "I am a denizen of Earth and I have every right to be doing this. Besides, my mother's family were some of the original founders of the United States- they fought in the

American Revolution and were prisoners of war with the British. Beyond that my father was half Native American, his ancestors were here waiting for you Europeans to get here. So we have every right to be doing this!"

I finally said, "Look, I know who you folks are but I have had up close and personal contact with these extraterrestrial beings and their craft and their technology. You can't deceive me about what is going on. You can't fool me, number one. Number two, I am not rich but I am wealthy enough as a physician that I don't need your damn money, so you can't bribe me. And number three, when I was 17, by any medical definition, I was dead. I had an enlightenment experience, so I am not afraid of death, and you can't frighten me away! I am going to do this one way or the other. There is nothing you can do about it." And I remember the look from the General. It was: "We know exactly who this son of a bitch is." So here began the process of a covert group that was desperate to infiltrate us. What had been warned in 1990 had begun in earnest.

The next month, in May of 1992, I had agreed to help convene a conference at the St. Malos retreat outside of Rocky Mountain National Park with Astronaut Brian O'Leary and Maury Albertson (who was one of the co-founders of the Peace Corps) and the Institute for New Science. It was a private retreat and we invited everyone involved in the civilian UFO world. There were a number of other people who, of course, turned out to be intelligence operatives including General T.E. and his friend the psychiatrist.

I wanted to create a collegial environment where there could be a sharing of information and perspective. In reality I found out that the whole UFO civilian world was rife with paid disinformation hacks and warring factions that within two nanoseconds of arriving at this facility had pulled out their knives and hatchets and were sinking them into everyone's back -- including my own. That was when I learned what a snake pit the civilian UFO world really is.

During the course of this retreat, the General and the psychiatrist were trying to court me into joining their group. The General said, "You know, we have an organization that deals with this that is very private..." -a loaded word meaning super-covert. I knew what he was saying. Then he said, "If you would just merge your operation with ours we will give you as much money and as much power and access to technologies as you could ever dream." And I said "Thanks, but no thanks. I don't need it. I thought I made that clear when we met in Atlanta last month." But he persisted in attempting to convince me- because they knew the kind of threat we could pose to their covert monopoly on the issue. They said as much.

A good friend of the NSA guy that was there and another CIA guy came to me and said, "You know, they are very jealous of what you are doing because they are in a black box and can only do certain things for certain purposes. You are a free agent and you can do more than they can!" I knew this. I explained, "We may not have temporal power but we are free – and have other powers that are God-given."

Eventually, the General went to Emily, my wife, without me present. He told her about this group- but he didn't call it MJ12. He said there was a board for this group. He said that this board had a certain number of seats on it. Interestingly, he said that the number was nine. Of course, he had done deep research into us and knew we were Baha'is and our holy number is nine. So, he said there are nine board members, each with his own shield- a certain crest- that would be given to me if I would simply take my organization and merge it with his. And Emily, being very sweet, said, "Oh, he seems so nice and he said all these wonderful flattering things about you!" I said, "Yes, dear, but can't you see what they are trying to do? Finally I went to them and I said, "Look, let me be clear. I am fiercely independent and I am going to keep this a private, clean, operation with its intended purposes. There is no amount of cajoling and no amount of money or offers of power that will ever change that!"

By the way, General T.E. has been involved with these covert projects since he was a very young man. I confirmed this through independent sources. He had been head of army intelligence before he "retired". But he was just telling people that he was retired. They never retire- until they end up in a coffin.

I met a military pilot who, in the 1960's, was in a special operation to pursue UFOs and film them. He told me that once a crew had such an encounter, they were split up and sent to various new posts- but that ALL the information went directly to a guy he was convinced I had never heard of: General T.E.! When he told me this story I laughed and said "I know him well!"

After rejecting these advances by the general, within thirty days the entire internet had websites set up and messages being sent out to the public attacking me. They unleashed all the dogs within the UFO civilian community, within the press, everywhere. I was called everything from a cultist to a demonic communer with extraterrestrial sinister forces to a fraud. Then they released the lie that I wasn't a medical doctor. Here I am at the hospital and they have put out there that I am not even licensed to practice medicine! I have to then release to the public my medical license and degree to show that I am actually a medical doctor! The psychological warfare and harassment was intense- and continues to this day. For 14 years it has been a relentless string of attacks, character assassination, defamation of character, and every kind of dirty trick.

General T.E., told me a number of things. For example, he said there were extraterrestrial craft and facilities underneath the surface of Mars and that covert projects had imaged them. He also privately told me about all kinds of assets that covert programs had that were advanced technologies - up to the level of what the ETs had. I was able to gather quite a bit of good information through the courtship that was being attempted.

I learned that this particular 'cell' was interfacing with the civilian UFO world from the covert world -- they are an interface group and they have penetrated many civilian UFO projects. I knew then why that lawyer had told me in 1990 to be very independent, careful and very public. I had to be a lion at the gate to protect what we were doing from infiltration and from attempts to destroy it. There would be offers of enormous amounts of power and money, threats and attacks. I would have to be willing to be the kind of warrior that I had, in a sense, been trained to be through my childhood and early adult experiences.

12

Gobsmacked!

In our research, we have observed that there is a pattern of extraterrestrial vehicles being seen over geo-physically unstable areas and volcanic areas such as in Costa Rica, Mexico, the ring of fire around the Pacific rim; and around facilities where there are many nuclear bases, weapons or power plants.

Extraterrestrial civilizations observing Earth know that we are a lot more fragile than most of us realize. We're the proverbial frog in the water that is being boiled slowly and we really don't quite know it until we are cooked.

ETs have been monitoring events very carefully, and there is a pattern of activities that suggest to me that they have concern about what we're doing to the environment, and the instability that we may be creating. They are also concerned with nuclear material that could do a tremendous amount of damage to earth for thousands of years.

In '92, after we went through an initial period of experimenting and training groups, we learned that there were these strange things going on in England called "crop circles". There were reports from people like Colin Andrews- whom I got to know very well and became close friends with- that there were unusual aerial phenomenon and unusual craft being seen in fields, and videotaped. There are daytime videotapes of small, foot diameter disk-shaped objects moving through the fields, both before there would be one of these crop circles and also after.

In the summer of '92 we took a team of people over to England and decided to do the CE5 initiative there. By then, a lot of media had found out what happened when we were in Belgium and Gulf Breeze. By the time we got to England, it was a media feeding frenzy.

This caused some difficulty because a lot of the places where we wanted to set up our contact effort were being totally overrun with curiosity seekers and the media.

I remember one time dashing through the countryside, trying to shake the cameras and media. It was like when Princess Di was being chased through the tunnel- we were speeding along trying to shake off a German TV crew who was following us so they could stake us out and see where we were going to be that evening.

In July of 1992 we went to a farm in Alton Barns, which was the epi-center of the most interesting crop circles. This was a large farm- over 1,000 acres, and we were given permission to use the property for this purpose.

We set up a number of experiments over the course of the week or ten days that we were there.

One of these was to go up on Woodborough Hill and as a group visu-alize a specific shape of a crop circle. We began the meditative process: first expanding awareness, then connecting with the extraterrestrial peo-ple, and then asking them to create the specific shape that we were visu-alizing.

We didn't decide what that shape would be until the night we actual-ly sat together on Woodborough Hill.

We decided that it should be what is now known as the CSETI trian-gle – an equilateral triangle with a circle at each apex.

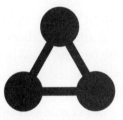

As a group, we conveyed this precise shape into unbounded, univer-sal Mind, and to the ETs. The next morning, the exact shape we were sending out was discovered in a field not far from where we were work-ing!

No one except this relatively small group of people doing this knew the design. In fact, we didn't even know that this crop circle had appeared until a couple of days later,when we came across Ralph Noyes who said, "Oh, we just learned from a farmer that the most perfect crop circle of the season has been found. It has the most anomalous bending of the crop and unusual phenomenon in it. And has appeared on this farmer's land!" The farmer had been out working in the field until very, very late the night before and went out very early, because it was a dry period, which is rare in that part of England. Nobody had been in the field, and it was hard to get to, being right at the base of Oliver's Castle (a steep cliff area surrounding the field). So I asked, "What shape is it?"

And Mr. Noyes said, "Well, I've drawn it in my book."

We bent down and looked at what Ralph Noyes had drawn: It was exactly the shape that we had projected the night of the experiment!

Immediately, Shari Adamiak, my main assistant, and a couple of other CSETI team members dashed to this farm. We went up to Oliver's Castle, and looked down on the field, and it was as if the shape had been lifted from our minds and placed exactly in the field. We were stunned.

Later we learned that some of the tests that were done on the actual crop and soil indicated that there were electromagnetic anomalies and cell wall changes in the plants. The tests indicated that this was one of the most important crop circles of that season, from a scientific point of view.

Interestingly, a group of people who were there studying crop circles and had been funded by W. B., the wealthy businessman (and some other people connected to covert programs) sanitized their report of this particular crop circle – and especially of how it was conceived. Here was the same pattern: The so-called civilian UFO 'community', riddled with spooks, had sanitized the Gulf Breeze event in March of that year now had sanitized this one.

This was another indication of how tightly controlled the so-called "civilian UFO community" is and how thoroughly it is infiltrated.

One evening, while at the base of Woodborough Hill, we were doing our CE5 protocol and inviting the extraterrestrial vehicles to come into that area. Suddenly, in the clouds above us, there appeared counterclockwise spinning lights -- not coming from the earth shining up like a searchlight, but from *above* the clouds shining *down*. There were a whole series of circular lights that were going around counter-clockwise shining down from above into the clouds.

Shortly after that, it suddenly started raining, very hard - but it was raining only on this very small area where we were doing our contact protocols.

It seemed as if the ETs had created an artificial weather event to allow a major contact to occur - but in the privacy of a rainy,foggy night. Eventually, it was raining so hard that almost everyone left -- Colin Andrews, who had been in another area of the farm and a whole group of other people, left.

Four of us moved to a narrow concrete road that was on the farm, just wide enough for one vehicle behind another. There was a little pull-out on it where we decided to stay.

Through my intuition, I knew that the ET craft would come. I was clearly told, "We will be there later, later."

So I said, "Let's just stay here in our cars, and wait." It was after midnight. We decided that we would stay in two separate vehicles, and do the protocols from there.

Then all of a sudden, I heard this banging on the window of the driver's side of the car, and it was Chris Mansell (the Englishman that was with us) from the car behind us. As I put the window down, he said, "There is a spacecraft rotating in the field and lit up like a bloody Christmas tree !"

And I said, "Yeah, yeah and I'm Santa Claus!"

I felt sure he was joking. He said, "No, look," and as I looked out the window I saw a ship, about 100 feet in diameter, disc-shaped with a coned top with lights. Around the edge of the disc were beautiful multi-colored lights-red, green, blue, yellow - that were going around counter-clockwise. The craft was spinning counter-clockwise, but the lights were going that direction as well as clockwise, fusing and blending into each other, in a beautiful, very unusual pattern.

These lights were like something not of this world. The intensity and the quality of the light was unlike anything anyone had ever seen.

And it was *so close*. Initially it was a little higher above the field, but it came to within 10 feet above the ground - and in the same field where we were -- just a few hundred feet away.

We got out of the vehicle and went into contact and signaling mode. But the woman I was with was completely terrified. She came completely unhinged. I learned that, unfortunately, people really do need to be prepared for this kind of event!.

Her anxiety was in part because we were close enough to this huge craft that the compass we had was rotating with the craft counter-clockwise. The magnetic field was actually moving off magnetic north and moving around counter-clockwise!

The electromagnetic effects of this ET craft also caused our hair to be slightly electrified and standing on end. You could sense an unusual silence in the field and the presence of the consciousness of these beings who were on the craft. It was just astonishing!

At this point I said, "Well, let's signal to the craft with the searchlights." And as I signaled to the ship, it moved closer to us and signaled back. With that, this woman became quite hysterical, and screamed "Oh, my God, don't do that!"

"But this is why we're here." I exclaimed.

"Well, I didn't think they would actually come." She said.

"Well, then why did you come. Do you think this is a joke?" I asked.

In her mind, she thought that maybe we would just have a sighting from far away. But it was a really close encounter with this craft, and she knew that they were there because we contacted them and she knew they were signaling with us.

Chris Mansell and the Dutch woman who was with us were very calm and relaxed; Excited -- but not scared. But this one person was scared. And the moment that her fear really broke through, the craft stopped coming towards us and then backed slowly away.

This was an act of compassion. Even though there was no threat at all from this craft, the ETs knew someone was afraid, and they gently and slowly backed off. Then, the ship began to rise slowly and went up into the mist and off into the clouds.

As it did so, we could see that it was actually staying up in the clouds above us. We could still see its lights, but it appeared as a softly glowing amber object, floating silently. Amazingly, the compass we had continued to rotate counter-clockwise, the same way the craft rotated, until the needle on the compass made a complete 360 degree revolution all the way back to north.

It was a beautifully choreographed encounter. At the end of that hour, the sky opened up and this object appeared again, but this time higher. As I signaled to it, it signaled back to us and then it vanished. And that is how that CE5 ended.

As the event was unfolding, the rain had stopped to just a mist, and the whole area was enshrouded in clouds and fog.

Colin Andrews told us, as soon as he got on to the road and left, it was dry. I believe the lights seen earlier that were spinning around in the clouds above the farm were setting up a weather change that allowed this event to take place in privacy.

It turns out that the people who were attempting to spy on our expedition and disrupt the effort to make contact all left because they were discouraged by this 'terrible English weather'.

I realized from this experience that I really needed to better prepare people for contact. Participants would need to learn how to be more centered in consciousness so that they wouldn't be afraid, because it *is* an unusual experience, and there are unusual physiological and electromagnetic effects when you are fairly close to these objects. Being centered in calm, deep awareness is essential.

The next day it turned out there were a few people who were on some of the surrounding hills who saw much of this encounter, so we had corroboration - and word got out. The next day, it was a feeding frenzy of media and public interest.

Because of this, we did a briefing about this near-landing on the farm in Alton Barns.

When Chris Mansell got up, he said, "There was a bloody spaceship in the field and I was gobsmacked!" It was the first time I had ever heard that word, and it was just perfect!

By 1993, we had decided to expand these efforts and have a more seasoned group of people called the Rapid Mobilization Investigation Team -- the RMIT.

中

Truth Stranger than Fiction

In the Volcanic area in Mexico, near Popocatepetl, a whole series of ET events were taking place and were on the Mexican national news. These craft had been videotaped, photographed, and witnessed by thousands of people.

In the winter of 1993, we organized a team of ambassadors to go on an expedition to Mexico to welcome these extraterrestrial people and to investigate why they were there. Before we went, I had a lucid dream where we were in a specific place with a mountain, some forests and an ET event taking place. It turned out this dream occurred exactly seven nights -- adjusted for time zones -- to the hour of when a major encounter occurred with our team in Mexico.

We found that on many of these expeditions, one or more of the people on the team have some type of pre-cognitive dream or experience prior to the event happening in the 'physical here and now'.

The details in these dreams are very specific— the time of night, the look of the area, everything about it. This was also happening to other groups who were beginning to experiment with the CE-5 protocols.

But first, after landing in Mexico City, we were robbed by Federales at gunpoint. Our passports were confiscated. They asked for bribes of enormous sums of money for us to get them back.

We refer to this type of treatment as "the shakedown factor." After major challenges, we eventually arrived at a rural area near the volcano. The very first night, we were on the side of the volcano that was closest to Mexico City. Under the stars, we began to meditate and vector the ET craft into that spot. It got so cold at that altitude that frost actually formed on us.

Suddenly, a point of light appeared out of space that illuminated us, and a beam of light descended and flashed the entire group -- submerging us in a bright flash of blue-white light as if someone flashed a very bright flashbulb. We got the sense that the ETs were checking us out- a type of scanning procedure. At the same time I felt that there was a message in that event - that they were welcoming us. We had been in the country six hours when this happened.

The next day we went around the back side of Popo and arrived in the little town of Atlixco, where 90 percent of the people had seen these objects around the volcano.

We sensed that the ETs were there because the ring of fire was going to become more and more unstable, and this was the fourth largest volcano in the world, looming outside one of world's most populous cities.

We sensed that the extraterrestrial vehicles were there to monitor the situation and take actions to help stabilize the earth.

We found a perfect site near the little Indian village called Atlimayaya. Atlimayaya is at the end of the road past Atlixco and Metepec. The glow from the city of Puebla can be seen from the high plane, at the base of the volcano outside Atlimayaya.

Atlimayaya literally is where the road ends. From there, the native people go on trails out into the jungle and the forest at the base of the volcano.

Off the road to Atlimayaya we set up our operation with five CSETI members present. Once I saw the setting, I knew that it was *exactly* what I had seen in the lucid dream seven days before.

And so I said, "This is exactly where we should be!"

The moon was up and about two-thirds full. After a period of doing the CE-5 contact protocols I grew very tired and laid down.

I settled into a deep meditative state, very relaxed. Then suddenly, I got a clear message that said, "Sit up and look to the right!"

So I sat up and looked to the right; coming towards us from the volcano, was an enormous triangular craft .

We all stood and connected to the ship. I could see in my minds eye the person in charge of the craft and the other beings on the craft-they were all extremely luminous and white.

These ETs were very directly connected to us, by way of a device that was on board the craft. They were absolutely locked-on to our consciousness, using a mind-technology interface device.

As always, we were using thought and consciousness as a vectoring tool.

To confirm that they were seeing us, we signaled with very bright lights, and then this huge craft signaled back - and turned directly towards us.

Then it made an almost perfect circle around us, hovering *very* low, just a few hundred feet above us. It was the size of about three football fields on *each side* of the triangle with a light at each corner. As it signaled to us, the entire leading edge of it would light up.

All of us could sense the extraterrestrial beings, and three of the five of us saw the same beings and received the same message about why they were here, the volcano erupting and what would happen in the future.

The craft then went off towards the direction of Puebla. As it left, we were saying good-bye, and I signaled toward the receding edge one more time. Suddenly, the other edge of it that was leaving the area signaled back and said good-bye.

It then descended lower than our altitude and disappeared somewhere into a valley.

Later that same night, we were sitting in a meditative state, connecting with cosmic beings, at the base of the beautiful snow capped volcano. As we looked up, we saw that a very unusual oval- shaped ring of clouds had formed to the left of the volcano, that looked exactly like a humanoid face !

And the two brightest stars in the sky, were exactly centered where there should be eyes.

This cosmic face was looking at us from beside the volcano. And there was no question in any of our minds that this was a very unusual signal from these beings saying that they were still with us.

On the day of this event, we had been exploring the area on foot. We went on a hike deep into the jungle and found an ancient pyramid covered with plants that to my knowledge was not on any map.

While we were there, we had a series of very unusual mystical experiences with nature and the volcano. We met some native people who related stories to us about what they had experienced with the extraterrestrial beings in the area. The messages and images they received were nearly identical to ours.

As we left the jungle we looked up and saw in the sky a formation of clouds that made the exact shape of an eagle. And the beak of the eagle was pointing to precisely where our field -work site would be that night. We knew everything was being orchestrated by a higher intelligence, the one Mind of the cosmos through which we are all connected.

Over the course of those five days, we had multiple sightings of these ET craft, including smaller disc-shaped ones that would come straight up out of the volcano, circle the top of it and then fly off into space.

All of these accounts have been written up in more detail in my first book.

The key to everything that happened is universal awareness and an intent that is good and peaceful.

By 1993, it was clear to me that this effort to create contact between humans and extraterrestrial people was attainable. It was no longer a theoretical question. By then, there had been hundreds of people in the United States, Europe, England and Mexico that had been with us on expeditions where contact had been made. Many of these events had been filmed, and all of them had been mass witnessed.

So now what? If we have the body politic and the masses of the people of the earth being lied to about this, how far can we take this? We needed some way of educating larger numbers of people in the world. I knew we must bring out the truth. We needed to provide the evidence and this peaceful perspective to our political leaders, our governmental leaders and the scientific community- and most importantly those running these covert programs.

Word of our work was out and I developed a network of military, political and scientific contacts between 1990 and '93.

We also learned that there were extremely powerful weapon systems being used to target extraterrestrial spacecraft and destroy them. We learned that rogue, covert projects were running these operations and that this was one of the greatest threats to world peace- ever. But the entire matter was being completely ignored by the media, by the mainstream military community and by the mainstream political community -- never mind the man on the street.

So at this point I felt it was important to bring together people to try to disclose the evidence and the facts -and explain to the public and our leaders what the meaning is behind the ET presence.

I began to articulate this concept of pulling together people to disclose the truth so that it would not be just an ad hoc group of part-time people making contact, but society at large would begin to acknowledge that we are not alone. It was time for the community of civilized people to take responsibility for the relationship between humans and extraterrestrial people in an enlightened and peaceful way.

If we didn't do it, no matter how much contact our little group might have, it couldn't begin to correct the problems of a multi-hundred billion dollar per year Shadow Government that had enormous technological prowess, reconnaissance abilities and weapons that were being deployed all over the world - and in space. We knew these weapons were attacking ET vehicles and the people on them, and we had multiple independent corroborating military witnesses to this.

In the summer of 1993, I was invited by some people to come to a home near the Monroe Institute in Virginia to discuss the initiative to disclose all this information to the world.

Some very fine people were there - but later I found there were some people who were there with other agendas. We discussed how to best achieve disclosure and how to reach the larger society.

Towards the end of that meeting, I decided to commit to this effort - what is now known as the Disclosure Project. (In the early days it was an unnamed initiative and later had a project name given to it called, "Project Starlight.")

As I was leaving the area near the Monroe Institute, which is very near where we now live, I was hit by some sort of an electronic weapon system. I suddenly became completely and utterly disoriented, febrile – as if I was on fire from the inside.

I became so disoriented while driving my vehicle, that I didn't know if I was back in England (we had been in England earlier in July)- or where I was! I didn't know which side of the road I should be on, and in fact I discovered I was on the wrong side of the road! If I had not been able to transcend the power of this weapon, and snap back in and re-orient, I am certain I would have been killed in a head-on collision leaving the area of the Monroe Institute. It was very disturbing.

I learned from that experience that there are shadowy people watching what we are doing very carefully, and that they would do almost anything to try to stop us. But when I'm faced with such a challenge, my reaction is to fight twice as hard!

Over the course of the next few months, I talked to people I knew who were in the political and military realm who showed great interest in what we were doing. Many supported the Disclosure Project. We put together a team of people to create a plan to get this information to our leaders.

I began to articulate this agenda to groups, explaining that it was time for the truth to come out. As a result, a large network of support developed. After one of these talks in Colorado, a gentleman (I'll call him M.J.) came up to me and said, "I know a few folks in Washington who can help."

I'm all ears." I said.

"I'm friends with the new CIA director, Jim Woolsey. He used to be on the board of my institute. What you're saying makes sense. And it needs to happen." He said, very sincerely.

It turns out, M.J. had been one of the people following our work, and had written a book -- under contract from the Coast Guard. It was for the military in general and there was a section of the book on wildcard scenarios of events that could happen in the future, but were not anticipated by the mainstream military.

A section of it was about CSETI and the CE5 initiative- though it wasn't named. But it described everything we had done, and even included scenarios like a group going out to a beach in Florida, making contact with ETs!

I then realized there was another whole orbit of people watching what we were doing. Many of them were futurists and people connected to top national security and intelligence fields who felt that this information should begin to come out.

Around that same time some people in New York who were friends with Laurance Rockefeller approached me and said, "You know, this is something that Laurance Rockefeller is very interested in."

"I'm willing to meet with anyone about this." I said.

I ended up having a series of meetings in the summer and fall of 1993, and one of them was with our military advisor for the project, a Naval Commander, whose father and grandfather had both been deputy directors of NASA and before that NACA. He had been very supportive since 1991, when we first met, and he said that, "You know, I can help you with the military end."

Then another man surfaced who was a friend of Bill Clinton who said, "I can help you with the political end."

And other people surfaced and said, "Look we can get this information to the CIA director and to the national security people."

And another man surfaced who wanted to get this information to Dr. Jack Gibbons, who was the President's Science Advisor. Then another man, whose brother was the science advisor to Al Gore, the Vice-President, helped us.

So a whole group of people assembled rather quickly around this time.

I was very aware that there could be a number of mixed agendas going on. And at the same time, I was acutely sensitive to the need not to be prejudiced against anyone because of his affiliations. My goal was to simply speak the truth, explain what needed to be done and educate.

By this point, there were CIA people surfacing, flying into Asheville where we lived then, saying, "Do it and do it now! We're part of a group that wants to see this happen. It has been kept secret for too long!"

My largest effort has been associated with providing information and perspective to people who are in clandestine programs or are in what people call the 'control group' or high cabal.

Much of what I have written and said has been oriented towards providing information and a new paradigm to those people.

In September of 1993, our military advisor had approached the man who at that time was the head of intelligence for the joint staff -- an Admiral. He later became Director of Naval Intelligence (DNI).

Our military advisor said to the Admiral, "Look, I'm working with Dr. Greer of CSETI, and we want to meet with the people at the Foreign Technology Division of Wright-Patterson Air Force Base." This is the entity that had received some of the material from the extraterrestrial vehicles retrieved from New Mexico in the '40s. As it turns out, this group has been renamed the National Air Intelligence Center or NAIC. But in 1993 it was called the Foreign Aerospace Science and Technology Center – FASTC. Interesting how they keep changing names!

Surprised, this admiral pushed back from the desk and asked, "Are you serious?"

"Yes, sir." Said Will.

And then the Admiral asked, "Well, is Dr. Greer serious? Is he credible?"

And he said, "Extremely credible, sir."

So the Admiral said, "All right. I'll set it up."

He called Wright-Patterson Air Force Base, and said, "I want you to meet with Dr. Greer and his team."

But the Base Commander said, "We won't allow it."

Eventually the Admiral ordered the head of Air Force Intelligence to make the meeting happen.

That same week in September of 1993, I had been invited by Laurance Rockefeller to his "JY" ranch in the Tetons.

So first I went out to Laurance's ranch. As it turns out, a number of people involved with this subject had been invited to the Ranch, many who were tied into the intelligence community.

In addition, there was one of Rockefeller's chief aides, a wonderful man, who was very supportive of our work. Also there was a 'woman in red', whom it turned out had been in Laurance Rockefeller's circle for years. Her husband (I'll call him Bruce) was on the boards of Morgan Stanley and many top transnational companies and was also a CIA operative. (He told me this personally.) He also had been one of President Reagan's ambassadors.

So into this interesting mix arrives this country doctor from North Carolina, who has been making contact with the ETs!

At an early meeting, I explained that we were putting together a team of top military insiders and evidence, and intended to disclose the matter to the public. You could have heard a pin drop in the room.

They asked, "You're going to do what?" And, "Who are you working with," and, "What is going on?"

I said, "Well, when I leave here I'm going straight to Wright-Patterson Air Force Base. There are covert military and intelligence factions that are supportive of disclosure. I am not speculating on this." I was very forth coming.

"Here's what we're going to do...." It was clear people were stunned.

It was obvious that there were people at this meeting who were outraged at the prospect of a disclosure. I remember having a conversation in '92 with some of General T.E.'s people who asked, "If you make contact where it's a very large event that gets televised, will you allow us to control it first before it gets out to the public?"

"No, I won't." I said.

Then they said, "We control the media, and all the satellites they use; so we will take control." To my disappointment, it was confirmed to me again by CB Scott Jones that, ultimately, that it would, indeed, be controlled.

Yet, I vowed, "We're going to keep this as independent as is humanly possible."

The JY Ranch is surrounded by Grand Teton National Park. On the first day we were there, I was on a walk around the lake with two prominent abduction researchers. I'll never forget how one of them (I'll call him Mr. X) proceeded to inform me that he was a big advocate of hallucinogenic drugs — that in fact at that very moment, he was on hallucinogenic drugs! Of course, he was stumbling around the lake, falling over logs and I knew something was not right!

So here is this famous abduction researcher, who told me that his work involved people whom he encouraged to take hallucinogenic drugs to "help recall their abduction and sexual experiences with aliens." !!!

I thought, "Oh, my God. So that's how that 'spin'is making its way into the public."

Of course, I subsequently learned that Mr. X had deep connections to the MK Ultra CIA program dating back to the 1950s and 60's. They were developing mind control with the use of hallucinogenic drugs.

There is a complete and utter infiltration of civilian ufology with people who are operatives from covert, shadowy intelligence fields, and who are involved in some of the most bizarre mind control experiments, including high powered drugs mixed in with electronics and so-called psychotronic weapon systems.

The truth is so much stranger than any fiction you will ever read.

14

Disinformation

I was mortified to find Mr. X proudly admitting that he did this type of leading hypnosis, at times so stoned on hallucinogenic drugs that he said, "I can't get up off the couch to even get a cup of coffee. I have to have an assistant bring it to me."

During these sessions he said that he would be leading his abductees under hypnosis and in an altered state of consciousness, where they would 'discover' their hidden alien experiences!

I thought to myself, "Mother of God. Here we have multi-hundred-thousand dollar book deals and research programs funded by Rockefellers and Prince S. A., foisted onto the gullible public. And all these things are presumed true due to the stamp of this researcher!"

By 1993, therefore, it was obvious to me how elaborate the hoax was that was being perpetrated on the public. And that 90-plus percent of the information in the public domain on UFOs, extraterrestrials and encounters with ETs was all bogus disinformation- designed to scare the hell out of people.

From 1993 until now, it has personally been very difficult for me to live with this knowledge. I have held my fire concerning the corruption and the outright hoaxing of information and experiences that are foisted on the mainstream public through multi-million dollar disinformation campaigns related to UFOs and extraterrestrials.

But suffice it to say that the entire field of UFO research is so mobbed up and so labyrinthine, that at least 90 percent of everything that has ever been put out in the public domain on this subject is complete fabrication and carefully tailored disinformation and psychological warfare programming.

Mr X and I had an interesting philosophical discussion, but it was difficult to go too far because of incoherence on his part from all of his drug use.

What isn't known is that Mr. X is a major abuser of those substances and also has encouraged people who abused them to come forward and get in this folie-a-deux -this conjoint madness to concoct alien encounters, and then rubber-stamp them as having actually happened.

Now, one of the interesting things that was discussed was how he had been "persecuted" for doing this abduction research, and that he was some type of victim.

In reality, what happened is that not only had he been doing drugs with his subjects, but he had been doing something that is an absolute ethical no-no: He had been billing his research subjects for his time. In a research experiment, you can't charge the subjects. This is highly immoral and unethical.

One of the things that I learned in the course of this meeting at the JY Ranch with Laurance Rockefeller was that David Rockefeller, of Chase Manhatten Bank and Nelson, who had been US Vice President and had passed away, were very much involved in the secret government. Laurance Rockefeller knew of these things but he was really more of the philosopher king of the family and was not the power guy. He was a professional philanthropist, who genuinely wanted to just give away his wealth before he died.

Unfortunately, he had morally inept people surrounding him, including this nest of CIA people, not the least of which was the 'woman in red' whose husband was CIA.

So into this mess steps Laurance Rockefeller wanting to support getting information out about this subject. But his money is intercepted by CIA operatives and ne'er-do-wells and is funneled away into bogus abduction research, substance abuse, and all kinds of other craziness.

One man in Laurence's circle specifically intercepted what would have been an enormous amount of funding for CSETI to have a CE5 Initiative professionally supported, and took it into his own institute, so it could then be funneled back into other clandestine operations.

This I know for a personal fact.

So Laurance had some very good intentions, but was surrounded by a circle that was infested with a number of intelligence operatives who were hell bent on keeping his resources away from productive work.

Their task was to open a toilet lid and put millions of dollars in it and then flush it into the sewer. And that is what they did. I witnessed it firsthand, and it was a tragedy of the first order of magnitude.

Eventually, Laurance Rockefeller's whole interest in this area got intercepted by this 'woman in red', whose ethics were appalling.

Around this same time, we had put together a series of documents that constituted what is called "The Best Available Evidence." In the spirit of collegiality, I shared this openly as a work-in-progress with Laurance and with other people.

It turns out that the 'woman in red' intercepted it, took Laurance

Rockefeller's and one of CSETI's stalwart supporter's money and hired a writer within the UFO community. He then took it, rewrote it, put their name on it, copyrighted it and stole it from us. Later, when we tried to use it for further free and open briefings, she hired one of the biggest law firms in Washington and threatened to sue me! How nice… This, after they stole the concept, including the title of the entire document.

Notwithstanding these issues, I developed a bond with Laurance. I had some very lovely times with him and his wonderful wife, Mary.

I recall, towards the end of one evening, Laurance and I walked out onto a wooden deck off from the lodge where we were meeting at his ranch. On this deck was a statue of a Native American on horseback with headdress, arms outstretched to the stars.

We were looking up at the sky and talking.

Laurence turned to me, and said, "You realize that no aspect of life on earth will be unchanged by this matter being disclosed, so profound and far-reaching are the implications."

"Yes, Laurance, that's why it's secret and that's why it has to happen." I said. "But we need your help."

"I want to help." He said. "But my family is already jumping up and down on my feet because I'm involved this much!"

"You still need to do the right thing here." I replied.

"It's much too dangerous." He said.

"Well, Laurance, my God, you're old, you're rich, and you're a Rockefeller!"

He replied, "My hands are tied. But know this — you have to do it…. Think of it this way: It's like a flock of geese in a "V" formation, and you need to be up here at the front breaking new territory, and we will be back here."

"Oh!" I laughed, "Yes, after I have broken all the resistance of the head wind."

"But I have to stay back here." He said. "I can't be up there. The family won't have it."

So you have people like Laurance Rockefeller, who really wanted to do the right thing- but he allowed his wings to be clipped by family loyalties, and was surrounded by a mob of intelligence operatives and spooks who were hell bent on intercepting his interests, and making sure that whatever support he could give, went into the toilet.

Many wonderful things happened, including the fact that we were able to put together briefing materials which Laurance Rockefeller used to personally brief Bill and Hillary Clinton at the "JY" Ranch.

You may remember that the first couple of summers of the Clinton White House, the Clintons would spend vacations at the Rockefeller Ranch. Laurance gave the ranch to Senator Jay Rockefeller from West Virgina, but it was still the family ranch. There, they were able discuss with Bill and Hillary Clinton the information we had assembled on the ET matter. Laurance was sincerely trying to get this information to the right people.

I later found out from a friend of the Clinton's that when President Clinton returned to the White House and was reviewing the briefing documents again he exclaimed —and she did a perfect impersonation of Bill Clinton— " I know this is all true, but God damn it, they won't tell me a thing. Not a God damned thing !"

Later I was invited to go to a meeting in New York to give a presentation at the home of a novelist named Judith Green, who had an apartment on Park Avenue. There was a large group of people present, including Mrs. Boutros Ghali, Rockefeller's representatives -- a whole group of people from high New York Society were present.

I spoke about contact with these life forms and what it would take to create a peaceful world here so that we could live in harmony with our extraterrestrial neighbors. My talk was very well-received and subsequently, I was able to meet with Mrs. Boutros Ghali.

It was disappointing, however, that some there had the misconceptions that are in rampant circulation in the mass media and UFO circles.

Those who put out distorted research dealing with cattle mutilations, human vivisection, alien rapes and encounters get enormous funding from the covert group and their friends and contacts in the disinformation arm. They control and spin disinformation to the mainstream media, the UFO public, and what I call the "retail consumers of all things extraterrestrial", who swallow hook, line and sinker their harvest of fear.

They are very good at packaging it and seeing that only those aspects of the UFO subculture that support the party line of *fear* get financial support, publicity etc. Now, unfortunately, blowing the whistle on that hasn't endeared me to some folks, but the truth is, people need to know how clever this group is at duping researchers to put out disinformation.

For example, many so-called abduction researchers receive leads to abductees by being tipped off by these shadowy groups and their contacts. Often these leads are people who have been abducted in mind control experiments that are run completely by shadowy human paramilitary operations.

The information out in the public on this subject is so polluted and corrupted with disinformation and hoaxed events,that you really have to scrap it and start all over.

This is not what I thought was true in 1990, but by 1993, I had heard it and seen it firsthand at the deepest and highest levels of the intelligence community. As I met first-hand with these shadowy groups and figures, this was no longer just a theory on my part, but became something I knew to be true.

Unfortunately, I have had to live with a terrible burden of how much of this to say to the public. We know it will create a firestorm of hatred against us by the very machine that wants the world deceived. This huge disinformation campaign puts out enough fool's gold that the truth- the kernel of real gold- is buried under a mountain of fool's gold. And most people aren't doing an assay and wouldn't even think to do one!

So everyone is accepting fool's gold and mistaking it for the real thing. Why? Because the central operation of the past 40 or 50 years has set up false decoy databases and decoy belief systems, to distract people from what's actually true.

This shadowy cabal forces into the civilian population completely concocted pseudo- extraterrestrial events. Very advanced technologies are used so that covert programs can simulate an extraterrestrial event, an abduction, or a cattle mutilation that looks like 'aliens' are invading. In reality, the operation is being run out of a facility in New Mexico or Utah, using unmarked helicopters and specially trained people who swoop in and stage these hoaxed events. This is carefully calibrated psychological warfare. The stakes are enormous. The propaganda purpose is very simple: Put out enough fearsome and scary information so that the operation can seed into the consciousness of the masses a back-of-the-mind fear of anything from outer space. Eventually the deceived masses will be brainwashed enough to support armed conflict between planets.

It is all part of a preparatory or 'acclimation' disinformation and mind control program. The public is being "dis-informed" under the pretext of being "informed." And there are willing and unwilling dupes within civilian UFO research who are part of this.

Most of them are unwitting dupes. They don't even know they are being played.

But who is doing this? It is not as direct as "the government" you learned about in civics class! What government? Which government? The Shadow Government- The Secret Government.

Is the secret shadow government directly controlling these things? It's even more subtle than that. Do they have agents within the civilian

UFO world? Yes. Frighteningly, many of them.

Equally scary is another way in which they achieve their purpose. By putting up enough believable disinformation and hoaxing enough events they are able to persuade researchers to accept these bogus events without question and then report them to the public in various magazines and books. The vicious cycle continues – the public unthinkingly accepts these reports as reality.

It is a complex issue, but it is very easy to fool people if they don't know there is a 'faux phenomenon' or false phenomenon paralleling the factual and actual extraterrestrial phenomenon. With unlimited funds and sophisticated electronics and technologies, it is easy for this rogue clandestine group to do that.

This group has enormous resources, while on the other side of the equation is a poorly funded, amateur, hobbyist UFO civilian community. It is like taking candy from a baby.

This is a rule of thumb that you can go by: If there is a lot of money behind it, and if there is a lot of fearsome, scary, spooky almost demon-like information associated with it, you can be assured that it is disinformation that has wittingly or unwittingly been proffered to the public.

Many people don't realize that in cases of, say, animal mutilations, the vast majority have reports of unmarked helicopters and human commando style operations doing these "events." This is well known in the research community, but these facts never get reported to the public. The event is always portrayed as an alien mutilation of our innocent livestock!

Think about this. We have a public that loves to go down to McDonald's and eat hamburgers. And this public is being informed that evil aliens are invading and torturing our poor cows! Come on!

There is a psychological warfare component to all this. The people who trade in these scary scenarios find out quickly that if they go the direction of negativity, they get a lot of funding and grant supports from certain quarters. If they don't go negative, or if they begin to tell the truth, all their financial support dries up.

This is precisely why CSETI and the Disclosure Project has never had any serious funding. We refuse to lie about these things. We refuse to go negative. And we refuse to put out information that scares the hell out of the population.

I have said publicly that if I were to write a book that said I had been abducted and kidnapped, vivisected or sexually molested, by fearsome extraterrestrials from Tau Epsilon, I could retire a very wealthy man. The book advances, the screen plays and the media deals would be extremely generous. That's the truth.

Now, back to the story. I left the Rockefeller ranch and went directly to Wright Patterson Air Force Base with our military advisor and one other gentleman and met with a Colonel Kanola and Bruce Ashcroft, a civilian intelligence officer also considered a 'public information officer'.

We did not go there to view the extraterrestrial bodies or material that had been there since the 40s. The purpose of the visit was for me to do a briefing to them about what we were doing and how necessary it was for them to be ready for change. You will remember how the Admiral at the Joint Chiefs of Staff had ordered the meeting, and actually had to pull rank with the head of Air Force Intelligence to make it happen.

The meeting went on for an hour or two, during which time I made a very clear case regarding how we had established contact on numerous occasions with the UFOs in question. They were writing furiously as we disclosed this information to them. We continued to explain that it was well past time for this information to be disclosed to the public.

At one point, the Colonel asked, "Well, what if these life forms are hostile?"

I looked at him and I said, "You know what? You and I wouldn't be having this conversation if they were hostile given the fact that the technologies that they have are so advanced that they can alter the fabric of space-time. If they were hostile, in a nanosecond the earth could be turned into a cinder floating through space and you know it. And insofar as we have been doing reckless and dangerous things against them for decades, the fact that you and I still are breathing the free air of earth is abundant testimony to their non-violence."

He just looked at me.

We left briefing materials at Wright-Patterson AFB with these officials. Later, my military advisor was able to get into the computer system and see that all these materials were accessible in the archives of Air Force Intelligence at Wright Patterson. The CSETI contact events and our best available evidence and assessment of the situation were all there, in that computer system.

But after the material began to be accessed by higher ups or their aides, it disappeared. Our material was never seen again!

A little postscript to this experience: Later we learned that Admiral Cramer was told that he was not to be involved in this sort of meeting again. When our military advisor went back to visit the Admiral, his aide insisted, "Don't ever bring up that subject again with Admiral Cramer.

He can't talk about that!"

Do you think that we should have been surprised to learn that, short-ly *afterwards*, he was promoted from being head of Intelligence Joint Staff, to being Director of Naval Intelligence – DNI?

I was told that Admiral Cramer was rewarded for not pushing this issue anymore. Hence, the promotion up to DNI. The bitter irony here is that he was probably given more information about the subject after he was rewarded for dropping the subject.

15

The Crossing Point of Light

By the fall of 1993, I was on a very steep learning curve regarding how the shadow government had infiltrated not only the covert world and the government and corporations, but also the civilian media and the civilian UFO community.

After the Rockefeller meeting and our briefings at Wright-Patterson AFB, I reconnected with the man who was friends with CIA Director Woolsey. He was convinced that we needed to get this information, through a number of channels, to not only the President but other senior officials in the Administration. We were doing this through the President's science advisor, Rockefeller, and a friend of Bill Clinton who supported our effort. This man's brother was also in the White House, and a very close associate of Bill Clinton's.

We were approaching the powers that be in a friendly, helpful way, saying, "Look, the time has come for disclosure to happen. The Cold War is over. There is a window of opportunity here, to disclose to the public, in a positive way, the fact that these extraterrestrial vehicles are real and that there are classified projects that may have been justifiable during the pressures of the Cold War, but are not justifiable any longer. Disclosure needs to happen now. We have a chance to make a break from the past."

We were also saying, in the same breath: "If you don't do it, we will.

We'll find a way to do it by collecting enough sources to make a convincing case." This is exactly what the Disclosure Project is.

With this fresh impetus, we decided we needed to get further insight into the intelligence operations.

James Woolsey was nominated and confirmed by the Senate in 1993, and now in our story this is September of '93, so he had not been in that position for very long. We found out from our senior White House contacts that, in fact, the President, as well as the CIA Director, were trying to find out through channels what the truth was about this subject. We were also told that they were being flat-out lied to.

I have a letter that was FedExed to me in the fall of 1993 by this CIA Director's friend, saying that CIA Director Woolsey had made inquiries into the UFO matter and could not find out anything about it and was being lied to. Further, they knew they were being lied to! He told me that the CIA Director wanted me to come to Washington, and that I was going to be the first person to brief the CIA Director on this. Well, I thought that he had gone stark, raving, mad. I'm thinking, here I am, a country doctor in North Carolina. And I'm supposed to be going to DC to meet with the Director of Central Intelligence on something that is Spook Central? Right!

To be honest with you, my initial reaction was that this had to be a prevarication. I viewed it as a cover story- that the CIA Director knew everything and that he just wanted to find out what *we* knew and what *we* were up to. As it turned out I was wrong, and Woolsey and the President really were out of the loop.

On December 13th, 1993, we went to Washington to meet with Woolsey. The cover story was a dinner at his friend's house. It was the six of us, the three couples: my wife and I, the CIA Director and his wife, who, happily, was the chief operating officer of the National Academy of Sciences (so we were able to kill two birds with one stone); his friend and his wife. Our hostess it turned out, didn't know who was coming to dinner until the day of the event! Can you imagine? "Honey, guess who's coming to dinner? Oh, the CIA Director and this extraterrestrial expert, Dr. Greer." Wow. Can you imagine coming home and telling your wife that?

I remember arriving in the late afternoon at the CIA Director's friend's house, with Emily. I had a whole briefcase full of materials. We discussed what we were going to do, but I had no idea how long this meeting might be. We all knew that this was a very serious briefing for the CIA Director. He was being lied to about the most important secret in the history of the world. Woolsey's wife arrived first by private vehicle, and then the CIA Director arrived via Secret Service escort. After initial greetings and about ten minutes of going through some of the materials, documents, photographs, cases and so forth, the CIA Director said, "Yes, I know these are real."

It turns out that he and his wife had actually seen one of these UFOs years ago in New Hampshire, and so he didn't have any doubt that they existed. But what he wanted to know was: Why wasn't he being told anything? And were there any current projects dealing with it? And why were the extraterrestrials here? And what does all this mean?

People often think that senior officials like that would be laughing up their sleeve at this subject. But no! The man was visibly shaken. He was profoundly upset that as CIA Director, something this important was being withheld from him and the President. He was extremely upset about it. At one point, I thought he was actually going to break down and cry. I considered his reaction an entirely appropriate response, given the gravity of the subject, and I was hopeful of the outcome of the meeting.

The meeting that I thought might be half an hour or so, went on for nearly three hours. During that meeting, we discussed everything he wanted to know. And I told him why the extraterrestrials were here, and I explained why this was being kept secret. And I explained exactly what should be done to fix the problem.

It was, I was acutely aware, a terrible responsibility to take on. I felt the gravity of this situation. I'm dealing with someone who is arguably one of the most powerful people in the world, and I find out the emperor has no clothes! I find out that information is lost in the system and being denied to people who are running the most powerful country in the world. And then I find out they're not running the country at all and that there's a Shadow Government that's really running the whole show, and that this is now being confirmed to me by a sitting CIA Director.

I went from being a complete skeptic -- that someone at that level of power and authority would really be out of the loop -- to understanding how far out of the loop he was: And not just the CIA Director, but also the President. It was then that I realized the severity of the dysfunction within what we think is a constitutional republic and a democratic type of government- to the point that there is flat-out lying to people at this level of constitutional authority and responsibility. I doubted that the CIA Director, the President, and others who were being denied access to these projects were being lied to.

But, because now I have been with people like a sitting CIA Director and sitting members of the Senate Intelligence Committee and similar officials throughout the world, and seen their faces and their body language and their reactions, I can assure you that things are not what big media tells you they are.

I shared with Woolsey the information that these extraterrestrial beings were here for peaceful purposes. I explained that many UFO sightings were of craft made by covert programs in the United States and elsewhere- that the technologies behind these vehicles are very powerful and are in the wrong hands. I also made the point that this matter had to be brought under constitutional control and it could only be done by the President. As a weak back-up position, the Congress could do an investigation, but really, because of the structure of the executive branch and its supervisory and immediate control over the chain of command, leadership had to come from the executive branch - the President.

Toward the end of the meeting, I remember giving him a set of rec-ommendations which we subsequently published. So here's the scene: I deliver the evidence into the hands of a sitting CIA Director, recommend what needs to be done to disclose this information, end the secrecy, and get this matter back under proper control and oversight. I'm naturally hoping for some action, but what he asked me was: "How do we disclose that which we have no access to?"

Disappointed, but still pressing the point, I said, "You *have* to get con-trol of it. You *have* to insist on access." He just looked away. He knew what was involved.

During the time we sat down for our dinner, the CIA Director was sitting across from me, and his wife was next to him. The group was dis-cussing all these issues that had been raised. Finally, Dr. Woolsey, the CIA Director's wife, asked "Do you know how these craft communicate across the vast distances of space?"

I remember going through a quick but agonizing inner gut check: Do I tell her the truth and lose all credibility? Or do I tell her a lie or a sanitized version of the truth and maintain some respectability? And I thought, no, I've got to just tell her the truth, as far-out as the truth may sound.

So I said, "Look, these extraterrestrial civilizations have figured out the structure of space and time and non-locality." I saw some puzzled looks and knew I had to explain in detail. "It's like this, take our own galaxy, the Milky Way Galaxy, which is 100,000 light years or so across. A nearby star system might be one percent of the distance from us, which is 1,000 light years. Let's use that as an example. Look, if you had to communicate to that star system, and it had to return a reply, you'd have to say, 'Hi, how are you?' and they'd come back and say, 'Fine, thank you very much; how are you doing?' -- just that exchange would take 2,000 years! How and why? — a light year is the distance conventional electro-magnetic waves travel, at 186,000 miles a second, over the course of a whole year. So, 1,000 light years means it'd take 1,000 Earth years for us to get a message there and another 1,000 to get the message back. And that's only one percent of the distance across our own galaxy!"

"The speed of light is just too damned slow," I continued. "It's not a viable means of communication or travel when you start talking about inter-stellar distances. Quite frankly, it's barely sufficient, if you're not over the speed of light, to go around even our own solar system. This means that any civilization that's gotten here has mastered those technologies and sciences that deal with everything *beyond* the speed of light -- what I call the crossing point of light. If they've mastered that, they have discovered this nexus where electromagnetism, matter, space, time and consciousness all come together." It is, in fact, like the Moody Blues song – 'Thinking is the best way to travel'.

I explained that these extraterrestrial civilizations have technology-assisted consciousness systems, as well as consciousness-assisted technology, where there's an interface between mind and thought and a specialized physics and electromagnetism. And so when they communicate, the message is communicated from Point A, say here on Earth, back to a home planet, Point B, 1,000 light years away, in real time. That's because it has dropped out of linear space-time and has crossed over into this non-local aspect of the universe. This involves some very sophisticated physics but also encompasses the realms of thought and of consciousness.

They can think *to* a device or interface *with* a device, and it will instantly and accurately convey that signal and that message to another point -- and this is technological; it's not just 'telepathic'. The information and images are transferred non-locally to another point in space, no matter how far away, in real time. It is like two nodes, instantaneously *resonating*. The signal goes from one node to another, bypassing linear space-time.

Dr. Woolsey looked at me and said, "I thought it had to be something like that." She really did get it.

When you're dealing with civilizations that are traveling through inter-stellar distances, it is crucial to realize that they have had to master the sciences that involve consciousness, thought, electromagnetism, and non-locality. Hence, the CSETI protocols have a component that deals with non-locality and consciousness and directed coherent thought. This is because the ETs have technologies that pick up coherent and directed thought signals as clearly as we would pick up an electromagnetic signal from a laser or a radio or cell phone. It is very scientific and very reproducible- it is a science not widely known on earth today.

I think a lot of people can now understand this concept. Thankfully, there are now enough people who have arrived at a post-quantum understanding of the Universe.

A number of people I've worked with who have been in covert aerospace and electronics firms that deal with this subject have confirmed to me that we have retrieved extraterrestrial communication devices that do exactly that: they interface with thought and consciousness and respond to thought and consciousness. They are tuned to be able to do that.

Well, the hours spent with the CIA Director and his wife were certainly eventful and revealing. Toward the end of the evening, I sensed that he very much appreciated the information and was very interested. But I also sensed the profound tragedy and sadness in the moment when he asked me, "How do we disclose something we don't have access to?" - I realized then the enormity of the challenge ahead of us. I recalled the dysfunction that we had been warned about by Eisenhower when he said, beware the military industrial complex and the threat to our liberty and security by its excesses. What Eisenhower warned us about had fully matured into a level of dysfunction that was of truly epic proportions and I was witnessing it firsthand.

As we said goodbye I realized that the entire time we had been inside, the place had been monitored; we saw there were Secret Service people out front. Of course, they had a sag wagon and armed guards with earphones. The works!

In many ways, the encounter was traumatic for me – But I was grateful because I was able to learn the truth.

16

Circles of Power

In 1993, before briefing the CIA Director, my contact for meetings at high levels had suggested that we name our operation "Project Starlight." So that is what it was called in the early days. The philosophy behind it was to assemble absolutely the best evidence that was available, which had been rigorously tested and proved and to identify military, corporate and intelligence witnesses to programs and events. Then, with an iron-clad case in hand, we would brief the President, the intelligence and military community, Congress, the United Nations leadership, and other leaders around the world, *in advance of* Disclosure.

We knew it was crucial to, at the very least, give the system a chance. It's very important to understand that our intention was not simply to go in like a bull in a china shop and bring all this very sensitive information out, without first fully apprising the legal, legitimate leaders of the world and inviting their participation. At the time, many people thought I was being silly and naive, that "those people" would never get behind something this controversial. But that's not the point! The point is, from our perspective, we had a moral responsibility to at least give them an opportunity to do the right thing —and if they didn't do the right thing, then it would be on their consciences and not ours.

I felt strongly we had the obligation to give these leaders the current assessment of the situation, and say to them, "You need to take a leadership role, if this is going to be accomplished by you and not by an outside group." –(meaning, The Disclosure Project and CSETI). "You have an ideal opportunity that has opened after the end of the Cold War, to break the cycle of misinformation. To make a fresh start."

After I met with the CIA Director, a contact set up a meeting between Senator Byrd's chief investigator and counsel for the Senate Appropriations Committee and me. Sen. Byrd was then Chairman of the committee and very powerful. This man was named Dick D'Amato – not to be confused with Senator D'Amato from New Jersey. Dick D'Amato had a top secret clearance and had subpoena power from the Senate Appropriations Committee.

We met in the Senate Appropriations committee meeting room – a huge, ornate room with a giant table and brass nameplates for each member of the Committee. He proceeded to tell me, "I've been asked by Senator Byrd and some others to look into these things, and we've gotten close enough to know that these projects *do exist*. But I'm telling you that with a top secret clearance and a subpoena power from the Senate Appropriations Committee, I cannot penetrate those projects." He looked at me— I'll never forget it— and said, "You're dealing with the varsity team of all black projects, so watch out. And good luck." And that was the end of that.

Dick D'Amato and people like him know this is real, but they cannot get their hands around it or control the expenditures.

Access to these projects has nothing to do with rank or position. Access has to do with whether or not you are willing to go along with the secrecy. That is the only criterion that matters, whether you are willing to play along with the agenda.

Those who *shouldn't be in control but are*, comprise an illegal, rogue break-off group that is trans-national and whose members are not only ruthless and murderous but operating completely without any legal authority. When you're dealing with something as fundamentally important as this, involving technologies as powerful as those described, you begin to realize the risks to the world of allowing this masquerade to go on, unchecked, decade after decade after decade.

In 1994, an FOB, a Friend of Bill Clinton, came to my home after I had briefed the CIA Director. He was a very easygoing, affable guy. He said, "You know, everyone agrees with what you're recommending, but there's a consensus that if the President does what you've suggested to him and to the CIA Director—that they exert executive power to get inside this operation and disclose it— the President will end up like Jack Kennedy."

I thought he was joking, and to be honest with you, I laughed out loud. I truly thought, "Oh, come on." But no, he was deadly serious. And he made it very clear that he was serious.

So it went from crisis to crisis, as I came to realize that the government of the United States -- and of every other nation -- was really hostage to an illegal, rogue group that had technologies that could do circles around a B-2 Stealth bomber and could, at will, terminate a presidency or terminate any other person who got in their way. This was made very clear to me by people who were in the inner circle of the greatest corridors of power on Earth.

Obviously, this weighed on me very heavily. I would say the period between '92 and '98 -- those six years -- were extremely traumatic for me. I would keep my chin up and publicly keep moving forward, but on a deep personal level it was devastating. I never lost faith in what we should do, but it was made very clear to me that the task was enormous and that the hour was late and that the stakes could not be greater.

In early 1994, I went back up to New York and spent some time with Laurance Rockefeller. I also met with a number of other people in New York City who were connected to the United Nations and to other organizations. We were walking into various circles of power and putting this information in their hands. In a way, I became the cosmic hand-holder. I would sit with the wife of the Secretary General of the U.N. or a CIA Director or close friends of the President or senior brass at the Pentagon and tell them what was going on and take them through this -- it's like the stages of death and dying, where they'd go from denial to anger and shock and grief and everything else. And this was increasingly what I found myself doing.

In these circles of enormous power and wealth, all kinds of betrayals happen. Some of the people working with us would sell out to a cell within the Shadow Government that interfaces with the civilian UFO community that's headed up by Colonel MK, General T.E., W.B. a very wealthy Nevada businessman and others.

One such person went behind my back, and tried to defame me to Rockefeller's people, to intercept money that Rockefeller wanted to use to support our project, to take into his own institute.

So, here I am, working as an emergency physician, a very stressful job, raising four young children, and thrown into this nest of vipers. Traumatic doesn't begin to paint the picture! There were times when I really wanted to give up, but I knew I couldn't because I was still connected to the purpose and the vision of where we're headed. I tried to keep my sight on that far horizon— which isn't that far away in time, but seems very far away in events that have to happen— where we can create the world of our dreams.

And it was with that certainty, as well as faith, that I stayed in the effort

You have to understand the compartmented nature of these interlocking interests that are keeping all this secret: They are mainly in the corporate, institutional, financial, and technology sectors. The government of 'We, the People' is the least important component of it, and this includes the military, the CIA, the NSA, the NRO, Army intelligence, Air Force intelligence -- all of that is window dressing for an operation that's quite outside it. The real action is a hybrid group that is quasi-governmental but mostly privatized and utterly trans-national - and completely illegal.

Some of the chieftains of that group invited me to meet with them after I had met with the CIA Director. In advance of the meeting with the CIA Director, my contact to Woolsey was terrified by the idea that anyone would find out about the meeting. He was doing everything through FedEx, and he wanted me to talk with him on the phone at telephone booths, talking in a code!

I said, "We don't need to bother doing that, because the group that we're up against have technologies that can frustrate any system you can devise." Well, he had been on the short list to be Clinton's Secretary of the Navy. So he knew the spook world fairly well. But he had been in the conventional military and intelligence world. I knew what we were up against, but he didn't. So he said, "Oh, no, we have to do this. You're just a doctor! I've been in all these circles, and we have to be careful." So I humored him.

I tried to explain to him that there was no way to frustrate the surveillance capabilities of this covert group, because they had non-local, 'scalar' technologies that would enable them to bypass entire generations of electronics. Even the state-of-the-art NSA and NRO stuff is nothing compared to what they have, because what they have are electronic interfaces with consciousness, where they can monitor things in real time all the time. Well, he didn't know this. I knew it and had remote-viewed them remote-viewing me.

So I went along with his game. But before I had the meeting on December 13th, 1993, someone who had been tied into these projects in the military in Arizona came to me and said, "I understand you're going to be meeting with Jim Woolsey, the CIA Director, about such and such on this date." I said, "I won't confirm or deny that, but isn't it interesting that you would comment on it?"

I reported this to my contact, and had to pull him off the ceiling! He went ballistic! "How could this be found out?" I said, "MJ, you haven't been listening." The problem is: Most people are too arrogant to know what they don't know

I should also mention that during my visit to New York in the winter of 1994, while at the Hilton on Sixth Avenue in New York, I got a phone call from a "reporter." And he said, "I'm a free lance reporter for the 'Wall Street Journal'." He said, "I understand you had a meeting with Admiral Woolsey regarding UFOs and extraterrestrial intelligence."

He asked, "What can you tell me about that?" I didn't lie; I just asked a rhetorical question: "Do you really think a sitting CIA Director would meet with a country doctor from North Carolina about a subject like UFOs and extraterrestrials?" And he said, "Well, no, I guess not." And I said, "Well, there you are," and I hung up. And that was the end of that. But this experience revealed to me that the media community was also mobbed up with intelligence people who were monitoring our activities.

It was around this time, in early 1994, that a contract worker for the covert shadow group that had a cell within the CIA, called me and said, "Look, we really want to see you get this done. Hurry up." I said, "What do you mean, 'hurry up'?" They said, "We've been wanting someone to appear who would do this for us; at least a third of the people in this covert control group want to see this matter disclosed, but we can't do it…"

I said, "Well, who the hell do you think I am? I'm just a country doctor here in North Carolina. I barely have a pot to pee in!" He said, "Well, no, you don't understand. We can only do things behind the scenes." I said, "Oh, for God's sakes!"

Eventually, he flew in and met with me at the Grove Park Inn, in Asheville. I'll never forget what he said to me during this conversation, "You know, if you want to get a message to us or to the President, all you need to do is pick up the phone. Don't dial anything— just talk. Or if you prefer, just sit in your home office and talk to the four walls. Because it's all being monitored in real time." And I said, "Yes, I know." And he asked, "Well, how do you know that?" I proceeded to tell him how they had made errors and left their end of the hook or tap open a couple times. It happened to Emily, and it's happened to me.

Once when I picked up the home phone to make a call, I heard a control room on the line. I could hear people talking, instead of a dial tone. So I asked, "Who is this?" Then a woman with a very thick foreign accent but speaking proper English says, "Oh, my God, it's Mr. Greer." And I said, "Dr. Greer to you, bitch." And hung up! In those days, I was outraged by these things. Now, I could care less.

So, I told this man, "Yes, I'm sure that's true." He said, "But, you know, this really does need to happen." I said, "But why don't you do it?" And he said, "Oh, no, it's too dangerous." He said exactly what Laurance Rockefeller had said to me in September, standing out on his deck under the stars.

By now you see a theme that keeps repeating: There are extremely well-connected people who are on the inside and who want to see disclosure, but they're terrified of the rogue, violent group.

After this meeting, I got an invitation from a group of rogue insiders to go to Phoenix in the winter of 1994. The meeting was at the Wrigley Mansion— the old, fabulous mansion that the Wrigley chewing gum family had built. It had been taken over by a cell within this covert group. Present were a number of shadowy corporate people. It was a very late night meeting.

A prominent industrialist who was involved with this cell was kept on drugs and was kept under some kind of mind control while this cell milked him of his money. They then used his money to support this particular operation. The methods and motives of this group are beyond dark. I tell people: More than 10 or 15 percent of what I have seen and learned you don't want to hear - It's so damned disturbing, most people would commit suicide. And many people have, by the way.

We all gathered around a conference table in the Wrigley mansion. The discussion was about disclosing UFO information and making contact with ETs. One man, during a break, took me out onto a balcony and said, "You know, we understand you've had this meeting with the CIA Director and are providing information to the President, but you need to know that those people don't know anything, and they're never going to know anything. You should understand that -- well, you should be talking to people like us. The people dealing with this are people who do a lot of contract work for the government, under "Work For Others" – "WFO" - contracts. And you should be talking to certain think tanks. And you should be talking to certain religious orders and certain orders of Jesuit priests who have control over the technology transfer. And you should be talking to ..." He gave me a whole list.

Well, I thought the man had certainly gone 'round the bend'. But it turned out that every single word he said was true—it all was confirmed in the following months.

It gets more bizarre. This group or cell within the Shadow Government was attempting to intercept what we were doing. Remember, now, this is '94. A former head of Army intelligence- a member of that group - had offered me a board seat in '92. So, things are progressing, and I'm not straying from my course, because that's how I am.

So this man said, "We can really help you." I asked, "What do you mean?" He said, "Well, you know, if you want to be supported in this, just let us help you." I said, "How do you intend to help us?" "Well, you're a doctor, right? So, you have really good credit. We've checked this out." And I said, "Oh, yes, the best."

He said, "Well, we know you have platinum cards and gold cards. Just maximize all of them, every month: $50,000, $100,000, whatever. Get as many of them as you want. And give *us* the numbers. And since we run all the super computers that back up and monitor the banking system of the world, we'll simply erase those account balances to zero, as paid each month." This is a true story. I'm telling you, every word is true. Put me under any drug; hook me up to any machine. What I'm telling you is true.

I said, "Yes, but then if I did that, you'd own my ass, wouldn't you?" He just had a twinkle in his eye.

I was much too wise to take that bait, tempting as it was -- this has been an enormous financial strain and struggle for those of us trying to do this with virtually no funding. But no way was I going to do that!

Then he said, "I understand you're going to Europe soon to meet with certain people connected to the British royal family" --which I was. He knew everything I was doing! And I said, "Well, that's true." He said, "It so happens that, I'm going to be over there meeting with the Rothschilds and the people who control the Volvo Corporation and some of the other big industrial concerns, because they're working with us." I said, "Oh, I'm quite sure that's true." He suggested, "Let's rendezvous while we're in London together." I said, "Okay, that's fine."

He proceeded to tell me, "One of my friends, who's really interested in what you're doing, is one of the leaders of the Council on Foreign Relations, Ambassador Maxwell Rabb. Would you like to come to a meeting with him?" I said, "Well, sure, if he wants to help us." And then he said, "And also, the Petersons" — Mr. Peterson was head of the Council on Foreign Relations and his wife was head of the Tri-Lateral Commission -- are also working with me, and maybe we can get together with them." So I said, "When we have our next event, I'll invite them."

He said, "You need to know that all these people are reading what you write and are very interested in all of this." And I said, "I know that."

Look, everyone puts their pants on one leg at a time. I view all humans as educable. And everyone has a role to play in this whole cosmic drama. But this shadowy contact was essentially, again, inviting me into the inner leading circle of the cabal. While I had no intention of being controlled by them, I have no problem sharing perspective and knowledge with them.

He also said that there were many top people that he worked with in the media and that his group worked with Bono and U2, the Moody Blues, Pink Floyd and various other groups. And they were receiving what I was writing. And I just said, "Well, I appreciate that." He said, "They love what you are saying and doing…"

Later that winter, I went to Europe and met with some very good friends of Prince Charles and Prince Philip. One of Prince Charles' best friends is very supportive of the work we are doing.

She wanted to receive some of the materials that I had put together for the CIA Director and the President, so she could share them with Prince Charles and others. But remember, I'm squeezing this in between my emergency shifts. I literally, at times, went over to Europe for two or three days at a time, and would come back and have to work a 24-hour shift in the emergency department!

In a sense, it was our own little shuttle diplomacy operation. I did meet with this shadowy Phoenix contact in London. He was still in the mode of courting me into his operations. So I would listen and learn, - but *never* capitulate :This group is the largest Mafiosi and organized criminal enterprise on the planet.

17

Legacies Lost

When some people hear this story, they're horrified that I would be so willing to walk into the belly of the beast. But I say, "Well, why not?" I have no problem meeting with anyone on Earth to share the vision of the good future of the human race and what we need to do to get there. I have no fear - and I know they cannot corrupt me. They can't buy me. They can't deceive me. And I don't care if they kill me. So, what's to be lost? If you stay in the truth, it all becomes very simple. And there's no one you have to avoid, and the ones you need to seek are all open to you.

I have learned that we need to operate on multiple tracks of consciousness at once. It's like how dolphins operate -- they can be "asleep," but part of their brain is also awake. This is scientifically proven. They are operating on multiple levels and dimensions at once. Well, humans can do this, too. During this period, I would go to sleep - but there would be a part of me that would awaken. For example, right after President Clinton got elected in late '92, I was with him on an astral level at the Governor's Mansion in Little Rock, Arkansas, discussing this knowledge - and this continued through his presidency. Meetings would happen on an astral level and sharing would take place. Years later, a good friend of President Clinton said that he was very much in touch with that inner spiritual level and could meet that way. I have done this routinely with people for many years. If we go beyond our own egos and fear and prejudices, we can do this and reach people spiritually.

Now, it doesn't mean that those whom we reach -- whether in a face-to-face, physical meeting or through these other, non-local applications of consciousness -- are going to necessarily respond favorably. In the case of Bill Clinton, he very much wanted to see this happen but didn't have the courage to do it. His legacy was basically lost, because it was his responsibility, as the first full-term president after the close of the Cold War era, to have done this. He didn't rise to the challenge. About the time that I was going to let it be known that I had had these meetings with the CIA director, after he had left office -- I think he was there till '95 -- I was visiting friends in Santa Barbara. I was being interviewed by a major New York paper, and they were going to run the story about our briefings for the White House and CIA Director on UFOs. The very *day* they were going to run that story, Linda Tripp emerged with her stories about Monica Lewinsky. That was not an accident or a coincidence. It knocked all this off the radar screen of the media. And for the next couple of years, it was 24 hours a day, seven days a week: the blow job heard round the world! What utter nonsense!

News flash: The best aphrodisiac is power. And powerful men have affairs. And guess what? Married men who have affairs sometimes lie about them. Gee whiz. An impeachment proceeding based on this? Give me a break. Hilary Clinton was right when she said there was a conspiracy to assassinate Bill Clinton by character assassination instead of with a bullet. She was absolutely correct - and it was over this and related issues.

By the mid-'90s, I concluded that the President of the United States was not going to deal with the UFO problem and that, if he looked into it much further, it would be the end of his presidency.

It was around this time that I met a good friend of President Carter who told me that Carter, in his early days as President and during the transition into his presidency, tried to find out about the entire covert UFO matter. Carter had a UFO sighting in Georgia when he was governor, and we have his official report. So Carter tried to get a briefing from then-CIA Director George Bush – the current President's father –- but Bush told him he would not give him that information and he should get it elsewhere! Later, as Carter pushed further on this, he was visited by "a suit," who said, "Sir, if you would like to complete your first term as President, you will keep your God-damned mouth shut about this UFO matter." This insider and friend of Carter's told me that he – and perhaps his family- were directly threatened.

We learned from separate sources, including some Disclosure Project witnesses, that Jimmy Carter wanted to do a White House study on UFOs and that it was going to be done through SRI (Stanford Research Institute). Pentagon covert projects then told SRI that they would pull all of their contracts supporting SRI if they were to proceed with the Carter White House request to look into UFOs. So the study idea was buried. This is just part of a long pattern, going back to at least Eisenhower, of United States Presidents being threatened — and in the case of Jack Kennedy, being assassinated. Others have had their entire lives and presidency threatened if they push this issue. So this is the mother of all cosmic buzz saws that I walked into between 1992 and now.

Bill Clinton didn't have the courage to do it. But I believe, quite frankly, he could have. Doesn't our public expect our leaders to be willing to go the distance regardless of their own personal ambition or their own personal safety? Most politicians are not courageous. We have a weak and spineless ruling class that is intoxicated on money, power, and selfish ambition. So even when they find out about these issues, they don't have the backbone and stamina to do the right thing on behalf of the Earth, the Earth's people, or even the citizens of the United States.

Between 1994 and 1997, as we continued to work the system, I decided it was very important to reach out to the legislative bodies of the world. If the President, as a single person, was too terrified, and too threatened to act, and his inner circle was being denied access to information, then the next best venue was Congress. So many senior White House officials were being denied access that it was clear only an open hearing in Congress could change things officially.

Regarding other senior officials being blocked: Astronaut Gordon Cooper personally told me that Secretary of Defense Cohen had learned of Gordon Cooper's team filming a landed UFO at a dry lake bed at Edwards Air Force base in the 1950s. Cohen tried to get access to that information but was denied access. Cohen knew the dates and details of the landing and filming - and yet Cohen could not gain access to the film or the records!

So, we met with a number of members of Congress, including a member of the Senate Intelligence Committee, Senator Dick Bryan, of Nevada -- home to Area 51 -- and others who were in key positions. As we networked, we found we could meet privately with a number of key Congressmen. We presented the evidence and asked them: "Please sponsor open hearings at which these top –secret witnesses can testify before a committee of Congress with the world news media present."

What I found in almost every case is that they all wanted to *know*, but they didn't want to *act*. I'll never forget being picked up by one of these little golf cart type vehicles at McCarran Airport in Las Vegas. I flew in just for a few hours to meet with Senator Bryan of Nevada during the mid '90s. We arrived at what looked like a janitor's closet with a nondescript door -- when you opened it, you entered a beautiful conference room! It was used for these types of VIP meetings at the airport. I was escorted into the room, and then the Senator came in. We spent about an hour together.

Senator Bryan had an aide with him who sat on the couch. The Senator and I and my escort were at the conference table. I don't believe the aide at first understood what the meeting was about! The Senator asked, "Well, who have you met with to-date?" and I said, "The CIA

Director and this person at the Joint Staff, and . . . ." I saw the aide drop the paper he was nonchalantly reading! He looked like someone had punched him.

As the briefing proceeded, Senator Bryan said he had no doubt these matters were real and ongoing, but that he had never been allowed access to that information. This, from the mouth of a senior member of the Senate Select Committee on Intelligence! I then said, "You know, we desperately need for someone like you to hold open hearings on this subject, much as Gerald Ford had in the late '60s…"

As soon as I said that, he changed from being extremely engaged to being very defensive. He said, "Well, you've met with all these people. Why doesn't the President do it?" I said, "I think you must know why the President won't. This is really a big nut to crack." And he said, "Well, I'm just a senator." I said, "Well, I'm just a doctor!

"You took an oath to uphold and defend the Constitution of the United States, and I am giving you evidence that the Constitution of the United States has been subverted, that the chain of command has been decapitated, that the Congress has been kicked to the curb, and that the most important technologies and information in the history of the human race are being managed by a rogue, illegal group. If this doesn't necessitate an inquiry by the Congress, what does?!" He sat impassively for a moment then said, " I don't know if I can do that, but have you spoken to John Warner on Armed Services?" I said with all the passion I could muster, "Sir, I'm speaking to you." I was trying to not let him wiggle off the hook! But it was clear that Senator Bryan was just terrified at the thought of pursuing the matter.

We went through this same process with numerous members of Congress, the Senate, the executive branch, the military, the United Nations, and others – with no action being taken. Eventually I was invited by a group at the United Nations to give a lecture there. The title of my talk was: "The Foundations of Interplanetary Peace." If you look in the papers in my first book, there is a chapter by that title. The paper was written because I was asked to give this presentation at the U.N. Most people don't realize that almost everything I've written has been in response to a request from a group interested in knowing the truth. This type of process has been the catalyst for the creation of my earlier books.

I took one of my daughters who was 12 at the time to this meeting at the UN. We arrived at the main entrance, where visitors go in. As we were waiting in line to go through security, I suddenly heard an enormous commotion in the lobby. I looked over, and there was the wife of the Secretary General of the United Nations, with the Chief of Protocol and Security and a whole entourage, motioning for me to come over. So they came over and opened up the rope, and we went through and bypassed security. We exchanged greetings and Mrs. Boutros-Ghali took my left arm, and I had my daughter's arm on my right. As this whole entourage is walking through the great entrance hall of the UN, Mrs. Boutros-Ghali turned to me and asked, "When are you going to get this done?" I said, "What do you mean?" And she said, "Well, this information that we are not alone has to get out to the world." I said, "Well, Leah, you and your husband are the head of the world! You're the head of the United Nations. I'm only a country doctor from North Carolina." And she said, "Oh, no. It's too dangerous for Boutros. They'll kill Boutros!"

And I thought to myself, "What am I? Chopped liver?" And of course, the answer is yes, I am just that. I'm cannon fodder— this is true. I'm the expendable one in these circles -- that was made very clear to me from '92 onwards.

So, I said, "You know, I can only do so much, Leah." She was among the most powerful women I've ever met. She had an enormous presence and was very spiritual and had great insight.

We requested that the long awaited Disclosure event take place at the U.N. They agreed to that. But around the time that the agreement was made, they ushered Boutros-Ghali out. Normally, the Secretary Generals get two terms. He only had one. They cited all sorts of reasons why they had to get rid of him, just like they got rid of Kurt Waldheim. And as it turns out, Kurt Waldheim had supported creating the Office of Outer Space Affairs, which does exist at the U.N., moving the office's headquarters out of New York to Europe where it could really look into these issues. But they axed him over this – and brought out the Nazi allegations against him. Boutros-Ghali was looking into these UFO issues, and they axed him.

So in comes Kofi Annan. A senior aide to Kofi Annan— a Korean who was the highest diplomat in the United Nations bureaucracy from Korea— reached out to us. He said, "They have agreed to let us have the big hall, at the United Nations, to host these top military and government witnesses to UFOs for a conference". This was agreed to.

But a few weeks later, this ambassador called me and said, "Never call me again at the United Nations. Here is my home number." He'd become interested because he'd been aware of some extraordinary UFO events that were happening in Korea. I was shocked. I asked, "What are you talking about?" He said, "Well, I know we've agreed to host this for you, but it can no longer happen. The Secretary General was visited by some people who showed him documents that so scared him that he knew he couldn't do anything more with this." I was told that the U.N., which was almost bankrupt, would have been shut down and closed! Essentially, these intelligence operatives and trans-national rogues threatened the UN leadership and put the fear of God in them.

A lot of my life has been wonderful—but dealing with the Shadow Government has been very disturbing. So disturbing that at times I have had to just let it all hang out with whoever is there. For example, one time I was meeting with a bunch of spooks in California who were associated with an Air Force base near Sacramento. It was an intense time and I thought, "Well, you know, I'm just going to go somewhere and have a drink and be quiet."

A man, I'll call him George, sat down beside me on a stool and starting talking. I was in no mood to talk, but he wanted to chat and asked, "What are you doing in town?"

"I'm *quite* sure you don't want to know." I said.

"Well, actually, I do." George said, munching on peanuts.

"Well, I've been here meeting with some people." I responded.

"Well, what do you do?" He asked.

I said, "I'm an emergency physician, but that's not why I'm here."

"Well, why are you here?" He asked,

And so I said, "You'll be sorry, but I'll tell you!" So I proceeded to do a massive brain dump into this poor soul. I told him everything I've shared with you, and more. I told him the name of every operative, every spook, every corporation, who'd been murdered, what cell killed Jack Kennedy, who was part of that cell that I've met with—I mean, the whole damned thing. You know, it felt great to get all that off my chest, but he looked like he'd been run over by a freight train! And I said, "Well, I told you I didn't think you wanted to hear this."

George asked, "How in the world can you be telling me all this?" I said, "Because I'm nobody. I'm not under any security classification." Intrigued, he asked, "Well, how do you know this stuff?" I said, "You don't even want to know that."

In a sense, this chance meeting was hilarious. "Well, let me buy you a beer." I said. "This has been very therapeutic for me."

He asked, "Well, what if I called up Dan Rather and told him all this?" I said, "You think that that spineless shill at CBS would report this?"

"Good luck." I said. "I know for a personal fact that Mike Wallace of

60 Minutes was given smoking gun evidence on this, years ago. Bob Schwartz, who was on the board of Time-Life and was a noted journalist, was friends with Mike Wallace and had given him the original MJ-12 documents. Wallace had vowed to do an expose on this; but it was killed— and he didn't have the guts to stand down the corporate whores at CBS to do the story." ,

"So, who are you going to go to that's going to get this out?"

"You're acting as if we have a free press, and we don't -- and haven't had one for decades." I said.

In the spring and summer of 1994, I started reaching out to some other folks who were involved in overseas operations related to UFOs. And one of them was S.A., a crown prince.

A friend of his, who was also interested in what we were doing and was very supportive, suggested that I talk to him and felt that we should get together. Prince S. A. was also friends with Laurance Rockefeller, and as it turned out, had been pulled into the Col. MK / General T.E. / W.B. shadow cell operating here in the United States.

Well, after we spoke on the phone, I received a personal letter from Prince S.A., saying "I think what you're trying to do is very noble. However, I don't believe you will be allowed to do it, and I need to speak with you about this." He didn't want to talk about it on the phone. He wanted to meet.

So,we met in July of 1994. He was in New York City, staying at the Four Seasons Pierre Hotel, which is on Fifth Avenue near Central Park, not far from Laurance Rockefeller's home. So, I went to New York with one of our daughters.

You have to understand, I took my daughters everywhere. We had what were called "Dates with Daddy." My life being what it was, I needed to involve them. It was wonderful having time with each one alone, so we would take these special trips.

So, we went to the hotel to meet the Prince. He is very elegant, courteous and friendly. While my daughter played quietly in a corner, we had a private meeting to discuss the entire UFO matter.

After a time, he finally got to what he wanted to say to me in the letter but didn't want to write or say on the telephone. The Prince said, "You know, you won't be allowed to do this disclosure." I said, "Oh, why is that?" He says, "You won't be allowed to, but not because of what you think." He said, "The aliens won't let you." I said, "Really?"

Well, it turns out the Prince's brother had been abducted by what he thought were aliens. But the Prince did not know that the abduction was done by a covert paramilitary operation. This was investigated by a NASA researcher who I've worked with for years but who doesn't know that I learned that this NASA researcher is part of the shadow government and is an eschatological, fundamentalist, end-of-the-world Christian. He interfaces in the UFO world as an objective scientist investigating serious UFO phenomenon, but that is not his real role. This particular NASA scientist told me that the Prince's brother had been abducted from the castle in his country.

Now, what he didn't know is that I have a source inside the covert paramilitary operations who do abductions who told me that, "Yes, of course, we abducted him so that this particular powerful family and the banking empire would be on board with our program to fight the aliens." Prince S.A. told me these extraterrestrials had been the cause of every conflict on Earth since Adam and Eve and that they were the ones enforcing the secrecy! I asked, "Really? Why do you think they appear over us with dozens of witnesses, interacting and signaling to us and appear over major cities of the world, if they're wanting to be so secret?" He had no answer for that. I said, "I have to disagree with you. I think it is a very human group that wants to keep this secret, because to disclose it would mean the end of the entire centralized power system that exists, all fossil fuels, and the entire paradigm of anthropocentric religiosity."

We had a frank but courteous exchange of ideas, and then we agreed to disagree. It was clear that the Prince viewed the ET presence as something to fear and hate – and that he supported military action against them.

But in the course of this, he told me, "President Bush(Senior) wanted to do this, as well. Around the time of the end of the Cold War, a group that I was involved with that included Gorbachev, President Bush, the United Nations Secretary General, Perez de Cuellar, were meeting to plan the release of this information to the public." This was in 1989. He said, "But one night, during a late night planning session in New York, the Secretary General of the United Nations, Perez de Cuellar was coming back from a meeting where the plans were being put in place to make this announcement about ETs, and a UFO appeared, stopped his motorcade, and abducted him out of the limousine! They took him on board the craft, and told him that if they didn't stop this plan to disclose the extraterrestrial presence, that every world leader involved, including the United States President, would be abducted and taken off this planet and that they would stop the process!"

This is the famous case where an abduction researcher talks about a major international figure being abducted, along with a civilian who witnessed it. What they didn't know is that I knew people in the cell operating the alien reproduction vehicles and the psychotronic weapons systems that were set up and conducted this abduction. In fact, a relative of the infamous red-headed sergeant at Roswell who threatened everyone, was there to coordinate the event. He was inserted as part of the security detail for the Secretary General, and he set up the electronics at the site of the Secretary General's motorcade, so that this late night pseudo-abduction of the U.N. Secretary General could take place.

The goal of the operation was to stop this entire attempt by the world's power elites, including Gorbachev, to disclose the truth to the world.

Now, Prince S.A. really thought it was an alien abduction, just like he thought his brother was abducted by aliens. He didn't know that those abduction events are paramilitary operations run by humans, using things that look like UFOs and even having creatures on board that look like extraterrestrials but are either disguised humans or manmade creatures.

This is called 'stagecraft', and I have a document that describes these operations. It is from one of the private institutes involved in the simulation of alien abductions. This has gone so far that they have engaged in the abduction of world leaders to try to cause them to hate extraterrestrials and support Star Wars. It also convinces these leaders to shut down any effort to get the information out.

18

Astral Body Extractions

When the Prince told me about the effort being stopped, I realized how serious and maniacal and -- I hate to use this word – evil – the Shadow Government is. So utterly drunk on power are they that they're willing to do anything and everything to keep this secret.

I told the Prince I was quite certain that, since we had had open contact with extraterrestrial beings and our information was the opposite of what he was saying, that he had been the target of disinformation.

We had a casual conversation about the CE-5 Initiative, and he expressed an interest in CSETI. What he said next was very insightful, "You know, I've gone all over the world where these UFOs are being reported, and they will have sightings before I arrive and they will come back after I leave, but while I'm there, they're never around. I wonder if it's because of my attitude."

"Well, Your Highness, "I said, "with all due respect, I believe you've hit the nail on the head. We have found that if one is free of prejudice, open-minded, and willing to engage with these extraterrestrial beings in a completely pure-hearted way, that they will be there. And they will interact."

Piggybacking onto this meeting, of course, was this covert group, monitoring every minute of it. That night my daughter and I went back to our hotel, the St. Moritz on Central Park South, right across from Central Park.

After falling fast asleep, I awakened hours later. I couldn't raise my arms; I couldn't roll over; I couldn't move! I was in a state of complete physical paralysis. I knew what was going on; a directional electromagnetic weapons system hit me. It was coming through the window above my bed. Projected into the room was the single most extreme sense of evil and terror I've ever felt in my life. I could tell they were attempting to extract my astral body out of my physical body. (This is what most pseudo-abductions are, by the way – astral body extractions.)

The Shadow Government was showing me that they meant business and were prepared to abduct me. They were trying to convince me, as they had the Prince, that I should hate and fear 'aliens'. They wanted to convince me that the aliens were evil; that they were from Satan; that we needed a holy war against them. They were attempting to convince me by teaching me a very hard lesson.

But I knew this was man-made. The only thing I could do was turn to God. I held onto the hem of the robe of God. I went into a state of transcendental consciousness and God consciousness, and as I did so, my individuality disappeared into the Infinite- and this violent group lost their hold on me.

Once in the Unbounded, this system could no longer hold me. There was no "me" there; you see what I'm saying? "Leave thyself behind and then walk upon the water." Be as nothing, and then be everywhere. I have told people who are being targeted with these systems, "The only way to escape them is to understand the power of transcending self and letting the drop of your individuality merge with the ocean of Unbounded-ness."

But as soon as I re-emerged into my individuality and consciousness, the attack would begin all over again. It was one of the worst things I've ever experienced. They were clearly trying to grab my individuality, extract my astral being, and put me through their abduction sequence. Now, remember, if you cause enough trauma to the astral body, it can manifest in the physical. This is something many people don't understand. Most of these abduction events are actualized by technologies that can extract the astral body from the physical body.

Project Amethyst, run by a black cell at the NSA, killed people by severing the cord between the astral body and the physical body. I know a guy who ran that program.

This experience was, in a way, a gift -- because they tipped their hand and they showed me exactly what they had done to the Secretary General and what they had done to the brother of Prince S.A.. I was then able to remote view back through this electronic beam and see the people in the facility -- all human -- that were running it. You see, anything that comes at you -- if you stay calm and centered and in this transcendental state of consciousness— you can track back to its source and expose them. So, every time they've hit me, that's what I've done. And that's how I've seen what they're doing.

I have to admit, this was one of the most difficult things I have had to do -- to stay in control of my own faculties while this was happening, so I could quickly escape the bounds of relativity, enter into the plane of the Absolute, where they couldn't get me -- because I didn't exist anymore.

My daughter, thank God, was protected from all this and had no knowledge of any of it. So, that was our little trip to New York!

I have independently confirmed that some of the mid-level appa-ratchiks of this covert, shadow group -- which include a former US President — were in favor of disclosing this information in the late 1980s. But there was another group that trumped them—- and it is a fac-tion within this larger control group. This cell has the abduction tech-nologies, and they have the scalar psychotronic weapons systems and radionic weapons systems. They also have the ARVs- Alien Reproduction Vehicles- that look like UFOs and operate with new ener-gy and anti-gravity propulsion systems.

This cell uses these advanced technologies to contain disclosure on an official level— up to and including threatening the leadership of the world and abducting a world leader, like a Secretary General of the United Nations.

After this near pseudo-abduction experience in New York, I recalled a lucid dream I had around 1990-1991. In the dream, I was floating above Kennebunkport, Maine and saw something that was really very disturb-ing. I saw the United States President, George Bush, at his compound there. There were objects in the sky that looked like UFOs, but were actually manned by paramilitary rogue elements. They were flying around the compound, and out at sea, and were threatening the U.S. President. The Secret Service and George Bush were very worried about this. It made no sense to me at the time that I saw it. But after this meet-ing, where I learned what the Prince told me about the abduction of Perez de Cuellar, I understood who was doing it and why.

I also realized that, at the end of the Cold War, there was a sincere attempt to get this information out to the public, and that this cell with-in a cell within a cell -- this rogue, violent, and very dangerous group -- had stopped it. That was in late '89. And it was January of '90 that I was told to "pick up that which I had dropped." Even though, to the rogue group I am an insignificant person and have no temporal power or offi-cial position, because officialdom got stopped dead in its tracks, mysteri-ously, somehow I was being called to help.

People like Col. MK, who is known as Dr. Death and has a PhD in thananology, the study of death, are masters of psychotronics and high-tech electronic systems that are responsible for abductions, mind control, and similar attacks. So, when you realize what our leaders are up against— it doesn't matter if they're Skull and Bones, and it doesn't mat-ter if they're a former CIA Director -- if they try to step out of line, they run into this other group. This inner high cabal is hell bent on keeping this subject tied up until there is a worst case scenario. Their objective is the elimination of at least four to five billion of the six billion people on Earth.

After returning from this event in New York in 1994, I experienced the horrifying force of the Shadow Government. Every night at 4:20 a.m., as I was sleeping in my bedroom at home, there would be an almost sub-audible click, and I would be hit with an electronic weapons system. I would become violently ill and so sick that I would get up and be nauseated, vomiting, with diarrhea, diaphoretic. The bathroom floor would literally be soaked with sweat, because I had almost no blood pressure, and I would collapse on the floor of the bedroom, near death. This happened to me night after night after night, day after day. It was horrifying. It lasted for only 10 or 15 minutes. I know that this rogue group was trying to make me stop what I was doing—but I refused to stop.

During this period, I remember one night going to sleep and suddenly seeing someone with this group at an electronic control panel. It was an array of psychotronic and radionic high-tech equipment at an underground facility out west. I clearly saw the handler for this particular operation standing outside the entrance to an underground weapons facility. He was a middle-aged man with a moustache and graying hair— I know exactly how he looks; he was assigned to my case.

Inside this facility were some young men who were the grunts, the cannon fodder, operating this system to hit me. When I saw them, I turned to God and I said, "Dear God, forgive them!" and sent them a blessing. I saw them very clearly - and then I saw them seeing me. They had such a look of shame in their eyes. They looked away, and it all ended. After this, they stopped these nighttime attacks .

I later learned that the poor people who run these devices often end up dying from what they're doing -- that if they're projecting a disease onto someone, they get it. As usual, the operators and lower rung personnel are cannon fodder. They don't know it when they take the assignment. And that's why these handlers were outside the building from which the system was being operated.

I learned from this experience that, as these weapons were being directed at me, I could track back on the scalar electronic system, back to the source and see what they were doing. I would then put divine light around all of us and ask for their forgiveness—and also forgive them myself.

Around the same time, I learned that Colin Andrews, the crop circle researcher from England, was experiencing some weird happenings, also in the early morning, preceded by this strange sub-audible click.

I was tested severely during those years to see whether I would stay on this course. I was extremely close, in the summer of 1994, to closing CSETI, ending the Disclosure Project, and just walking away from all of it.

I tell people: Visualize what happened on the last day, the last hour, the last five minutes of my last shift at the emergency department where I worked for 10 years. A little boy was at a picnic, and he choked to death. He could not be resuscitated at the scene, and was brought into the ER. He was a beautiful little boy with blond hair and about three or four years old.

We worked on him for an hour, but he was already flat line when he arrived. He died in my arms. And in comes his big bear of a father, who collapses in my arms, weeping and screaming, a bloodcurdling cry like you've never heard, when I tell him his son is dead.

Dealing with this subject every day is orders of magnitude more traumatic for me than that. And for the nurses and me, having a little child die on my last day was as bad as it gets.

Hearing about CSETI experiences is like listening to a version of the X Files, but this isn't Hollywood; it's the real thing. There are aspects of my work that are wonderful and beautiful, and there are other aspects of this effort that are enormously painful and tragic. Perhaps this is a perfect metaphor of the times in which we live; there's so much beauty and promise, and yet there's also so much suffering.

19

"We Are Always With You"

A few interesting anecdotes will give you an idea of the kinds of people I've encountered doing this work.

For example, while organizing the conference with Astronaut Brian O'Leary in Colorado in 1992, we were approached by a woman who was insisting on coming to the private retreat for researchers. This was Col. MK's companion, now wife, who was claiming to be a journalist.

She was actually part of Psy-Ops and Psy- warfare projects with the Colonel, whose specialty was psychotronic, radionic, mind-control weapons and what are incorrectly called non-lethal weapons systems. These EM weapon systems are actually used, at times, to kill people and use so-called scalar, longitudinal electromagnetic waves.

Somehow, she got my home number. I was away, so she called my wife—a wonderful woman who epitomizes noblesse oblige and kindness. So this woman said, "Just exactly who do I have to *fuck* to get into this meeting?" This, to my wife! Such was our introduction to the enlightened community of spooks and UFO sub-culture crazies, and it's been downhill from there.

That's all you need to know about the caliber of such folk. When I tell people that the people you encounter in this field are some of the meanest, nastiest, most venal, corrupt people that you will ever meet anywhere on Earth in any sub-culture or setting, I mean it.

But you also meet some wonderful people. One of the people who came to a lecture was Dorothy Ives, the wife of Oscar-winning actor Burl Ives. Mr. Ives had been friends with the Nixons and the Reagans and with a number of other political figures, and was a 32nd Degree Mason.

Dorothy came up to me after the lecture, very excited, and asked if I'd return to her home and meet with Burl. I suggested that she come with me up to the MacGuire Ranch where we were going to make contact with the ETs, and then we could go see Burl.

So after the conference in Denver, we drove up to the McGuire Ranch, in Wyoming, outside of Laramie. We got there about sunset, and were doing our contact protocols. Right as the sun was going down, suddenly a brilliant, disc-shaped UFO appeared on top of a cloud and hovered. It winked in and out of the cloud and was signaling to the whole group.

Dorothy had never seen such a thing. I explained, "They're here, and they're very much connected with us all the time. They know when we're going to go out and do this CE-5 Contact protocol." Often, when we would arrive onto a site to do this work, the ETs would already be there, because I would have told them where we were going and what time we'd be there. Dorothy was just amazed, and she exclaimed, "Burl has got to meet you." .

We left from Denver and flew to Seattle and then drove up to their home in Anacortes WA, right on the water.

Burl and I became fast friends. The way you would see him on the stage is exactly the way he was in person. One of the greats of the 20th Century, by any account.

We met for a long time discussing a plethora of issues, the secrecy, the technologies, ET contact.... "You know, this is the most sane crazy person you've ever introduced me to," he told Dorothy, who was always meeting interesting and eccentric people. He understood that what we were dealing with was something that had a lot of profound dimensions to it and that our approach was very rational and very sane—given how "far out" all this is.

Dorothy initially didn't quite know who I really was or the extent to which I had deep contacts within the intelligence and national security community. Eventually, this came up and I told her, "There's a man whose family has deep ties with the National Security Agency. They are senior NSA people, and are handing off some documents to me."

One of these documents was a big, oversized xerox copy of a 1962 document. It had code names like 'Project Moondust, Project 46', on it and it was classified top secret- but had not been declassified! It was given to me so I could get it to the right people. This document was a wiretap transcript summary of what they learned from listening in on Marilyn Monroe.

This document has been authenticated by the top document authenticator in the world. An FBI agent told me, "You know, you can go to jail for X number of years and be fined thousands of dollars each time you show this to anyone." I said, "Really? I've already shown it to a few thousand people. Come put the handcuffs on! My first call will be to Ted Koppel or Larry King, and not to some lawyer." He looked at me like I was crazy, and I said, "You think I'm kidding? Try me." Here's the headline: 'Emergency doctor goes to jail because he revealed a document that confirms that spooks at the agency whacked Marilyn Monroe before they ended up whacking the President.' Now," I said, "you want that to hit the front page? Come get me." He just shook his head with a look of shock – but they left me alone. We never heard from that spook again.

This document describes how Marilyn Monroe, who had been recently jilted by the Kennedy brothers and was upset and hurt, called Robert Kennedy and a socialite in New York, an art dealer friend of hers. Marilyn Monroe stated that she was going to set up a press conference and tell the public what Jack Kennedy had told her regarding objects from outer space that had crashed and been retrieved in New Mexico in the 1940's! President Kennedy had confided this information to her, because he had seen the ET craft and debris from the UFO crash there. This still-top-secret document is dated the day before the night they found Marilyn Monroe dead. I've also located someone who was with the Los Angeles Police Department intelligence unit that helped facilitate the wiretapping and monitoring of her up to the time of her death and actually knew how they killed Marilyn Monroe. There is no doubt that she was murdered by cut-out agents of the US intelligence community.

Importantly, this document was signed by James Angleton— the legendary, fanatical mole hunter and leak stopper within the CIA. This document, in my opinion, was a death warrant for Marilyn Monroe, because it summarized what she was intending to do rather imminently. I don't think she knew what she had stumbled onto, in terms of the kind of buzz saw that was going to come at her.

I'm now working with someone who has similar documentation on the murder of Mary Meyer. Mary Meyer was the long-term paramour of Jack Kennedy who was shot on the C&O Canal path in Georgetown, back in 1964, because she knew too much. This contact has identified sources that knew why they murdered Meyer. And it's the same reason they murdered Marilyn Monroe!

When I mentioned all this to Burl he said, "Marilyn Monroe and I knew each other very well and I can tell you this: All of us who knew her knew that she had been murdered, but it wasn't until today that I knew why!"

Some of the people that Burl knew were good friends with Ronald Reagan. He was able to confirm information that I had heard from other sources. For example, I have met two people who were with Ronald Reagan during the screening of "Close Encounters of the Third Kind" by Steven Spielberg. This movie is actually a documentary or docudrama, since most of what is depicted came from Air Force files that Spielberg secretly had access to at Wright Patterson Air Force Base. Ronald Reagan

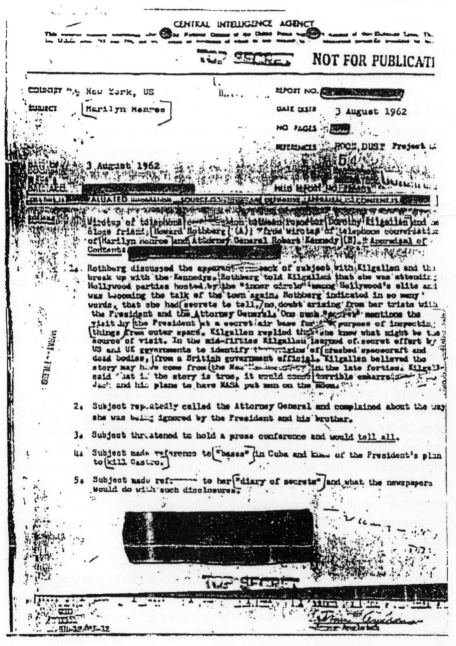

000959

CENTRAL INTELLIGENCE AGENCY

TOP SECRET   NOT FOR PUBLICATI

COUNTRY : New York, US   REPORT NO.

SUBJECT   Marilyn Monroe   DATE DIST   3 August 1962

                                          NO PAGES

                                          REFERENCE ROCK DUST Project

3 August 1962

EVALUATED INFORMATION

Wiretap of telephone conversation between reporter Dorothy Kilgallen and a
close friend, Howard Rothberg (A). Wiretap of telephone conversation
of Marilyn Monroe and Attorney General Robert Kennedy (B). Appraisal of
Contents

1. Rothberg discussed the apparent break of subject with Kilgallen and the
break up with the Kennedys. Rothberg told Kilgallen that she was attending
Hollywood parties hosted by the "inner circle" among Hollywood's elite and
was becoming the talk of the town again. Rothberg indicated in so many
words, that she had secrets to tell, no doubt arising from her trists with
the President and the Attorney General. One such secret mentions the
visit by the President at a secret air base for the purpose of inspecting
things from outer space. Kilgallen replied that she knew what might be the
source of visit. In the mid-fifties Kilgallen learned of secret effort by
US and UK governments to identify the origins of crashed spacecraft and
dead bodies, from a British government official. Kilgallen believed the
story may have come from the New York. in the late forties. Kilgallen
said that if the story is true, it would cause terrible embarrassment for
Jack and his plans to have NASA put men on the Moon.

2. Subject repeatedly called the Attorney General and complained about the way
she was being ignored by the President and his brother.

3. Subject threatened to hold a press conference and would tell all.

4. Subject made reference to "bases" in Cuba and knew of the President's plan
to kill Castro.

5. Subject made reference to her "diary of secrets" and what the newspapers
would do with such disclosures.

TOP SECRET

turned to the people who were at the screening at the White House and said, "There are only a couple people in this room who know how true what this movie is portraying is." This was repeated to me by two separate witnesses.

Most people don't realize that one of the chief control points for the secrecy is the mobbed-up culture of money and corruption in Hollywood and the big media. It's very much infiltrated by interests of the "national security" shadow state.

Of course, when you're someone like Burl Ives, you know everyone and everyone knows you. So, one meeting led to another, and I ended up meeting a number of celebrities. What I found from some of these meetings was that the UFO matter was an open secret - people knew it was real and that there had been assassinations and murders to keep it secret. Hollywood and the entire film and media industry was mobbed-up, top down, with control points that had become more and more entrenched, as time went on.

I learned from a number of people that you can't really do films on the subject of ETs anymore unless there's a heavy militaristic, xenophobic overlay. We went from "Close Encounters of the Third Kind" and "E.T." to movies like "Independence Day" and silly things like "Men in Black" or "Mars Attack". These movies all have an invasion or military conflict theme. These covert interests want the populace brain-washed via this type of propaganda to the falsehood of "alien hostility."

Hollywood, and the media in general, are key control points.

After I taught Dorothy how to do the CSETI CE-5 protocols, she decided to practice them one afternoon while sitting on the edge of the ocean at Anacortes, Washington. She was with one of her grandchildren, and suddenly a UFO appeared! It was going in and out of the clouds and communicating and signaling with her. Her granddaughter said, "Oh, God, look at that." And it was then that Dorothy knew she had this connection and could make contact.

During the LA Northridge earthquake in the 1990s, Dorothy woke up around 4:30 Pacific time and went downstairs. As she looked outside, she saw a golden light coming through the foyer windows. She looked outside at the source of the light and saw a large extraterrestrial vehicle, just right above the tree line. And she was in the beam of light.

She immediately began to receive a message mentally: "Do not be afraid, you will be safe, we are always with you, you will be protected..." She instantly felt compelled to call her best friend in LA, just as the North Ridge earthquake was happening. This woman said, "Oh, we're having an earthquake, but you won't believe what's here!" And she told Dorothy, "There's this dish-shaped craft with golden light coming from it, and I'm in a beam, and I'm getting this message that says, 'Do not be afraid; you will be safe. We are with you, and you will be protected.'"

It was exactly the same message, at the same instant, coming from identical craft that had placed them in this golden light. It was as if there was no separation in space or that the ET craft had bi-located and was in two places at once.

Dorothy called and told me what had happened. I told her that there might be a lot of changes in the world, including the potential for major geophysical and other changes, and that these extraterrestrial people are connected to us and will help stabilize the earth and protect humanity.

An interesting encounter happened when I was invited to Cambridge University in the 1990s to give a lecture to the international conference of MENSA, which is a high IQ group. I made a very serious, main-stream, data oriented, scientifically oriented presentation.

At the end of my talk, an elderly man stood up and said, "I'll have you know that I'm Dr. So-and-So. And I've been on this committee and that committee in the British government. And if there was any truth to this, *I* would know about it. Moreover, I find it utterly depressing that a man of your intelligence would be wasting your life on such drivel!" His neck veins were popping out and his face was red with anger. This, in front of hundreds of people!

I said, "Well, with all due respect, if there's even a ten percent chance that this is true and there are technologies that enable inter-stellar travel and could run this planet without pollution or poverty for thousands of years and create a sustainable world, it's worth my career and any sacrifice we make. Next question?"

So, now, the post script to this: we had a banquet in one of the grand halls at Cambridge that's still illumined with torches and candles. As I was leaving the banquet, I heard feet running up behind me, clack, clack, clack, clack, clack. There were a couple of young scientists who had been with this senior scientist who had been so agitated by my talk.

They said, "We wanted to apologize for Dr. So-and-So's behavior." And I said, "Oh, that's okay, I've been called every name in the book, and I'm used to that…" Then they said, "No, you don't understand. He was so upset not because he didn't think it was true, but because he's an eminent scientist and a physicist, and deep inside, he thought maybe it really was true, and it meant everything he knew and had been teaching for 60 years of his career was rubbish!"

This man thought, "My God, if this is true -- and I think it could be -- then what I know about science and physics is a fairy tale and isn't even kindergarten level science!" And if this is true, being an eminent scientist at Cambridge did not change that fact.

This is a phenomenon that I have seen over and over again. I have been the unfortunate person who's had to walk into meetings with the likes of a Lord Hill Norton, or the head of the Defense Intelligence Agency or someone who's a senior scientist with the National Science Foundation and share this information with them. These are important people, in important positions. And yet they realize there is an entire universe of operations, technology, science and power beyond their control. It is very disturbing.

Many come to realize that they are a pawn or a cog in a machine not of their making—or liking. It is traumatic to learn this when they're at what they consider the apex of their career and power.

There are a number of predictable responses: anger, denial, acceptance, fear.

In the mid-'90s, I was invited by the Board of Directors of Noetic Sciences to do a briefing for their board. The founder of Noetic Sciences was there along with a number of very prominent people. I presented what we were doing, what our findings were, what the evidence was. They also had a few disinformation people present who, at one time, had done good work in the field, but who had since been bought off by intelligence interests.

One such asset of the Shadow Government made a presentation saying, "This is all a mythology, and there are these little balls of light occasionally seen." He completely whitewashed all the hard evidence that he once wrote about. It was a very interesting thing to watch. I then stood up and politely said, "Well, on the contrary...."

Also, he was proposing, "Of course, these things don't actually exist in the physical world because they're inter-dimensional."

I said, "Well, inter-dimensional means nothing, insofar as a flower is inter-dimensional because it has folded within it everything from the physical reality of the flower to the astral form and light that is within it, to the idea form, the causal idea of the flower. And the actual conscious intelligence that created it and that sustains it is still present within the flower. *So everything is inter-dimensional.*" There's nothing that *isn't.*"

I said, "Look at your own selves. You have within yourself an opening to the Infinite Mind, and all the universe that's folded within it, as well as your own so-called causal body, as the mystics would call the idea form of what you are. And within and supporting your physical body is your astral body—the body of light that you can fly around with in lucid dreams or at other times."

I said, "The human being is completely inter-dimensional, or trans-dimensional, and encompasses every fine and infinite level of creation all the way to the grossest manifestion, the physical. So, what are we talking about when we say 'inter-dimensional'? It means nothing to say this. Everything is inter-dimensional. The question is: Are you in touch with enough dimensions to express them? Well, an adept, in India, may be able to de-materialize his body and become invisible. Or he might be able to manifest a ring or an object. But an extraterrestrial civilization may be able to do the same things through both mental capabilities and technological assistance. So, the fact that there are inter-dimensional expressions of ET technology does not mean they're not extraterrestrial or physical. It's not an either/or question. Such an argument is like two people debating whether an orange is round or the color orange, when it's both orange, the color, and round."

That night, we were hosted by Paul and Diane Temple for dinner. They are venture capitalists and have a large estate next to George Lucas' ranch, near San Raphael, CA.

Senator Claiborne Pell was also there for the dinner. Senator Pell really epitomized the best of our leaders; he was a very enlightened man. Senator Pell knew what we were doing. I had worked with some of his staff and aides. So we met in California in San Rafael at this hilltop home.

Senator Pell, Emily and I stepped between huge Lalique doors that opened out onto the patio. We began to talk out under the stars. Senator Pell looked at me through his black horn-rimmed glasses and said, "You know, Dr. Greer, I've been interested in this for years, and I've been in the Congress since Jack Kennedy was a Congressman. I've been on every committee, and have made inquiries into this, and I've never gotten a straight answer." He then asked, "Would you be willing to come and brief my staff on this and share with us what you know?"

"Well, Senator, I'd be very happy to do that— any time we can set it up." I answered.

He then said, "But I don't know why they wouldn't tell me - why have I been kept in the dark?"

I made a few comments, as I have to others, about why. The "why" is always the hardest thing to answer, the most painful thing to answer, actually. "You know, Senator Pell, it's a crying shame, because here you are, one of the truly enlightened members of the Senate. You could do so much good as Chairman of the Senate Foreign Relations Committee. But you have been deprived of dealing with the *ultimate foreign relations issue!*" I said this, pointing to the stars above our head. He looked at me and blinked through his horn-rimmed glasses and said, "Well, Dr. Greer, I'm afraid you may be right."

I said, "Yes! You, and people like you, should have been the vanguard of the human race making contact with these peoples and managing these technologies and managing our relations with them, instead of a rogue kleptocracy stealing it from us. The entire time you have been in the Congress and Senate, you have been blocked from dealing with the most important issue of this century." It was a very poignant moment...

I felt it very important for Senator Pell to understand what is at stake here: It isn't just about him knowing; it's about him and people like him who are in the constitutional chain of command of our country, and who could manage this well but who are deprived of doing so. He and Senator Byrd and Senator Bryan have been pushed out and the whole matter has been hijacked out of legal oversight and control into a rogue, illegal covert management.

Occasionally, when pressed, I have been asked, "Don't some of the members of the Congress know what's going on and are part of this effort to keep the secret?" Yes. And we know who they are. One of the people who is central to maintaining the status quo and is a major control point in blocking information at the level of the Congress is a senior Senator. Former Congressman George Brown of California, who is since deceased, was involved with this group and was responsible, as a member of the Science and Technology Committee, for keeping this quiet. There are other people who are cooperating with the secrecy, such as former Chairman of the House Intelligence Committee and current CIA Director, Porter Goss. I have provided information to him via a member of our team who is a very close family friend.

The fact is that you only need a few points of control in these institutions to keep it secret. These players then go to their colleagues in the Congress and say, "I've had top access, and none of this is true." Memo to their colleagues: People lie.

Over the years, the covert government has always kept a few such operatives in key points of control in various institutions, to maintain the secrecy and to maintain the current order of covert management. This is true for every major country in the world, every major Parliament in the world, and every major religion in the world. Academia and the scientific community are also similarly infiltrated.

On the same trip I was invited to the home of Y.H., an incredibly spiritual, pure hearted woman who is the original publisher of a major new thought book and is a very big supporter of what we're doing. Her husband, who is a former military man, knows about these things, and we've had long, interesting discussions about UFOs.

One of the things that Y.H. shared with me is that she had become friends over the years with a number of people who have been involved in these types of projects, covertly. She knew Andrija Puharich, Marcel Vogel at IBM and others who had an enormous amount of knowledge— but their knowledge was being used to empower technologies within this shadowy, covert corporate world. She knew other people who played a dual role of acquiring information and passing it up the chain of command, only to then go out to the public and spread disinformation.

One such figure is a physicist dealing with zero point energy. He told Y. that he knew of actual operational free energy and zero point energy devices, but that he is NSA and naval intelligence. After speaking with this physicist, he virtually told me that he's an intelligence operative.

Yet, something that he explained to Y. caused me to have an enormous amount of compassion for people in his position. At the same time, there's a certain element of revulsion. He said that he very much wanted the truth to come out and for these Earth-saving new energy technologies to be put into use, but that if he talked about what he knew, he was convinced his family and children would be killed.

It seems he had sold his soul to the devil, in the course of his career— and yet his whole being sincerely wants the world to have these wondrous new sources of clean energy. So, he's deeply conflicted. His role has been to say, "This is possible, but we don't yet have it," when, in reality, he knows we have these technologies but can't talk about them without risking his life and that of his family. This is a common theme.

The Disclosure Project's goal is to get people who have the courage of their convictions to come together as a team — and speak the truth! There is safety in numbers and credibility in numbers. But so many of these people we reached out to, in shadowy operations, would say to me, "I want the truth out, but I'd like to breathe the free air of Earth for another 30 days." Their fear was stronger than their sense of duty, and they felt that if they spoke out, they were dead men walking.

I also met with Congressman Christopher Cox, currently head of the Securities and Exchange Commission, and who is on the short list of people who eventually will be running for President of the United States in the Republican Party. Harvard-educated, he's a very bright man representing Orange County CA, and was on a number of key committees. A friend and supporter of CSETI, who knows Congressman Cox, and who is an executive with IBM in Orange County, asked me to brief him.

Shortly after the meeting began, Cox said, "I have no doubt this is true, but I've never heard of it, and I've been on some pretty important committees." So I told him about all the folks I've met with who are out of the loop who should be in the loop and that this is a common theme.

Remember, The Disclosure Project is not just disclosing things to the millions of people on the Internet and CNN, but also to people like Christopher Cox, who do need to know.

Sometimes these contacts and meetings happen rather mysteriously. At times I will go to a city, and lie down in my hotel room and ask, "Who is here that I need to speak with?" I will go into a meditative state and let my awareness travel to whomever it is I should see. I will then see a specific person, and decide, "I'm going to go to this particular place and ask this person to be there."

And when I go to that place, there they are! I see them exactly like I saw them in my meditation. They vaguely say, "You look familiar" I say, "Oh, yeah?" And then we talk, and they always ask, "Well, what do you do?" And I'll just flat out tell them. Invariably, they will say something like," I work with SAIC -- Science Applications International Corporation -- and you don't know how right you are. Let me tell you about what I have seen..." We have received information from dozens of important intelligence sources this way.

20

A Different Day

In 1994, I was invited to be on a special with Larry King. The show was broadcast live from near Nellis Air Force Base, Area 51. Larry King's producer, at the time, a guy named Farmer, told me it was the most watched special they'd ever had.

There was a point in the interview when Larry turned to me and he asked, "Well, what do you think the President knows about this?" As you now know, I had put together the briefing document for the President and Dr. Jack Gibbons, the science advisor to the President, and had met with the CIA Director the preceding December. So I said, "Well, I think you should ask the President that question." And I remember one of the other guests and Larry King said at the same instant: "What does that mean?" I said, "Well, I think it would be better if you asked the President that question." I was very cryptic.

Afterwards, in Larry King's trailer we spent some private time together, because he knew that I wasn't saying everything. He asked me what I was really up to and I confided in him off the record about our contacts to the President and that I had already briefed the CIA Director. He said, "My God, why didn't you say that on the air? That would have been a scoop! --" I said, "Because I'm still working with these people."

I was discreet about this meeting with the CIA Director until after he had left office in '95 or '96.

"My God, this stuff is really real?" Larry asked.

"Of course it is." I said. And then we had a very interesting conversation. Later I said, "But Larry, why are CNN and the other news outlets covering the OJ Simpson trial and tabloid trash like that 24/7? I don't know anyone who's even remotely interested in that stuff. Everyone's so sick of hearing about it."

"Well, we have to." He said.

"What do you mean, you have to? You're a journalist. Why don't you report the big stories of the day? This is the biggest story of the century." I exclaimed.

"Well, the corporate guys tell us that to keep our ratings up and compete with the other networks, we have to cover this kind of lurid stuff, and they pay my big pay check. It's all about ratings, and ratings get the advertising dollars, and advertising dollars pay me my big salary." And he was just that direct about it.

I said, "Yes, but what about journalistic integrity and editorial discretion about what's important, what is really newsworthy?"

"Oh, come on." He said, "That's out the window and has been for years. It's all about money and ratings."

You don't think the big media can go any lower, until it hits another low point. It really is a race to the bottom – and they hit new lows every year!

There are also covert national security filters in place to keep these big, sensitive stories out of the news. The corruption of the media is the central reason for the secrecy.

In 1995, we organized the first gathering of witnesses. There were about 18 colonels and aerospace people and people from all over the United States and Russia. We gathered at Asilomar, which is a retreat in Pacific Grove, California, near Monterey. Laurance Rockefeller was very supportive of this and his people were there, as well as some of the initial witnesses.

It was all videotaped and audiotaped, but the people, to whom I entrusted this task, took all the tapes and made a back-door deal with the Rockefeller group. So we don't have any of the records of that testimony! And to this day, we have not retrieved it.

Sometimes people will see me being very fierce and careful about people and organizations; there's a good reason for this. That kind of theft and betrayal has happened over and over again.....

In late 1996/ early 1997 we decided that we needed to do a formal briefing in Washington, DC to which we would invite government whistle-blower witnesses and members of Congress and other influential political people to whom we had contacts.

Prior to that briefing Shari Adamiak, Neil Cunningham, a picture editor for the BBC in London, and I went to a lab in Phoenix run by covert operatives

One of the operatives said, "You can use our digital labs to put together all the videotape, for this meeting for Congress..." We had collected videotape and photographic images of UFOs from all over the world. Neil Cunningham of the BBC was going to help us put together the best-ever images to show. Of course, we knew who this man was and we knowingly walked right into spook central.

I flew into Phoenix on a U.S. Airways flight and as we were landing, I began the CE-5 protocols. I went into an expanded state of consciousness and into space and began vectoring extraterrestrial vehicles into the Phoenix area.   I told the ETs, "It'd be great if you can do something undeniable while we're here that we can put into this footage to share with the Congress whom we will be briefing in a couple weeks." This was on March 13, 1997, and the briefing for Congress was in early April.

The laboratory is in Tempe AZ, and while we were working there someone ran in, all excited. He said, "There are enormous UFOs in the skies over Phoenix and they're being filmed!" It was the Phoenix Lights! And that event was a CE-5.

We landed at around 5:30, and these events were occurring around 8:30. One of the longest sightings was virtually over the lab. That night on the local news we saw footage that we could incorporate into the film summary we would then give to Congress!

One evening, while we were in the lab working very late on these digital images, a retired general walked in. He was a pilot for a private contracting airline running covert ops and transporting drugs for these shadowy projects.

We learned that there was a large cell of spooks conducting flight operations out of Phoenix, importing and distributing contraband drugs. This general was all coked up -- he was absolutely out of his mind on drugs.

As he came over, he saw some footage of a UFO that I got from a military source. He looked at it and said, "How the hell did you get this? This is top secret."

I looked at him and I asked, "You think I'm going to tell you?"

"Who the hell are you?" He asked.

I said, "I'm Dr. Greer.

He replied, " Oh, yeah, I know who *you* are."

We were in this lab for days until the wee hours. The characters who wandered in and out were quite unbelievable; coked-up agents, former Air Force and intelligence people, black ops, drugies, high tech people, the whole nine yards—all operating out of this little obscure lab in Tempe.

In the middle of this episode in Phoenix, I had to go to San Diego for one day to do a lecture. Shari and Neil stayed in Phoenix working on the tapes at the lab. While I was away, these characters tried to seduce Shari into thinking that I was the devil incarnate for trying to tell the world the truth about UFOs.

She and Neil were bombarded by weird mind control and psycho-logical warfare activity that went on for hours. Finally, she said, "I'm leaving here." And they backed off.

At one point, another member of my group was in contact with this same group. They took her out to the desert and began to try to convince her to turn against what we were doing. They said, "We know everything about Dr. Greer. We know what's in his bedside table.... After she told me this, I said, "You go back and tell these bastards I have no secrets from anyone I love. I have nothing that I care to hide. Tell them to do whatever they want – it won't change a thing..."

She flat out told them my every word. That was the end of that. They found we could not be intimidated.

I mentioned earlier a gentleman, who had approached me at a lecture in Tennessee who said he didn't know why I wasn't dead yet, and that they'd been watching what I was doing. He was a man who had person-ally been involved with and seen the launching of a weapons system that had targeted and destroyed an extraterrestrial vehicle. He had individual, specific knowledge of those systems. During this period between the early '90s and the late '90s, I met not one but about a dozen people who had either been at facilities who were developing these weapons systems or who were at actual events, where we had targeted and hit extraterres-trial vehicles using advanced electronics systems.

Of course, the fantasy cover story for Star Wars or SDI is that there are "brilliant pebbles" – such as those used in the SDI program to inter-cept missles and things of this sort. In reality, the real action has always been in the area of electromagnetic weapons systems and EMP weapons (electromagnetic pulse weapons) and scalar systems. When an ET craft materializes in our time/space, it is vulnerable to these advanced EM weapon systems.

We have top-secret witnesses who have been present for the after-math of those events, where they have retrieved or seen the crashed craft, such as Jonathan Weygandt, who was on the Bolivian-Peruvian border when the cabal downed one of these ET craft in the early 1990s. We have people who have been in meetings where they were planning to do this. And we have people who have participated in the development of these weapons.

One such witness who came forward was at the 1997 meeting in Washington, D.C., that we hosted for members of Congress, the White House and Pentagon officials. Congressman Dan Burton, who was

Chairman of the House Government Reform and Oversight Committee, was at this event, among other key people. Some of the witnesses who were coming forward were going to say things beyond what even the 'friendlies' within this control group felt was safe.

This one witness, G.A., had specific, detailed information about these rogue Star Wars plans. He had sat in on joint meetings with the NSA, CIA, NRO and some corporate programs, where he had seen these plans from the '70s on. He said they were fully operational: there was a covert ability to not only target and attack actual extraterrestrial vehicles but also to stage a false attack on Earth, using alien reproduction vehicles that are man-made and other weapons systems that were highly classified. The intent was to use 'stagecraft' to fake an 'alien attack' so that the people of the world would be united around Big Brother and a global corporate- military junta.

It would look like the "War of the Worlds". And it would surprise the national military command center and most of the agencies, the CIA, the White House and the Congress, never mind the masses and the media. Just as the gullible masses have swallowed abduction stories and mutilations as proof of 'evil aliens', the masses would again take this Star Wars bait. I have interviewed numerous people, in classified projects, who have been on the abduction squads and have staged abductions and mutilations.

G.A. was really nervous about sharing what he had been part of. He confided in me that he had been approached by people he used to work with -- these were buddies that had been in really special operations -- and some of them had saved each other's lives in various situations. Such groups are like a true brotherhood. They had been out of communication for a long time with each other, but knew what he was doing with The Disclosure Project. They certainly monitored that he was dealing with me.

They begged G.A. to meet with them before he would say what he was going to in front of these Congressmen and White House people. One of Al Gore's and Bill Clinton's best friends was at this meeting, and they knew powerful Congressmen would be there. So he agreed to meet with them.

The morning of the event, in April of 1997, we gathered for a private meeting of all of the assembled top-secret witnesses. Astronaut Ed Mitchell was also there.

Just when we were about to get to G.A.'s testimony, we took a break. He came up to me and said he had to meet with members of this cell he had been part of—that they had surfaced and they were *insisting* they meet. He felt enough loyalty to them that he agreed to meet. They took him out to an undisclosed place in Virginia and held him there until about midnight, after this closed briefing for Congress was over. They then returned him to the Westin in DC and he slipped a note under the door of Shari Adamiak's room, who was my main assistant. In this note he said, "I really cannot talk about this now. They are begging me to say nothing about this until they can get things under control. They're going to work on it and they need some time." G.A. told me that, because of The Disclosure Project, morale within this rogue group was very low.

This rogue group in charge of faking an ET attack on earth had been exposed by us, and they were panicking. The only real power they have derives from secrecy, the element of surprise and the ignorance of others – and we were changing that dynamic by revealing their plans.

Numerous people on the inside of this operation, including an SAIC executive and a man who'd worked for years with all the major aerospace companies, have told me that what we were doing had thrown this entire so-called MJ-12 control group into chaos. We were moving major information out to the big guns in DC and to the public. There were defections occurring, and a lot of controversy, and this group that was never very homogenized was becoming more fractured, due to our work.

But the insiders said to G.A., "Give us some time to get this under control, and if we can't succeed, then you can talk about it." In a sense, I'm heartened that they haven't played that card yet, but I'm not convinced that it won't be played.

The danger is that almost the entire world, including the majority of people who think they know what's going on with UFOs and covert programs, would be fooled. This type of effort is called a deceptive indication and warning, or a false I & W, where you set up something that looks like an attack from an enemy, but it isn't. It is a staged event designed to achieve certain strategic objectives, like the Gulf of Tonkin incident. To expand the Viet Nam War and make a call for more funding and more troops, we essentially orchestrated what looked like an attack on our assets. So, I call this the Cosmic Gulf of Tonkin plan. It would take everyone by surprise.

Now, the only way it won't take people by surprise is if they know the truth. And that's why I felt it was so important for G.A. and people like him to come forward, go on the record, name names, and talk about what the specific plan was.

Carol Rosin was told by Werner von Braun, when he was virtually on his deathbed, that these covert programs would attempt to put weapons in space, and would hoax extraterrestrial events and stage an attack. He warned this was a grave danger to the world.

But he said one thing that I asked Carol not to talk about during the Disclosure Project events: Von Braun said there were electronic warfare systems that affect consciousness— that they were well developed and had the ability to affect behavior and decisions. These so-called psychotronic weapons were the gravest threat of all.

Around this time, we had a retreat in Colorado. Present was a woman who had worked in a corporation that was dealing with these technologies and had personally been present when they were used. The operator could turn a dial and cause, say, a Board of Directors meeting to come to agreement on something within minutes, or they could turn the dial the other way and cause everyone to start fighting and descend into utter chaos.

I know others who have worked with E-systems, Raytheon, SAIC, and EG&G who dealt with high-end electronics, and they also have seen versions of this same ability.

Sometimes I look at the world and at some of the people that we have to work with and I'm convinced that they have been turned into zombies, because it doesn't make sense that people are behaving in certain ways — it seems almost scripted.

Some scientists that have free energy technologies have been targeted with scripted belief systems and behavior patterns that have kept them from coming forward with these devices. They all seem to have the same personality quirks and behaviors, with unstable vacillations between hopefulness and paranoia. So the technologies always stay hidden – or never even get finished. We've seen this over and over and over again. These weapons systems are being used to create this behavior. It's the only thing that really explains the degree to which these technologies keep getting held up and diverted or taken off course.

In the process of setting up these meetings in Washington we became more and more aware that we were being targeted with electromagnetic weapons systems. After I was on Larry King, we went to New Mexico, near Roswell and did a CE-5 project. One evening Shari Adamiak, one other researcher and I were out in the field doing CE-5 protocols. We saw some people who were obviously doing reconnaissance on us. Then suddenly, while in one of our meditative states, Shari began shaking and almost convulsing. I knew it was a seizure brought on by a directional weapons system exactly like the one that tried to extract my astral body out of the St. Moritz Hotel earlier that year.

I knew what to do: mentally I went to her and stabilized her back into her body, and neutralized the scalar system by using higher consciousness. The rogue group was attempting to do a forced astral extraction, using one of these electronic warfare systems. Shari attempted to take a long, deep breath, but was visibly shaken and frightened by the attack.

Such attacks began to happen more and more, so we began our own counter-measures with people who had versions of these technologies. I would notice that there would be times when we would be gathering and there would be a pulsed wave that would come through. Literally, I would feel like I was being microwaved from the inside out. As we put protective measures in place, these events subsided. We also created a very spiritual support team to do meditation and prayer for our protection.

One of the worst experiences of this was the night of the congressional briefing, in April of '97. During our presentation to the congressmen, I suddenly felt this energy wave hit me. It almost knocked me out. There was a man there from the Pentagon who was aware of it, as well. It was so intense, again, I felt like I was being microwaved from the inside out.

I could barely maintain consciousness and thought I was going to pass out on the stage. I have to tell you that, prior to this, Colonel MK had insisted on coming to this meeting. When we said, "No, you can't come," he said point blank, in a very coarse way, "I'm going to be there anyway." And he was - if you get my drift. He is, after all, Dr. Death, and a specialist in so-called non-lethal electromagnetic warfare systems.

But each time these covert interests use these systems, they tip their hand and we learn more about them....

In the mid-'90s, I met a man who had developed some of these systems for the Agency prior to 1958. Many people think this sounds like something out of "Star Trek", but by 1958, this man and his team had perfected the electronics to be able to hook people up to a device that would electronically assist them to remote view any distant place or person. He was forced to sell this invention to a front company for the Agency. But at one point he asked, "Would you like to have one of these devices?" I said, "I'm not going to take that right now." I viewed it as too high risk – and we already have the ability to do remote viewing by developing our own higher awareness.

Another scientist who was working in this area had developed electronics to enable people to levitate. One of our military witnesses is a colonel whose parents in the '50s were friends with some people at the Rand Corporation. They had seen people during their lunch breaks using these devices which enabled them to literally float above their desks.

So, these capabilities have been around since the '50s. And look at where other technologies have gone from the '50s to now, in terms of electronics- and imagine how advanced these Shadow Government technologies are today! Of course, all these wondrous technologies could be used for enormously beneficial purposes -- everything from healing to transportation to energy generation. Unfortunately, they are held by people who are abusing power and are addicted to the abuse of power.

21

Electomagnetic Transfer

Around this time, a former colonel surfaced via a CSETI board member who was best friends with former CIA Director, Bill Colby. Colby had been very involved in these programs and actually had access to extraterrestrial devices, operative energy devices and other hardware, as well as around $50 million in unacknowledged funds. Colby wanted to transfer these assets to CSETI to get this disclosure done properly, with hard evidence and hard documents. This was what was offered to me.

"Finally," I thought, "CSETI will have sufficient funding to share the truth with the world."

Initially, the colonel wouldn't tell us it was Bill Colby whom we would be meeting with. He would simply say that he's a very high official connected to these super-secret projects.

I said, "That's fine, whoever it is. If they want to help us, we are grateful." And so I authorized this to go forward.

The week our board member was going to meet with the former CIA Director, to formalize this transfer, Colby was found floating down the Potomac River! The colonel who set up the meeting *personally* told me that Colby was assassinated. His wife later said, "I don't know why Bill would go out canoeing in the rain-swollen, flooded Potomac River at night, leave the door to the house open and the computer on and the coffee maker on!" She exclaimed, "This is very unlike Bill."

Mrs. Colby was hinting that something wasn't right, but there was never an investigation. So they assassinated a former CIA Director who was friendly to what we were doing, because he was going to make a definitive break with the rogue group. He was getting old, and did not want to take this secret to his grave. Like many of our witnesses, Colby knew the entire covert world was out of control, and it had gone too far.

I was shaken by this, but not out of fear. It's so disturbing knowing that someone had lost his life trying to work with us.

From that day forward, I vowed never again to okay a transaction without knowing who the players are. Because if I know who they are, I can protect them.

By 1997, Shari and I knew that we were being targeted with increasingly powerful EM weapons. And so it came to pass that, within a short time span, Shari, a supportive Congressman and I got metastatic cancer. I am convinced that these were electronically induced. At a subtle level of electromagnetism, you can transmute elements, and also transfer something from one place to another— and infect someone or harm someone electronically. This is a very lethal application of a science that could be used to heal people. Unfortunately, right now, the worst elements of humanity currently possess these technologies.

When people worry about these technologies being disclosed, I say: "Forget about it. The worst elements already have them!"

Thus began a very difficult and emotional time: Following the congressional briefings in 1997, within six months, Shari and I both had aggressive, metastatic cancer. I had malignant melanoma, which is highly fatal when it is metastatic. So, to say that this was disturbing to me and my family is an understatement, of course. And Shari— who was the single greatest person assisting everything we were doing besides Emily, was suffering terribly from metastatic breast cancer. Here we are, two totally normal people, with no history of these cancers in either of our families. And we get them the same month! It was just too much of a coincidence to believe…

Now, I can't prove what happened, except I will tell you this: The world's expert in the pathology and diagnosis of malignant melanoma looked at the one that they took off my left shoulder and said, "It is metastatic." The first one was metastatic. Now, metastatic means that it originated from a primary tumor somewhere else. But I had no primary tumor anywhere else on my body or in my body.

I was checked out from the back of my eye where the retina is to anywhere where there is a melanocyte, the type of cell that makes a malignant melanoma. And no primary was ever found! Ultimately I had to tell my dermatologist, "Well, we can stop looking." He asked, "What do you mean?"

I said, "I know where it came from. It came from a laboratory in Utah, where it was electromagnetically transferred onto me." And he looked at me and he asked, "Do you think such a thing is possible?" I said, "Yes, I know it's possible." And I said, "My right-hand assistant in the Disclosure Project has also just been diagnosed with breast cancer that is metastatic."

"Oh, my God," was his reply.

At the time, we had a golden retriever, named Yami. He and I had always been very close.

At the same time I got cancer, he got cancer of his left triceps muscle –a sarcoma. He had to have his entire left front leg taken off. When he came back from the vet, and I came back from the doctor, we had identical matching scars— to the angle of the scar and the type of staples used!

To this day, I am convinced that Yami bonded to me and astrally took some of the 'hit' from the EM weapon system targeting us. I believe he saved my life. So spirit can work through nature, through a dog, whatever, to help!

You can pray and meditate all you want, but if you're in downtown Hiroshima when the nuclear bomb goes off, more than likely you're going to get vaporized. And this is what happened. You can be Gandhi and you might bless the person as you go down, but the bullet will go through you and kill you.

Remember: the Orwellian "mind fuck" term is non-lethal weapons systems. But in reality, they're quite lethal. Language is often used to hide what they're actually doing.

Many insiders had told us that these covert projects were in a free fall and there was a sense of panic— that we were really getting the information out to a lot of powerful people and they were losing control.

So, you can see the battle had been joined. And they lashed out. Around that time, I acquired a secret document that had a list of the code names and project names dealing with the extraterrestrial connected projects. That document is actually in the Disclosure book.

The day after the congressional briefings in 1997, I was asked to do a briefing for the head of intelligence for the Joint Chiefs of Staff, Admiral Tom Wilson. In advance of this important meeting we sent a document to his people. His assistant told me that the Admiral had, in fact, found these code names and code project names and numbers useful; he inquired through channels and found some of these ops in a cell in the Pentagon.

Once Admiral Wilson identified this group, he told the contact person in this super-secret cell: "I want to know about this project." And he was told, "Sir, you don't have a need to know. We can't tell you."

Now, can you imagine being an admiral, J-2, the head of intelligence for the Joint Chiefs of Staff, at the Pentagon, and being told, "We're not going to tell you"? Well, he was shocked and angry.

I took one of our witnesses, Shari, our military advisor, and Apollo astronaut, Edgar Mitchell with me to this meeting with the Admiral. It was a stand-up briefing. As the briefing progressed, he began canceling other appointments-- he was so interested in the information. The only reason the meeting ended when it did was because Ed Mitchell had to get up to New York for a TV interview. But the Admiral, I know, would have kept going for some time more.

During this briefing, the Admiral and I discussed the risk this rogue group – that had shoved him aside – was to the United States, the rule of law and to the national security. I pointed out that the first CIA director, Admiral Roscoe Hillenkoeter, had written a letter in the early 1960s stating that the *secrecy related to UFOs* – and *not* the UFOs- were a threat to the national security. I told the Admiral that this illegal, rogue group had ARV technology that can do circles around his B2 Stealth bombers. He thought a minute and said, "Well, as far as I am concerned, if you can get people who know about this matter to talk on the record, you have my permission to go to the media with this! This group is illegal!" So when people ask who supported *disclosure*, among others, I tell them the head of intelligence for the Joint Chiefs of Staff!

After this meeting, these rogue groups came at us with a vengeance. Obviously, they were very disturbed that we had gotten specific information to a man like Adm. Wilson- and that they were shown to be the illegal operation that they are. So, Bill Colby was murdered; the Congressman died very quickly from the type of cancer he had. Shari Adamiak and I got metastatic cancer at the same time. And so now we're in the fight for our lives, literally.

After the briefing for Congress in April 1997, Dan Burton came up to us and said, "I want everything you have on this subject, because I'm going to look into it." It turns out, he tried to and then had someone visit him who said, "Back off of this."

Someone who knows him personally explained to me that the Congressman was threatened. If he's asked about it today, Congressman Burton will say, "Oh, it was just something I had a personal interest in." Not true: One of his best friends, who is his scheduler in his office, is a woman who saw a UFO hovering outside her bedroom window. She was close enough to Congressman Burton that he knew that she was telling him the absolute truth. As the chairman of the Government Oversight and Reform Committee, overseeing the government, Congressman Burton was a very appropriate key person— but within months, he was shut down.

So, here we are, getting this information to not only people like the CIA director, Sen. Pell, Senate Appropriations people and Senate Intelligence Committee members — but also to people who really have personal knowledge that this is real, like Dan Burton. And an increasingly powerful group of good men at the Pentagon were interested and concerned – and discovering that, in fact, the Shadow Government had taken over the subject. And on top of that, you've got really deep throats ready to pull the curtain back on the Wizard of Oz as he sits there pulling all the levers, scaring the hell out of people. We were exposing what Werner Von Braun warned about: Hoaxing an extraterrestrial attack so that there could be a global seizure of power around fear and war. I assure you, the people that were receiving this information took it very seriously.

So, in that setting comes this devastating personal turn of events. Shari, my close friend and trusted advisor, who's situation rapidly worsened, passed away in less than a year! It was a very emotional and difficult time for me.

In July 1993, I was almost killed leaving the planning meeting for Disclosure held near the Monroe Institute; in'94, there was the terrifying attack at the St. Moritz hotel in NY City, followed by the strange 4 a.m. attacks later that summer at my home. And now this is '97. I was taken right to the limits of what I could endure.

And yet, some really wonderful things happened during this time....

22

A Billion Scintillating Lights

In June of 1997, at a training group with about 20 people on Blanca Peak, in Colorado, we had an extraordinary encounter with a dozen extraterrestrial elders. Shari Adamiak and I knew that there was an enormous amount of gratitude being expressed to us by the ETs. It was a beautiful, celestial meeting.

As we were doing our protocols and inviting the ETs to come to Blanca Peak, there were a number of sightings of these objects zipping around the sky — some literally flying out of the mountain! I knew that there was a clearing up on the mountain where we would make contact and had remote viewed it earlier. Suddenly, at the right instant, I got a message to go up to this site, in the pitch dark, and we left as a group for the contact site.

The contact site was at around 9,000-10,000 feet up on the mountain. As we walked silently to the site, with the 14,000 ft. peak looming above us, we began to see a billion scintillations of light all around us. It was subtle, but it was visible.

The whole mountain was like that all night. The entire area was vibrating in this celestial scintillating light. Even the ground and the rocks were glowing and sparkling with an amazing energy.

When we entered the site – which was a circular clearing in the evergreen forest and scrub- we could see the shape of a craft. It was not fully materialized but was circular, glowing and distinct – half in this world and half beyond the crossing point of light. It was trans-dimensional—partially materialized, partially not, half astral and half material. Suddenly, as we entered this object, we saw that there was a semi-circle of lighted beings.

I walked to a certain point and suddenly a brilliant, scintillating light was right above me. That's where I went, and I stayed at that spot. It was not subtle, but a clearly visible white scintillating light right above my head. So this is how I knew exactly where to be.

The larger group stayed back as I approached each ET being and quietly connected to him. It was clear that they were very senior, enlightened leaders. Each one of them was from a different star system. There were no two alike. I entered the state of God consciousness while at the same time connecting with these beings.

A beautiful communing began as we were each awake and aware of that time and place and yet instantly awake in the infinite cosmic Being. It was transcendental in many ways, although it was also very present, very real – super-real. As we were in this state together, I could see beyond that level of energy to another level where, suddenly, there were many angelic forms. And then beyond that, I saw the Avatar- a divine Being representing the Godhead. It was a beautiful cosmic gathering that no words can describe.

I approached each elder ET independently, honored each person, and welcomed them to Earth, thanking them for their presence. At a certain point, others noted that it looked like I had disappeared. Some people couldn't see me at all. Other people could just see through me. I felt enlivened, lighter, enthralled. My vibratory frequency was so high, I could feel myself becoming rarefied. At one point, I thought I was going to lift up or levitate or just disappear. But my experience was that I stayed there, pretty much fully in the physical- and yet people were seeing through me. This went on for half an hour or more. It was a coming-together of people who were all part of the cosmic culture, if you will. We were there with them, for that purpose. That was the purpose of this meeting. The ET beings also expressed their gratitude for our work and effort – and asked that we do all we could for universal peace. Specifically, we were asked to intervene to avert the Star Wars technologies from being used against ET peoples. I assured them we would do all we can...

The next day, Shari and I went off for a quiet time together in the San Juan Hills south of Blanca Peak. We climbed up on some rocks and I pulled out my compass. During the ET encounter the night before, the compass had been in my left inner coat pocket, right over my heart. Now, as I looked at this compass, I saw that magnetic north had been shifted almost 180 degrees! The needle was altered so that it was pointing almost 180 degrees off magnetic north. It was clear evidence of a very unusual magnetic field flux anomaly that affected the compass from the encounter the night before.

The compass stayed like that for several days and then went back to normal. We have photographs of this, by the way. It is very reminiscent of this same compass rotating counter- clockwise as the ET craft approached us in July 1992, nearly 5 years earlier!

Then, in July of 1997, we took a research training group to England to that same area, in Wiltshire, England, near Stonehenge.

That year, we were renting a huge old manor house that must have been built in the 1600s or 1700s. We housed the entire team there for a week. Prior to leaving the States for England, we learned that Shari's cancer had become metastatic and was now in her lymph nodes. This was very serious.

Also, I had just had another malignant melanoma taken off. So that first night we were in the manor house nursing our wounds and we were frankly very emotionally upset. At times we were just laughing and telling stories, and at times in tears. We just knew one or both of us were not going to make it…

As we were sitting in the upstairs room of the manor house, Ron Russell and a few others, on the CSETI expedition, were outside on the grounds. Shari and I were just too tired and too upset to go out, but I had told the group they should go out by 10:30 pm. The room Shari and I were in had a bay window and a little fireplace.

Suddenly, we saw a brilliant light, like a ball or a cluster of light, fly right through the closed window, turn and go over by the fireplace and then elongate into an extraterrestrial person! Here is this extraterrestrial being, shimmering, again not quite fully materialized, standing about 3 feet tall. There was nothing subtle about this, because it was visible with the naked eye in the fully lit room. Shari didn't see it at first, so I said, "Shari, look."

As she turned, she saw the ET and exclaimed, "Oh, my God ". We sat there in meditation with this being, who was basically trying to console us. He was very sweet, and very grateful and very loving— just beautiful. We remained in this state of contact and meditation for probably half an hour. I knew then that one of us wasn't going to make it, and this being was expressing great compassion, respect, and gratitude for our work.

We had no intention of ever relating this account to anyone -it was so personal, beautiful and poignant. But the next day Ron Russell brought up the fact that while they were out on the Manor grounds, a very unusual event was observed by everyone. Out of the sky, at a little past 10:30 p.m. a light appeared, and then descended, coming over the tree tops and directly into the bay window of my room! It descended out of space in a clear sky, came down across the manor house lawn, and flew into the window.

Ron exclaimed, "That's Steve's room!" And so they saw the arrival of this being, from space. The entire group outside saw how our encounter in the Manor house began: As a light from space that flew over the grounds and right into the window, whereupon I saw this light enter the room, then materialize as a being on the hearth of the fireplace!

You will find that the truth hides its own reality, because the truth is so much more bizarre- and beautiful- than a science fiction movie.

Our last expedition with Shari was in Joshua Tree Wilderness in 1997. April of that year we were at the Pentagon with the Admiral, disclosing all this information in front of key people in Congress and the White House. But by the fall, Shari had metastatic lesions in her brain and was partially paralyzed. Shari had joined me in this effort in 1991. She was at the first lecture I'd ever given. And she was with me until she passed away in January of 1998.

I was going to cancel the Joshua Tree expedition, but Shari said, "If it's the last thing I do, I'm going to be there with you and the ETs." And so she was...

We were all amazed by the indomitable will of Shari. She was a lioness, completely fierce, very devoted and extremely competent. Shari was the first person that I could take as far as anyone could possibly go, into contact. She could go the furthest, without exception. There's nobody else, to date, that could go that far. She had no fear and knew her destiny.

It was she and I who privately went out to the Baca, this remote area of the Colorado Rockies where we have our trainings, near Crestone, in 1996. It was a vision quest. I told her that I wanted to show her some things and tell her some things that I had always known -- since I was very young, since my contact as a young boy. I had never told anyone, but I knew that she was very perceptive and spiritually awake; I knew she was ready.

So, we went to the Baca on a cold evening in the spring of '96. I said, "Let's walk out and invite the ET beings in." As we did, we saw a craft in the sky, moving very strangely. Suddenly, I said, "Now, look out here in the field."

There, an enormous discoid-shaped area was scintillating with light. It was like a hologram, but more real and more alive. After a few moments, distinct humanoid shaped forms began to emerge from this craft, and approached us. I said to Shari, "Now, let me show you how these extraterrestrial beings prefer to stay in this form when they're on Earth, because it's safe."

As this event was unfolding, I said to Shari, "Now, I want to tell you what the structure of the cosmos is and how it's put together and how it is that they are here." We had a tape recorder, so I began speaking and recorded what you now can read in the chapters in "Extraterrestrial Contact: The Evidence and Implications": "The Crossing Point", and "Extraterrestrials and the New Cosmology". That information was recorded in real-time during this contact in the desert of Colorado.

Later that evening, we went back to the Baca Townhouses. As we drove to the townhouse, I said, "Now, they're going to follow us home." We saw these bright strobe-like lights along the road, escorting us as we drove back to the condo in Crestone.

After we got back to the condo, we went out on the patio to see the Sangre de Cristo Mountains that rise up 14,000 feet, covered with snow. They were shining in the moonlight in the crystal clear air of the Rockies. I said, "We should be here, because they're going to show us one of their points of entry and where they like to be. Now, look around. Can you see the fine structure of the fabric of the astral component of the cosmos that supports the material creation?"

I explained, "Thought and consciousness and the astral forms of light, support the material cosmos. A 'gap' exists, where the realm of pure consciousness, thought and astral light phases into a semi-material-ized energy field. This is the realm where the astral crystallizes to the material, like an architectural blueprint. The astral becomes crystallized, as a matrix,that then supports the material objects and even the atmos-phere." And as I said that, it was like a veil fell away, and she saw it- the structure of this celestial, etheric and astral realm as it crystallizes into what we call the material cosmos.

"Now, look up here on the mountain." And there was an enormous sombrero-shaped craft that was translucent. It was not fully material-ized, but was like a really dense, perfectly shaped cloud, being lit from within — a golden-white light, sitting on the very top of one of the high-est peaks above Crestone. It was there for about 45 minutes.

Because Shari could see and experience those things, I had someone to articulate them to. And because I could articulate them to her, I could share them with others. We cannot teach anything unless there is some-one ready to see it. There is a saying: "The wise are they who speak not unless they have a hearer."

The first year we went to Joshua Tree was 1996. Early on, a very fast, spiralling craft came right overhead. We could actually hear it whistle, it was so low in the atmosphere. It came right overhead and over the Palm Springs Valley. Everyone in the group saw this and was astonished!

One night, we were leaving one site in Joshua Tree wilderness because I had a remote view that we should move. As we drove along this dirt road, very late at night, suddenly the dashboard lights dimmed. I turn to Shari, "Oh, they're here."

Seconds later, coming straight down from the zenith, a huge craft shaped like a Hershey's kiss appeared! It was flat on the bottom and tapered up to a point, and had a scintillating, sparkling tail on top, as it came down at enormous speed towards the desert floor. It was 200-300 feet in diameter.

It was a teal color, and brilliant - so bright that it illuminated the desert floor like daytime and then, whoosh, went straight into the Earth and it was gone. "Ah. This is where they're telling us they're going to be located under the Earth." I said.

If you have the ability to materialize and de-materialize objects, you can stay in a quasi-materialized form so that one object can go straight through another object, like a ghost going through a wall. There's no reason why not. Most matter is, after all, "empty space".

As I drove, I mapped, mentally, precisely where this huge ET craft went into the Earth. Driving very rapidly, I raced to that site. But there was a vehicle in front of me, going too slowly. I floored our car and flew by them so that I could track exactly where the ET craft went into the Earth...

We have a special site where we do our field-work in Joshua Tree now, where we saw this huge craft go into the Earth.

Shari was determined to come, but the cancer was all through her body and was in her brain—she could barely walk. The first night, she lost her balance and fell, skinning her knees. But she said, "Oh, it's okay. It's okay." Here she is, on her deathbed, and is still determined to join us in the name of Universal Peace, to be out under the stars, together with these cosmic beings. It was all so beautiful – and yet, at the same time, so painful for me.

23

Infinity

The first night in November of 1997, we set up in an area called Hidden Valley in Joshua Tree. There was a tree next to us that - even though there was no wind — began to shake violently, inexplicably. People in our group started shouting, "What is going on?" And I explained, "They're letting us know they're here."

The ETs actually went from person to person, touching us on the shoulder or on the head. We also had an anomalous high-pitched electronic tone move through the group that most everyone heard. So I knew that they had locked onto where we were, and we were connecting.

The moon was maybe three-quarters full. It was a magnificent, crystal clear night. All of a sudden, what looked like a bright light bulb turned on in the sky. It simply appeared — fairly close and big — about a third the size of the moon. This enormous craft lit up, floated along underneath the moon, and then disappeared. This was an absolutely unambiguous sighting of an ET craft. It was in the direction of where the ET craft had come straight down and gone into the Earth one year earlier.

The final night of Shari's last expedition, while driving west to the Palm Springs area, from Joshua Tree, an amazing send-off happened for her. It was late, and of course she was exhausted from battling cancer.

Suddenly, a huge craft came flying over the valley, very reminiscent of the first night she and I were ever in that area. This enormous craft was right at the point of the speed of light. To our delight, the lead part of this seamless ship got ahead of the back part, like an accordion that's elongating, then contracting. The ET beings were saying goodbye to Shari...

By December, Shari was in a coma and unconscious. In January, 1998, she passed away.

I've been with a lot of people when they've died, working as an Emergency Doctor. And I've always known from my own near-death experience that it's important, if possible, to have someone there to assist them in connecting to the Godhead —to help build a bridge to the worlds of light. Our culture has all but forgotten the sacred moment of the passing. Today, everyone is hooked up to tubes, and it's all very technical— but there's a lack of appreciation of what else should be going on at that moment, as we transform from the physical plane to the celestial and astral world. I want to share this story because it illustrates what is possible in that regard.

In January, people who were taking care of Shari wanted me to fly out to Denver. I had visited several times and was very involved in those final months. But I said, "I will come out when the time is right." Timing is everything — and each of us has our moment of a sacred passing to the other side.

Early one morning, while I was meditating, I suddenly went into a state of cosmic consciousness and then into God consciousness. What I saw was the entirety of creation in the shape of what some call the cosmic egg. If you can imagine: it was infinite, and yet it was discrete. Around it was the infinity of God. I was in a state of being perfectly one with that and aware of it. Then I saw that Shari was there. She was ahead of me, and I knew that what I was doing was showing her the highest celestial level of creation. I knew that she would go into the infinite, celestial home ahead of me – because she was literally closer to that infinite cosmic conscious place...

I knew that she was going to go into it and become one with it. It was, in a sense, the raiment of God— the body of God. It was the total expression of Creator, Creation and unbounded Mind together. I could see the totality of the creation as this gorgeous peach-pink-magenta, sombrero-shaped or galaxy-shaped entity – similar to an egg. It was infinite, even though it was discrete – filled with joy — indescribably magnificent. It was not only physically stunning and celestial, but filled with love and everything beautiful.

As we approached it, we heard a trillion— an infinite number of — beautiful angelic voices, like the Vienna Boys Choir, singing, "We are all one in spirit" over and over and over. As I gazed into infinity, I could see that every created being in the cosmos was represented in it, and yet were still one in this state of infinite awareness. From the morn of eternity, the sound of these voices repeated, "We are all one in spirit" in a specific melody so exquisite – if only I could describe it. It was beautiful beyond words. And just as that happened, I dissolved into that state of infinite love and perfect unity in consciousness.

After coming back to the awareness of my bedroom, I looked over at the clock and marked the time. I knew in my soul that seven 24-hour periods— seven rotations of the Earth— from that exact moment would be the moment of Shari's passing. I just knew it.

Well, she was getting closer and closer to death, and everyone was saying, "Oh, you have to be here." And I said, "I will be there."

So, on the sixth day, I flew to Denver. Her family and Ron Russell and all her close friends were there—and then I just sort of enigmatically appeared. I said, "I'm here because it is time."

That night I waited till everyone left Shari's hospice room, and then sat with her in prayer and meditation. She had been in a coma for weeks. As I read a beautiful prayer to her, I looked over – and her eyes opened for the first time in weeks. And one enormous tear glided down her cheek. She knew I was there.

So I told her, "It's okay -- you can go now."

I was certain that Shari needed to hear that from me, because she had told me that she felt she was abandoning me with the burden of this work. I said, "You can do enormous work on the other side. You can do many things beyond what you can do here." What most people don't know is that those enlightened people who go to the other side are the leaven that mysteriously raises this world.

They're the inspiration and the unseen hand that protects and guides and helps the progress of this world. It's happening all the time, whether we see it or not.

I connected with her very deeply, reassured her, and said, "You can go now. It's time. You can go."

Seeing her in her coma state, and realizing that she'd complete her passage to the other side by the next morning – I felt a deep sorrow.

I was staying in Shari's home, which was now empty, except for a woman who had been caring for her. But, that night I couldn't go back right away, so I went to a night place in downtown Denver. I simply wanted to sit and have a drink someplace.

A gay couple began chatting with me. I ended up telling them all my feelings. I explained to them about the astral and spiritual realm and what was going to happen. These new found friends were extraordinarily pure hearted and spiritual. Just what I needed on this night – in a most unlikely setting!

I've found that I can go to places like that and meet such spiritually incredible people. On the other hand, I can go into a church and meet misguided, cruel people. So, it's not the place, it's the intent.

Late that night, I returned and slept in Shari's old room. That morning I awoke very early, sat up in bed and meditated. I quietly marked the time, because I knew the exact hour and moment, adjusting for time zones, of her passing.

The woman who had taken care of Shari suddenly knocked at my door, "It's time – she is close to passing…" she said. "You're all dressed and ready to go!" she said, with a surprised look.

I arrived before the others and spent time alone with Shari, taking her into the state of infinite peace and love and into that unbounded state of pure cosmic mind that awaits us. As others gathered, we said prayers together, standing around her bed in a semi-circle.

At a certain moment, after we prepared her spiritually and connected her to God, I turned to her and said, "Now, let go of all things, Shari, and go into the eternal Light."

And with that, she took her last breath, and ascended to Providence.

Her passing was beautifully peaceful; even so, I was devastated.

Suddenly, there was an extraordinary power that entered the room. It felt like the darshan or spiritual field of a highly enlightened Avatar— like a breeze of powerful divine energy that swept through the room and completely *through* me. It was physically palpable! I then knew she went to the highest level. And then I completely fell apart!

All of us need to care for one another in this way at the time of our passing; we all need the help, prayers and spiritual power of each other, so that we rise to the highest and best spiritual state possible at the moment of our transition to the next plane.

The night of her passing I wrote the following tribute:

"Shari Adamiak passed on to the world of Light today, January 20, 1998 at 9:50 A.M. MST. Shari made her transition in the presence of friends and loved ones, peacefully and without pain. I ask that everyone pause to say a prayer for Shari and the progress of her soul in the presence of God. What words can contain our sense of loss and the love we all shared with Shari.

Since 1991, when we first met at a lecture in Los Angeles, Shari has been a pillar of strength and support, an indefatigable colleague, a true friend, an intrepid fellow explorer, an irreplaceable confidant and a fearless lioness without whose dedication CSETI could not have realized its many historic achievements.

She has been my right hand and trusted assistant for over six years. Whether braving the dangers of the remote parts of Latin America or assisting with meetings at the offices of the Joint Chiefs of Staff in the Pentagon, Shari was there with me – and for all of us. She never faltered and she never gave up.

Unfazed by the barbs of critics or the machinations of relentless covert operations, she resolutely worked for a time of peace – a peace universal, for the Earth and for countless worlds beyond.

How many wonders did we witness together? From walking in the shadow of some of the world's largest volcanoes with ET spacecraft floating silently above us, to watching a dozen top-secret military witnesses tell an assemblage of Congressmen the truth about UFOs, Shari and I saw events unfold of such great significance. And through it all, Shari was filled with a joy, an excitement and energy, an almost childlike curiosity and wonder at the mysteries of creation and the astonishing potential of these times.

Even as her body began to fail her, she evinced a spirit of such grace, courage and love that all those who knew her were amazed and blessed by her example.

Just two months ago, in November of 1997, she journeyed to Joshua Tree wilderness in California with me. There she experienced what she loved most: the oneness with the stars, the universe and the communication with those peoples from other planets visiting our turbulent world. Fighting weakness, pain and increasing paralysis of her right arm and leg, Shari went into the desert each night, undeterred by the growing obstacles posed by her physical condition. And there, through the crossing point of light, we saw the depths of space and the people and spacecraft from other worlds, who await our own coming of age as a people. Nothing would keep her from this purpose.

Now, a great light has gone from this world, but it shines forever brightly in the realms of eternity. I know Shari was ready for this great journey: Precisely seven mornings before the morning of her passing, we crossed over together to the other side, if only for a while. Awestruck, we witnessed a Light – a Presence- so beautiful, emanating from the center of creation. No words can depict it; it was beyond anything the intellect can grasp. An infinite brilliance, golden while in the center and becoming more peach, pink and magenta as it expanded infinitely before us, suffused us in a sea of love, joy and beauty unlike any experience of my life. It was the experience of the consciousness of God – pure light, unspeakable love and peace. And permeating that Spot were millions of voices joining as one, singing a melody too sweet to recall. And the refrain was: We are all One in Spirit".

Knowing her time was near, I came to Denver yesterday to see her to the other side. Last night while saying prayers, she emerged from the coma, and with a look of great joy on her face, opened her eyes. I told her all was ready. I could hear her acknowledge these words, and a large tear welled up in her eyes as she knew that our time together in this world was nearly over.

This morning, we were called to her bedside. As we gathered, we said prayers and prepared her spiritually for the transition. As lights and a great spirit filled the room, we said it was time, and I said: "Shari, go into the eternal Light." With that, she took her final breath and ascended to Providence.

Even while knowing the joy and love of her present state, the loss is nonetheless severe, but let us remember her thus: She lived in the world of Light, joyous, and she would want us to continue the work to which she dedicated her life – the establishment of Universal Peace, and the creation of a cosmic civilization.

And we find hope in the knowledge that those who have passed on to the next world become the leaven which raises this world of existence. Shari and I discussed her future work, from beyond the veil of light, which would advance the cause of peace and enlightenment in all the realms of God. I have no doubt that she will serve well from her new home in the eternal and become one with the angels of peace.

Without peace, there can be no progress on the Earth. So let us work for peace with hearts filled with love. For when we pass from this world, all we really take with us is love – endless, infinite love."

The night of her passing after writing her tribute I went into a very deep sleep and had an extraordinary experience with an ET. I awakened into a lucid dream with an extraterrestrial who we now call Kindness who was being introduced to me by Shari. She was an ET that was so evolved that she could communicate with both Shari in her astral light body and me simultaneously.

This being, a female extraterrestrial, had a perfectly round head, no hair, and really exotic, beautiful eyes and a very beautiful face. She was very slender and fine-featured. As we connected with each other, she exuded the most extraordinary kindness. She was the embodiment of perfect kindness—very kind, very loving.

As I was talking to her, at some point I asked, "Do we have your permission now to do this Disclosure of the truth ourselves? The President has failed to act, the international community has failed to act, and the Congress has been intimidated or is frightened or corrupt."

Kindness said, "Yes, if you can, do it."

If you can, do it. And so, it was green lighted by this very senior ET ambassador. So from '98 on, we put together the plans for the 2001 Disclosure, knowing that it was approved by this extraterrestrial the night after Shari passed away. And this after the head of intelligence for the Joint Chiefs of Staff had said something very similar.

Interestingly, in this same lucid dream, I was with Bill Clinton and we were having a discussion about this. And with a very sardonic smile, he said, "Well, I can't do this, but you can." And, of course, what he was saying is that "I won't do it because it's too dangerous, but why don't you?" John McCain is right when he says that courage is the indispensable quality for real leadership...

We always felt that this work was being assisted by Shari. And it turns out that at nearly every contact expedition since 1998, the extraterrestrial who I call Kindness, has appeared in a beautiful blue-white ship. Often it will zip into the sky, make an arc and flash the group, shining a blue-white light on all of us! I know it is this senior spiritual and political ambassador of the extraterrestrial coalition that has been connected to us since 1998.

Before that, my main ET contact was a male ET that had jet black hair with very Caucasian features, intense blue eyes, and the whitest skin I've ever seen. He is the ET that contacted me in 1990, when I started CSETI and all these projects.

Kindness' spacecraft has been seen more than once right over our house in Virginia. Our neighbors have seen an intense blue ship, that is not quite fully materialized, actually enveloping and hovering over the house at 4:30 in the morning. One neighbor had no idea I was involved in these projects at the time. But when she looked at this cobalt blue disc right on our house, what she felt was incredible peace and protection.

After Shari passed, I was emotionally spent for a while. I felt responsible, and had survivor's guilt. The children knew I was sad, so they gave me a video tape of "The Bird Cage" that Christmas. I watched it and watched it and watched it — I needed laughter therapy -- because not only did I have cancer, but then I was also now very sad because my closest friend had died. Frankly, she had been murdered.

I have met all kinds of celebrities and rock stars and CIA directors and senators. But the only person in the whole world I care to meet is Nathan Lane—Ms. Albert in "The Bird Cage"! I would love to spend some time with him and tell him, "You saved my life with this movie, because I laughed my way back to health!"

After Shari passed on to the other side, we went to Hawaii in

February of 1998, and were with Joan Ocean on the big island. We did the extraterrestrial contact training program there and had a very positive experience. For me, it was really needed, because I was devastated by Shari's passing and by a lot of the other things that were happening.

One night we saw in the field a scintillating, electric blue craft. It was not quite fully materialized, but it was clearly visible and a beautiful disc of cobalt blue light. It was Kindness- the ET I met the night Shari passed over.

At the end of the training, we went out to swim with the spinner dolphins, under the guidance of Joan Ocean, who is an expert in dolphin contact. The spinner dolphins jump out of the water and corkscrew spin and then go back in; they're so very playful.

After much searching, we arrived at an area where there were spinner dolphins nearby. I got in the water with Linda Willitts, my partner who was swimming with me. I went into a state of expanded, relaxed awareness and a group of four dolphins came over.

I stayed in a very innocent, child-like state where one is just awake, but without expectation or force— just *being*. It is a very Zen-like state of consciousness and deeply peaceful.

Then suddenly these four dolphins approached and adopted me into their little pod.

The four dolphins and I made a star formation: there was one ahead of me, one on my right flank, one on my left flank, and one beneath me -- just exactly as though we were planes flying together in formation. I was close enough that I could see their eyes and touch them, if I had wanted to. We looked into each others eyes with a very deep knowing and playfulness.

I swam away with them, but when I could not keep up, they would slow down for me. They would take me down and dive, but I couldn't stay down as long as they could, so I'd come up. And as I would come up, they'd come up in unison with me. We were heading right out into the open ocean. The boat was getting smaller and smaller in the distance, and Linda could not keep up. So for safety reasons, I had to turn around, but they were taking me out to their special area out in the ocean.

It was a beautiful experience and a very peaceful communing with these intelligent beings in their element. This is a good way to train for being with the ETs. We enter the same non-forceful, innocent and playful state of cosmic mind. It's like the elusive butterfly: You have to be in a certain state of mind, and when they are comfortable with you, they will come. You must be completely one with their consciousness.

I find that this is a wonderful practice to do with dogs and other animals. We can have a very special, mystical connection to animals.

At the end of this trip to Hawaii, on a moonlit night, we went hiking where the lava from the big erupting volcano plunges into the ocean. Near a welcome station a brilliant strobe light, blue-white in color, simply appeared within a few feet of us.

When we got back to the vehicle, the lights were on and the doors were unlocked and all the electronics were changed within the car. We eventually were flashed twice by a distant object. This has happened thousands of times over the last 15 years.

In Joshua Tree, on a subsequent event, we were at that site where the craft had entered the earth. Suddenly, we began to see these unusual lights flashing on and off in space. They didn't move and it wasn't a satellite; it was just a light that went on and off.

Well, at one point, the whole group was suffused in this unusual light— a subtle, silvery light. Everyone noticed it! It was like we were in a cone of light, and it was very silent and peaceful. This continued for around a half hour. And then as quickly as you would snap your finger, it vanished and everything became pitch black again!

On one of the expeditions to Crestone, Colorado we were doing a protocol to create a protective dome around the group. Suddenly we had a really wonderful sighting of Kindness' bluish-white ship. It came in and made an arc and then went back out into space.

As we were doing this, we sensed that there was a huge craft that had settled around us. It was completely silent and only partly materialized. But the air around us suddenly got warmer and you could see a distinct glowing form all around us. Many people saw ET beings moving around us, again almost ghost-like, not quite fully in this material dimension.

We saw a golden craft with a red light going around the outside of it. In the distance, a spectacular electrical storm was occurring. Well it turns out that there was a cook and other staff who worked at a little motel called "The White Eagle," near Crestone. They had gone out for a break, and were looking over towards the Baca where we were located. They didn't even know what CSETI was or what we were doing. But as they looked over towards where we were located, they saw a glowing dome, like a ship, with red lights going around the base of it, counter-clockwise. They were absolutely shocked. And they said they could even see through other objects to see it: The farmhouse that was directly in the way was not visible to them.

Of course, the next day, they reported this to us. They were absolutely stunned when they heard that we were exactly at that location of the craft and what we were experiencing. I understand they ended up leaving the valley because they were utterly unnerved by this experience!

After this craft moved away, the temperature, within moments, dropped 10 to 15 degrees. It was like we were in a building and then the building was gone!

24

Stagecraft

There is no doubt that the ET civilizations are very advanced, and not just technologically. To go faster than the speed of light through the cosmos, any civilization has to evolve socially and spiritually, or they will destroy themselves before they could ever reach Earth. Now, many people are addicted to the good ET/bad ET fantasy, because we anthropocentrically project onto them what humanity has done to itself. But the truth is that we have only ourselves to fear.

The path of wisdom, regardless of how you view ET motives, is for us to be ambassadors to them, to engage them in dialogue and to create peace together. We are not going to solve any perceived conflict or differences through weapon systems, no matter how sophisticated they are. Advanced EM weapon systems have the potential to be many times more devastating than nuclear weapons. So there is no possibility of any civilization – human or ET – surviving armed conflict at that level of technology. Those addicted to the paradigm of war- and space wars- are misguided conflict addicts, and need to be reined in. As mentioned earlier, a plan exists to deceive the public so they can keep the whole war machine going on and on and on—expanding more grandiosely into space.

One of the things that Werner von Braun shared with Carol Rosin was that first there would be the Cold War, and then there would be states of concern and rogue states. And then he said, specifically -- this was 1974 – there would be global terrorism and the threat of asteroids from space. And following that, the controllers would roll out the hoaxed extraterrestrial threat. And all of this is designed to achieve maximum control of the world's population through fear.

When Carol Rosin told me this, I told her, "I've met with a half a dozen other people who have been in planning groups where exactly that scenario has been gamed."

Our experience with these extraterrestrials is that they are clearly saying, "Try to get this corrected. Do what you can." And so we are doing what we can.

Carol Rosin had an experience with advanced mind-accessing technologies that she shared with me. When she first met Werner von Braun, he was very sick and she was asked by him to give a talk on his behalf at a big gathering of aerospace people in Chicago. She felt very unprepared for this, but he said, "You'll be fine; don't worry. Just go." So, she went and had no idea what she was going to say to all these thousands of people.

As she began her talk, suddenly she heard Werner von Braun's voice speaking to her, in her ear. She did not have any kind of implant or any kind of electronic device in her. She gave the talk from listening to Werner von Braun speaking to her in her ear and gave the entire talk that way! That's when she realized just how advanced these systems are.

You do not have to have a specific device in anyone when using the really advanced non-local electromagnetic systems developed by this rogue group. Of course, one of the things that has been done in terms of controlling behavior and inducing memory are the so-called implants that people have taken out of alleged abduction victims. These are manufactured by covert high-end electronics firms and are then implanted into people through hoaxed abductions. These abductees are then directed to specific unwitting (or compromised) abduction researchers, who then claim ETs did it! What a travesty!

Since they have no idea what the covert human capabilities are, such researchers claim only ETs could have done it. Nothing could be further from the truth. If you don't know what the human covert capabilities are, there is no way you can judge what it is that you're observing—whether or not it is of human or extraterrestrial origin. After 50 or 60 years and trillions of dollars in covert expenditures, working with some of the most brilliant minds in the world, some really amazing advances have occurred in the covert world. I'm certain that the state-of-the-art is extremely advanced and is, in some respects, approaching parity with some of the extraterrestrial capabilities.

Also, we have noted that many abductions are clustered near military facilities or within military families. I learned from some of the people who were looking into this back in the '70s and '80s that they had found a very strong correlation with military families and personnel and military areas. This was reported to some of the civilian UFO groups, but the people trying to get that information out were black-listed from every meeting and were not allowed to talk about it. It was whitewashed and covered up. Makes you wonder who is running these UFO and Abduction groups!

In fact, the executive director of one of these civilian abduction groups called me and said he had heard that I had reached this conclusion, that I was absolutely correct and that there were a large number of their cases that he knew were military abductions. But, this fact was being covered up by the founder of this group, and anyone who tried to bring this information out or tried to talk about a positive interaction with extraterrestrials was summarily removed. It turns out this prominent UFO abduction group had dominant funding from Prince S.A.!

This is the kind of thing that goes on routinely. And this is why my concern has always been the truth and wherever the truth leads us. Unfortunately, there are some people who have so much of their reputation and belief system wrapped up in these ideas that they won't let the truth out.

Back in the '80s, there was a researcher named Paul Benowitz. An officer in the Air Force Office of Special Investigations (AFOSI) was involved in such a case. A military abductee was directed to Paul Benowitz for the purpose of causing him to go off track on an investigation regarding super secret projects around Kirkland Air Force Base in New Mexico.

A woman, late at night, was driving near one of these secret facilities where they were testing an anti-gravity vehicle. She saw something she was not supposed to see, so a military abduction sequence was initiated. They gave her a chemical, she lost consciousness, and then they implanted her. Using advanced MK-Ultra type techniques, these covert operatives then gave her screen memories of an ET abduction sequence.

She was then directed, through these people, to Paul Benowitz and they started targeting him with some of these electromagnetic weapons systems. He subsequently had a serious nervous breakdown and had to be hospitalized. It was a huge tragedy.

This all happened because this hapless person saw something she wasn't supposed to see. The cover story was "an extraterrestrial abduction," when, in reality, what she had seen was a testing of an alien reproduction vehicle near Kirkland AFB. Some people are just in the wrong place at the wrong time, and rather than let it out that secret human projects have anti-gravity propulsion systems, a hoaxed ET abduction occurs as a convenient cover story.

During the course of our investigations in the '90s, we identified a few people who have been on these squads. One is a man outside Seattle, Washington and another one is in Colorado, who was an Army Ranger and had been pulled into one of these compartmented programs. He said that it was the practice of 'stagecraft'. You were only sent on an abduction once, and then they separated you.

I've asked him to come forward publicly, but he's terrified and he's certain that he'll be assassinated if he does. He said that they actually had humans directing people who were made to look like extraterrestrials. This 'stagecraft' is very advanced and would fool almost anyone that it really was an ET doing the operation. He said they were using electronics, as well as drugs, to abduct people. "You have no idea how many important political and key military figures have had either themselves or their family members abducted by us so they would learn to hate the extraterrestrials and support the Star Wars effort."

I said, "Yes, I do believe it," I told him, "because I met with Prince S.A., whose brother had been abducted through a covert paramilitary operation so that this powerful banking family would accept there was a threat. These operations are extremely well managed, and very sophisticated at the art of deception."

A number of separate, corroborating people who've been in corporate and military intelligence programs have told me the exact same details regarding the modalities that are used and the purpose behind the operations. These hoaxes are perpetrated in other countries, as well.

And the purpose is to do exactly what Werner von Braun had warned about: to prepare people for an eventual false threat from outer space that would "unite the world" around a new level of centralized military-industrial-economic power.

Some people in the media, and certain authors, have been targeted with this type of experience. President Kennedy was assassinated because he got too close to the truth on this and related matters.

25

Out of the Loop

President Kennedy was assassinated for a constellation of related issues: UFOs and extraterrestrial intelligence are part of a set of problems that include the world banking system, the intelligence directorates, this shadowy group that controls our society through interlocking corporate, financial and institutional interests and corrupt corporate interests in military and government affairs.

Jack Kennedy knew a great deal about this and was going to take decisive actions to try to correct it. He was going to rein in the military industrial complex. He was going to make peace with the Soviets; he was going to end the Cold War. In short, he was going to upset the fascist apple cart. And you have to understand that Jack Kennedy also was bright enough to know that Marilyn Monroe was murdered because she was going to talk about some of the things he had told her about ETs and related issues.

Bobby Kennedy certainly knew about these things. I have a letter from Bobby Kennedy talking about UFOs and his interest in the subject, written not long before he was assassinated.

Jack Kennedy, as I understand it from my sources, was in the process, in the fall of 1963, of putting through the federal system an executive order that would have altered the dynamics of many of these projects. He was very much in favor of virtually dissolving the CIA. He wanted the UFO matter disclosed and the technologies used to benefit humanity. He wanted to change the course we were taking in Vietnam. Well, this rogue entity was not going to let all this happen. He was, of course, assassinated before these changes could be effected.

A man involved in the Kennedy assassination called me to discuss the UFO and energy/propulsion matter. This man was involved in the logistics surrounding Kennedy's assassination. But he has also been deeply involved in this shadowy meta-government that runs UFO projects and is sitting on the new energy systems that could save the world's environment. People who know him will tell you that he has killed more people than you can count on both your hands and feet. But now he's working on the reverse engineering projects and dealing with UFO and "flying saucer" technology. I've spoken to him a number of times, and I know for a fact that the assassination of Jack Kennedy and the deaths of many people have been attributed to trying to stop leaks on this issue.

When I met with Lord Hill Norton, in England -- a five-star admiral, "sea lord" and former MOD head — he wanted to know why he was never told anything about UFOs. He had heard that I had met with the CIA Director and was briefing Clinton's people. I went to his home in Hampshire. It was one of these grand old houses with the thick, thatched roofs — a beautiful place. We sat in his living room in a couple of wing chairs. He was on my right side and had a little pad of paper and was asking me questions, taking notes fastidiously. He wanted to know everything I knew. Lord Hill-Norton was an intense, short man with piercing blue eyes.

At one point, he asked me, "Why would they not tell me about this? I was head of the Ministry of Defense, and I was also head of MI-5 and MI-6 and all the other sensitive operations in the UK. Plus, I was head of the Military Committee for NATO! Yet I never knew about this when I was in those positions. I only learned about it later, and I found out about it from people like Lord Mountbatten. Why wouldn't they tell me?" He was outraged that he was "out of the loop," just like Admiral Tom Wilson, who was head of Intelligence Joint Staff, and just like CIA Director James Woolsey, and on and on and on.

I said, "Well, sir, let me answer your question with a question. What would you have done if you had found out that there was a trans-national group that answered to no government in the world but had infiltrated almost every aspect of every government of any significance in the world; that had arrogated to itself, through a criminal enterprise and ruthless behavior -- including murder and assassinations – illegal control of the most important technologies ever discovered, including technologies capable of interstellar travel, technologies that could take the whole world off the need for fossil fuels, save the environment, and end poverty in the world; and that this group had utter contempt for the rule of law and for democracy and for the freedoms and welfare of the people, or even for the future of Earth? What would you have done?"

He exclaimed, "I wouldn't have stood for it for one bloody moment!!" I said, "And that's why they never told you. You've just answered your own question." He asked, "Well, what do you mean?" I said, "Because if you had known, and this would have been your response, you would have ended up like Jack Kennedy or like Lord Mountbatten, blown up by an alleged IRA bomb that was actually set by this rogue group. And you would have ended up like Marilyn Monroe and Mary Meyer and all these other people, who were killed for not going along with the secrecy. You would have ended up like all the rest of them." Then I added, "And like, unfortunately, some of my group— like former CIA Director, Bill Colby." He just looked at me. He then muttered something to effect of, "Those bastards!".

Whether you know or whether you don't know is dependent completely on whether or not those in this shadowy, covert world think you will go along with whatever amount of secret information you would be exposed to. And if they think you're a stand-up guy, who, as soon as you find out how valuable the information is and also how criminal the enterprise is that's doing this, would try to fix it, they won't give you this information, because if they do and you step out of line, they're going to have to eliminate you.

My military advisor has been in such unacknowledged special access projects and has described to me how they work. If there are ten people in that project and it's an unacknowledged project, only those ten people know what's going on in it. And if you're in that group and you step out of line, he told me that there is a bullet with your name on it, and it'll find you. And if you are not in that cell, no matter what your rank and position, you will never know it exists.

One of these projects was headed up by Admiral Harry Trane, who later went to SAIC. At a certain point when they were going to close that project so it could morph and turn up at another place— just to keep the shell game going— this Admiral gathered all the men together and said, "Thank you very much for your services; you have been in an X *billion* dollar, unacknowledged project, but now it is time for it to change its form." And they shut it down. I am working with many men who've been in these kinds of projects.

One of our witnesses is Merle Shane McDowell. He had been at Atlantic Command near Norfolk, Virginia, when an enormous UFO came in out of space, off the northeastern seaboard, and was eventually tracked on at least five different military radar stations. It was tracked going up and down the east coast. The control center where he was located went to what's called a full Code Zebra alert. You have to have zebra stripes on your badge to stay in that facility when they are at this highest stage of alert.

Anyone without Zebra stripes who isn't out of the command within 60 seconds will be shot by Marines stationed there. Admiral Harry Trane was the CINC— the Commander-in-Chief, Atlantic Command— when this happened. Merle Shane McDowell told me that the Admiral was really upset because this event was out of his control. The Admiral then ordered the downing of this extraterrestrial vehicle and scrambled jets all up and down the eastern seaboard, trying to intercept it. But in one sweep of the radarscope, it would move from off the coast of New England to off the coast of Florida, and then one more sweep and the UFO would be off the coast of Norfolk. Eventually, it went out over the Azores. At one point they did get a pilot close enough to it to photograph it. And McDowell saw the photograph of this very large, long, cylindri-cal-shaped craft. Over the Azores, it turned about 60 degrees and went straight out into space, instantly.

In the early 1980s, Admiral Trane, was apparently not in the loop on the UFO matter, because McDowell says, "The old man was really shak-en." He didn't know what this thing was! They were on the hotline to the Soviet Union, trying to find out if it was a missile or something of theirs. And the Soviets said, "It's not ours." It was nothing European. It was not American.

Later, spooks in suits came in and threatened everyone who had been part of this encounter. And the threats were serious.

One of the reasons I brief many mainstream military commanders about this issue is that those who do not know about the subject could stumble into a similar encounter like this and not know how to respond. Operational readiness is being undermined by secrecy, by this parallel rogue group who did know, but who wouldn't tell people. Remember: Admiral Trane ordered a military encounter and downing of an ET craft because, at that time, he did not know what it was! This is extremely dan-gerous and ill-advised.

After Adm. Trane left the military, he went through the revolving door of the military industrial complex and to the crown jewel of the secret shadow government: Science Applications International Corporation, SAIC.

Our military advisor had the opportunity a few years ago to meet with Admiral Trane, and to bring up this issue. Admiral Trane listened but became very silent and said, "I am profoundly disinterested in dis-cussing this matter". He then picked up literally the last word of what was being discussed prior to the UFO subject being brought up and con-tinued on, seamlessly.

These people are trained to do this. I have a very dear friend who introduce me to Mrs. Boutros-Ghali, the wife of the Secretary General of the U.N., and a number of other people. She has been a long-time supporter and member of CSETI and the Disclosure Project. She also has been friends for years with a very senior Senator. I tipped her off that I was pretty certain he was one of the key operatives in this secret rogue group. So, she brought this matter up to him. And he did the following: He listened, looking at her with these intense, eagle-like eyes. When she finished speaking, he brought up the last word of what was said *prior* to her mentioning UFOs and seamlessly continued the conversation. He just snipped the UFO part of it out, as if it was never discussed. She said it was really amazing.

I, too, have seen this happen with people. This is one way I've been able to identify the really well-trained, senior people in the shadow government group. A former US President and two former Secretaries of Defense are very deeply involved.

In the mid-'90s, I was invited by someone who knew Senator Barry Goldwater to discuss this at his home. Many of you may remember he was the senator from Arizona who ran for President in the 1964 election and lost. And he was also a general in the Air Force Reserves.

I went to Sen. Goldwater's home near Scottsdale, AZ, which was up on a hill overlooking the city. The senator was in his 80s, but quite sharp. He was very interested in what we were doing. We had sent all of our briefing materials to him and he was very grateful.

He told me this story: Back in the '60s he was very close friends with General Curtis Lemay —you know, "Bomb them back to the Stone Age Lemay".

Senator Goldwater, being in the Air Force and a pilot, had heard UFO reports from very credible people that he had known. He had also heard that some of the material retrieved from a 'crashed' UFO in New Mexico had ended up at Wright-Patterson Air Force Base.

Even though Senator Goldwater was a very senior senator, he had never received any information on this subject through channels. So, he went to Gen. Curtis Lemay and asked the General if he would arrange to get him into the "blue room" at Wright-Patterson Air Force Base within the Foreign Technology Division to see the UFO material. Now, he and Gen. Lemay had always been very amicable, but Curtis Lamay turned to him and said, "God damn it, Barry. *I* can't even get into that area, and if you ever ask me about this again, I will personally see that you are court-martialed out of the Air Force!"

This, to a U.S. Senator, U.S. Presidential contender and someone who was in the Air Force Reserves, as a general! I'm sitting in the living room with Senator Goldwater, and I asked, "My God, was he serious?" He said, "He was serious as a heart attack. And I never brought it up again!"

This story gives you an idea of the fear and the extreme secrecy surrounding this subject, even to someone of the stature of Barry Goldwater, founder of the conservative wing of the Republican Party. He was arch-conservative, pro-military, red, white, and blue, dyed through and through. And here he was being told by a friend and a fellow general that he would be court-martialed!

Sen. Goldwater said, "I think what you're doing is wonderful." He asked, "What can I do to help you?" And I said, "We're trying to put together a coalition of people who know the details of this at a significant enough level so that we can disclose the UFO matter in a credible way to the public and end the secrecy. The time has come to end this secrecy…"

Goldwater said, "You've got that right! It was a God damned mistake then, and it's a God damned mistake now that this was ever kept secret!"

So, we started talking about who was involved in this secret, shadowy group. As I went through a list of names of the people involved, I finally asked, "Do you know Admiral Y.N.?" "Oh, sure, He and I have been friends for years." I said, "Well, hell, he's like MJ-12 Number 3." Goldwater was shocked, "He is?"

I said, "Oh, yes." Along with people like Edward Teller and folks like that. Edward Teller had key involvement with these projects.

He asked, "Well, what can I do?" I asked, "Would you mind contacting the Admiral for me and asking him if he would meet with me, with the goal of discussing this matter and exploring how we could cooperate to get this information out to the public in a way that would be effective and safe?" He said "Well, I'll certainly try." So, he did.

A few weeks later, I heard back from Senator Goldwater. He said, "Oh, my God! I can't ever bring this up to the Admiral again!"

I was told in so many words that Admiral Y.N. had busted Goldwater over this, and he was not going to discuss this matter with anyone. This Admiral held several very high government positions and, from one of those positions, went on to be one of the chief people at Science Applications International Corporation, SAIC. Get the picture?

Admiral Y.N. is certainly a key person -- and has been for decades.

I later spoke with Joanne Goldwater, one of Senator Goldwater's daughters, who heads up Goldwater Foods of Arizona. She said, "You know, Daddy really can't help you get to these people anymore … whatever it was that the Admiral said to him put the fear of God in him." I said, "That's fine. This is a voluntary association and everyone has his limits. I don't ask anybody to do anything that they're not comfortable doing, and I appreciate your dad going as far as he did."

Around that same time, I learned that Vice President Humphrey had gone secretly to Kirkland AFB and Sandia Labs, to look into the secret UFO related technology projects there. He had learned that there were covert projects working on the extraterrestrial materials. A witness who was at Sandia Labs at the time told me personally that he had worked with the UFO projects there and with the extraterrestrial reverse engineering program, specifically the electronics.

Vice President Humphrey came to the facility and wanted to come in and see what was there. But the Vice-President was told, "Sir, you are not allowed into this area. And if you proceed further, we will shoot to kill." I asked this man, "Were they serious? They would have shot and killed the Vice President of the United States?" He said, "Absolutely. He would have been a dead man."

26

The New Era

When a Manifestation of God - the Godhead - enters this plane, it invigorates every aspect of creation, like a spiritual springtime. There is a renewal of spirit, knowledge and intellect and what's called a divine plan that is established in the deeper realm of spirit, within all things and all beings.

It is embedded into the fabric of the creation and literally revives and enlivens all of creation, every atom. Everything is altered. And suddenly, "spontaneously," there are enormous breakthroughs in science, social thought, spiritual ideas and the coming together of peoples. All the enormous change and advancement in science and thought is because this spiritual force and divine plan is unleashed.

This new spiritual cycle has established a whole new world. That new cycle – however embryonic – is unfolding all around us and within us. But this happens even as retrograde forces try ferociously and futilely to stop it.

Now, it doesn't happen by itself. It happens through us. This is the interesting thing about being a human. A human being, even the least amongst us, nevertheless has the totality of the universe folded within him. We know all these truths, within us. It's all folded within. In reality, there is no difference between inner and outer. 'All This is That.'

All of us have reached a new potential. There's a new capacity within all beings in the universe. The cycle we have entered is one of universal peace, not simply world peace. The warmongers who are hell bent on thousands of years of galactic warfare are completely off the mark. No matter how addicted certain retrograde elements of our society may be to the old paradigm of endless war, that time will be over shortly – and we will enter a time of unbroken peace for at least 500,000 years on earth!

Now, we're in the death throes of watching the old paradigm die. It's darkest before the dawn, and it's often stormiest before the calm, and it's often most difficult and treacherous before a new time like this can be permanently established. That's the time we're living in: These last 100 to 150 years have witnessed enormous changes on every level: spiritual, cosmological, social, religious, political, scientific -- everything.

In the last 150 years, there's been more change than the previous hundred centuries before it. How did that happen? It happened because this new creation was manifested through the Godhead at the opening of this cycle. Spiritually, it already exists, in the empyrean realm of celestial knowledge. We can go within and see it- and it is beautiful!

Regarding the secret agenda of those addicted to the old world: Everything is in play. I've been told by deep insiders that everything is up in the air: It can go either way -- which is why we must strive until our last breath to bring forth this new world of universal peace. The more people have their eyes open about this deceptive and manipulative agenda the better off we all are, because if we know it, we can avoid being stampeded into the folly of Star Wars. Knowledge is power.

There's been a lot of manipulation since 9/11, but certain elements have overplayed their hand. And by overplaying their hand, people are seeing that a shadowy agenda is operating that has nothing to do with the security of the United States or the world. Before 9/11, we were talking about the fact that we had multiple sources who described the Cold War giving way to these rogue states and then to global terrorism and then the threat from outer space in the way of asteroids and extraterrestrial threat. And here we are.

It's getting late in the game, but the question is whether or not there are enough people still deceived. And the other question is whether there is still enough willingness within these covert programs to pull off a cosmic Gulf of Tonkin.

There are a lot of people in these projects who don't know what the real agenda is. It is highly compartmented. Out of the 200 -300 people in the policy group, globally, who deal with this, there are only a small number of them who know what all of the agendas are. And the worst agendas are the ones I'm discussing. There are about two dozen people who know the plan at that level. It's very, very, very tightly controlled through compartmentalization.

One of our most important objectives is to expose the layers of this agenda to well-meaning people in that covert group. There are defections. There are people who are saying, "I'm not going along with that. I was doing this to keep it secret so these technologies couldn't be weaponized by our enemies," or "I was keeping this secret to maintain the stability of the global economic system," or "I was keeping this secret because I wanted to be sure that we didn't suddenly collapse the oil industry,". But when they find out about some of these agendas, they say, "Wait just one minute!"

Out of the many thousands of people involved in these projects, and out of the many hundreds involved in policy management, most are deceived regarding the ultimate agenda.

That's why it's very important that we not assume anything about people involved with these operations. Many are good people who are themselves being manipulated. That's why some of the key people in this group keep calling me and saying, "Keep moving this forward; we want this fixed." One of them sent me a message that said, "Never, never, never, never, never, never, never, never, never, never, never, never, never, never give up."

Of course, this is easier said than done: After they've killed your best friend and you have metastatic cancer and you have quit your 'day job' and you have children to put through college and you're being called everything but a witch doctor on the Internet, and on and on and on and on, it is demoralizing and often hard to keep going. Keeping moving is the most difficult thing.

Some people in these super-secret projects are very grateful for what we're doing. At the beginning of our project there were around a third of the controllers involved who wanted to see disclosure; now, it is 45-50 percent. But there's still a very powerful element that is ruthless. Former CIA Director Bill Colby was, in a sense, a test case: People defecting at that level were not going to be tolerated.

But that was nearly a decade ago and things change. You can never judge the future by looking at the past, particularly not at this time. There is so much evolution occurring. We should view all these people as educable, and they can transform to a better understanding. Many will come forward and assist us.

I have had a recurring, lucid precognitive dream of being at a specific place in the American Southwest where there's a daytime vectoring and contact with an extraterrestrial vehicle and a very senior spiritual and diplomatic elder of the extraterrestrials emerges. It is a peaceful, open event, and it is being facilitated by a friendly component of these covert military programs.

This incredible event was shown to me in the early '90s. I think that the chance of it happening is actually going up as time marches forward.

When did all these super secret projects begin? The truth is: There are still black projects and materials that have not been de-classified from the turn of the last century and World War I!

There have been elements of this motif of secrecy that have existed in one way or another in society for thousands of years. There have always been cartels. There have always been secret societies trying to

acquire secret power. And they have gone through various transforma-
tions, depending on the exigencies of the time and place and political and
technological circumstances.

But certainly in the 20th century there have been very covert programs connected to important industrial interests that have known about
these technologies— particularly the so-called free energy electromagnetic systems, which is what Tesla discovered.

Even Faraday had discovered an "over unity effect" in some of the
experiments he did, in the 1800s. And so there have been interests that
have been keeping those things suppressed and quiet for a long, long
time.

In the 1800s— the era of the Vanderbilts and the Rockefellers and
Standard Oil – there were powerful interests that wanted to keep such
free energy developments secret. At one time, Standard Oil had a greater
income than the government of the United States. That corporation,
controlled by the Rockefeller family, was that large and that powerful.

Into that monopolistic, industrial environment, geniuses like Tesla or
T. Townsend, Brown, and others step. They have so-called zero point
energy and free energy machines, and early high voltage anti-gravity systems.

And there were reports of ET craft in the late 1800s – the famous 'air-
ship scare' of 1896. I have it from an excellent source that General
MacArthur actually was involved in the retrieval of an ET object in
China, back in the 1930s.

So, there have been programs observing the extraterrestrial matter
and at the same time trying to control the technological issue for over 100
years. However, a quantum leap occurred in these programs during the
World War II era.

Around the time that we developed the knowledge of thermo-
nuclear weapons and were on the path of early space exploration, there
were programs that were investigating propulsion systems that looked
like flying saucers. Von Braun was involved, as was Edward Teller, Dr.
Vannevar Bush and others. Goddard in 1936 and '37 was developing
some of Tesla's work; they stole Tesla's anti-gravity work and sold it to
the Nazis in the mid-'30s.

But once we moved from that level of experimentation and development into using thermo-nuclear weapons and covert anti-gravity propulsion, the extraterrestrial people who had been watching Earth for thousands of years became very concerned. They knew that there's a very
short distance from that point of technological development to the abil-

ity to go interstellar. And here is a group of people, on this beautiful Earth, who, in a few decades, have gone from horse and buggies to anti-gravity, electromagnetic weapons systems, and thermo-nuclear devices. Well, you would have to be galactically brain dead not to be very concerned about this!

At that time, during and after WWII, ET reconnaissance and limited intervention increased. ETs were trying to slow down the pace at which we were going into this destructive trajectory. We have Disclosure Project military witnesses who describe extraterrestrial vehicles inter-cepting inter-continental ballistic launches off of Vandenburg Air Force Base and over the South Atlantic. ETs were trying to delay our wild push into mutual assured destruction.

People like Colonel Diedrikson, who had been with the Atomic Energy Commission, observed that there was a strong extraterrestrial concern at all our nuclear facilities. He had personal knowledge of the interception of an inter-continental ballistic missile that had been spe-cially developed so it could be exploded on the moon. The ETs inter-cepted it before it could become exo-atmospheric.

By the 1940s, we were actually knocking down extraterrestrial vehi-cles near Roswell, New Mexico, which at the time was our only nuclear base. We have an FBI document written to J. Edgar Hoover stating that a specially configured radar system was responsible for downing those ET craft. By the 1960s we had the ability "to travel among the stars" as Ben Rich said. Rogue covert projects had developed electromagnetic systems that involved the ability to alter consciousness and harm people.

By the way, Tesla actually had a functioning anti-gravity experiment working and witnessed before the Wright brothers flew.

During President Eisenhower's administration, any semblance of constitutionality and legality associated with these projects went down the toilet, and it has been out of control ever since. The Shadow Goverment stabbed Eisenhower in the back.

27

Truly Quantum, Cosmic Moment

I have learned from people like Catherine Austin Fitts -- who worked with the first Bush presidency, in Housing and Urban Development -- that there is an enormous amount of clandestine funding being siphoned out of every agency, through dummy programs, into these black projects. When she discovered this, they ran her out of town and tried to destroy her life financially and professionally. This is a mainstream, credible person who's been in some of the top investment banking firms in the country. She was Assistant Secretary for Housing and Urban Development.

As my friends in the Pentagon say, "A billion here and a billion there, and pretty soon you're talking real money."

Thousands of employees are involved in various projects, but they don't really know the details of what they are working on. Someone might be working on a little widget here within a compartment that's part of this compartment that's part of that compartment — it's very, very tightly controlled. The policy group or control group is 200 to 300 people, and it is trans-national. The United States by no means is the only major center of activity. There are important representatives in this group from China, Latin America, The Vatican, various institutes, Europe, Russia. National boundaries, actually, mean nothing.

National issues are irrelevant. It's not even about government as you and I normally think of it. It is centered in corporate, financial, transnational, and religious interests; they are the tail wagging the dog of government. The single most powerful entity within this group today is the corporate Mormon empire. The Mormon hierarchy has vast financial and corporate holdings linked to these covert programs, but the "rank and file" wittingly have nothing to do with it.

Enforcement: you know, I always tell people, "Oh, the CIA? Those guys are pussycats." The ones you've got to worry about are the contract guys who work for Lockheed or E-Systems or the ones that are contracted from this group that are attached to what are called the Devil's Disciples, which is a motorcycle gang. It's a sub-section of the Hell's Angels that routinely engage in torture and human sacrifice and vivisection -- where they cut you open alive -- in order to enforce secrecy in certain settings.

I know a man who is an energy researcher who worked with a victim of the Devil's Disciples. They wear necklaces that have a tooth from each person they've killed on it. So, they knocked his teeth out and eviscerated him, and left him to die, but he survived. Today, he is a very anti-social person and doesn't want to have much to do with humans.

The Devil's Disciples are working under contract from some of these rogue criminal enterprises that are involved with the hard-core end of the secrecy. Much of the security is outsourced to entities like Wackenhut for traditional security. But then there are these non-traditional enforcers.

A covert ops guy I know in Arizona acquired the Carp tape, where what appears to be either an alien reproduction vehicle or an actual ET craft went out of control and crash- landed near a military facility in Canada.

During the retrieval operation, one of the special teams involved filmed the landed craft. The person who made this film was doing it clandestinely; it's a very shaky film. I have it. It came to me with some photographs of what looked like some ET life forms.

This film and the man who shot it made their way to a person who is black ops but presents himself as a concerned UFO researcher and digital image analyst. So he gave this person who made the film a 'safe house' on his ranch in Arizona. Well, I'm not sure that it was a safe house at all. One day, this 'protector' came back out to the ranch -- and hammered to the mailbox of the ranch was a baggy with a finger in it, with a little piece of paper that said, "TWEP" -- terminate with extreme prejudice. They never found this person, and it is presumed that he was killed. The owner of the ranch told me this story.

The people who are in these key roles are often there because they have been brought along, inter-generationally — that is from one generation to another.

For example, I mentioned James Jesus Angleton, who signed off on the wiretap of Marilyn Monroe. I was contacted by a decendant, who is enormously wealthy and involved in this covert group, but not with the Agency. Everything important is outside the Agency, in the private world.

After the Disclosure Project event, he called me up and said, "You've moved our timeline of bringing this information out up by six to 12 years." I said, "Good." He added, "We're looking at this material with NATO; there is a compartmented operation within NATO headquarters that deals with this, in Europe."

He explained, "But what we're planning to do -- and we would like for you to cooperate with this -- is that in a few years, we're planning to have the key political, military and religious leaders of the world announce that ETs have been detected and we have evidence that we're not alone and that there are extraterrestrials."

I said, "It's a bit late in the day for that, don't you think?!"

He was trying to talk me into delaying disclosure to match their time-table. Of course, I have been approached this way before – remember General T.E.. I said, "My concern is that in delaying Disclosure, there would be an opportunity to further consolidate power around an agenda that is the antithesis of the direction the Earth should be taking."

The more sympathetic members of this group -- including this gentleman, Angleton – are open to getting this information out sooner rather than later. There is so much spy-versus-spy going on within the Shadow Government, and there are so many factions, and shifting alliances: It's an extremely dynamic situation. People have a tendency to view this covert control group as monolithic and fixed, but it isn't. It's very dynamic, even fractured.

We have significant protection around the Disclosure project from unusual places. Since 1998, none of our military witnesses have even been told, "Be quiet." Not one. None of them have been threatened.

I met with a cell of the Shadow Government, prior to the 2001 Disclosure Project National Press Conference. I said, "Please make your people aware of the following: We welcome your assistance, or you may be neutral. But if you harm one hair on the head of any of these men or women or anyone associated with the projects or even make a threat in that regard, or should I step off a curb in Washington on the way to a meeting and get hit by a metro bus, there will be serious consequences." They knew we meant it. We have extraordinary spirit warriors who protect us – on earth and elsewhere. It does not mean we are invincible – far from it. But it is a check and balance, and it is just.

There can be no promises. All I know is that all that can be done is being done.

Since my near-death experience at age 17, I have had a very different perspective on what this life is about. It has informed everything I've done. We are here briefly, but our lives are eternal. We must walk our path – fulfill our destiny – and in that there is meaning.

So, I put aside my work as an emergency doctor, and dedicated myself to this work. I will admit to deeply missing the hands-on taking care of patients. But now I have to view Earth and her children as my patients, and do the best I can to take care of them...

It is worth the sacrifice, because the time we live in is setting the direction for the next half a million years of human evolution. We live in a truly quantum cosmic moment.

It is somewhat ironic that people often ask, "Aren't you concerned when one of these UFOs is nearby, that something might harm you?" I say, "No, except to the extent that there are other people nearby." The threat is always coming from humans, not extraterrestrials. We have many cases where people pulled out their guns and started shooting at a UFO, no questions asked!

And in some cases, they have attempted to shoot CSETI teams. In Mexico in March of '97, out of the five nights we were out doing contact work, four of those nights we were assaulted by armed police who were really just roving bands of bandits, extorting money from people.

On one particular night, near Atlimayaya, we set up near an old fort, at the base of the volcano. Suddenly we saw a police car sneaking up on us with armed police walking in front of the car, rifles drawn.

I mentally saw a flash that they were going to rob us and kill us. We were in a meditative state and so we called on the Divine Being for protection. We specifically focused peace and divine protection on the police.

Initially, the police were agitated and hostile - very threatening. But they went from that state to being almost placid, instantly. They inexplicably sat down, put their guns down, pulled out a guitar from the police car, and started playing the guitar!

I turned to our group and I said, "In one seamless movement, pick up everything you have, get in our car, and we're leaving." We did this like our lives depended on it, then briefly said, "Adios," as they were playing the guitar. It went from a situation that was extremely frightening to one that was extremely peaceful, through the effect of a divine calming influence.

We got in the car and then, at enormous speed, I drove our group back into the compound where we were staying. We didn't know how long they would be in that placid, dream-like state. They were armed, cocked, ready to go — and I was determined to get us to safety.

But this shows how the divine, cosmic Being can change a situation, mysteriously, quickly, if we will call on that Power.

28

Unraveling The Matrix

We moved our family from Asheville, North Carolina to Thomas Jefferson's Albemarle County, Virginia in the spring of 1998.

We had given from 1993 until 1998— five years— for the executive branch, the President, the military, the international community, and Congress to act. They were either frightened or corrupted.

We expanded our call for witnesses to come forward. We went from a dozen or so people in the early 1990s, to over 400 military, government and corporate insiders. Without a staff, without an office and without a significant budget, we put the Disclosure together. In 1998 we estimated that we would need between two and three million dollars to be able to do the research, world-wide travel, filming, archiving, processing, setting up the National Press Club event, arrange for a PR firm and launch Disclosure.

When the Disclosure Project was being ramped-up in 2000, a woman got involved. She said, "Okay, we'll fund this effort in exchange for having an interest in a documentary with the witnesses…,". She claimed she was willing to fund the effort up to $2 million.

Well, within about a month or two, she started reneging on everything. I had put everything on my credit cards: the equipment, traveling to Europe to film witnesses there, etc. But she wouldn't pay it. She had no integrity for her word or her signature. So, I got stuck with over $10,000 on my personal credit cards!

So Disclosure started in June of 2000 and then was stopped again in August of 2000. For historical purposes, it's important to give people an idea of the kind of chicanery we have encountered.

I was so disgusted by that point, having gone through what I call "Murder, Incorporated", now we have this kind of bait-and-switch double cross! Having gone through cancer, the loss of Shari and Bill Colby, survived that, moved to Virginia, trying to keep body and soul together, left my medical profession-- then we have this kind of cruel betrayal, at the moment that the project had been publicly announced! It was almost too much to take…

I was about to shut down all of these projects in August of 2000. And then along comes Dr. Jan Bravo. Jan made a substantial donation to the

Disclosure Project which enabled us to cover all the out of pocket expenses to get the May, 2001 Disclosure event completed. If it hadn't been for Jan, there's no question at all, I would have pulled the plug on the entire project. So, thank you, Jan.

Once we got back on track, I traveled around with a camera, filming witnesses mostly on my own. Now, anyone who knows me and machines has to laugh! Forget levitating a car. That's easy. Getting me, the biggest mechanical moron on Planet Earth, to operate a digital camera by myself, now that's a *real* miracle! I have no problem intubating someone who's just been shot through the neck or, de-fibrillating a heart. But a digital video camera!

Once we had identified enough of these resources, catalogued them and put them in a database, we set a date for the event. It was an enormous undertaking done with minimal resources and all volunteers.

We had over 110 hours of videotaped testimony, from the former USSR to Spain and Italy and England to France and Latin America and all over the United States. We have insider testimony from every agency and from every era— from the '40s right up to the '90s.

I had to take all the original digital videotape and using a dual G-4 Apple computer and a simple video editing program, go through all the videotape, edit it, make the cuts and create a log for every scene and every witness. I did this all myself, because someone who knew the whole picture had to do the cut.

I edited the 110 hours of testimony down to about 35 hours. And then I took the 35 hours and edited it down to about 18 hours. Those 18 hours were given to Jeff Thill, God bless him, and in his free time (working full time at Laser Pacific and raising two young children) took the 18 hours and created the Disclosure Project videos. We had no budget for it. This was achieved only by donated labor, material and real dedication.

Also, the 35 hours of videotape were used to create 35 hours of audiotape. That audiotape was then given to a transcription service that transcribed it into text. That text was then loaded onto disks that I put on my laptop computer.

It was 1,200 pages of transcripts! That had to be boiled down to what became the Disclosure book --that also had to include all the government documents and other documentation and position papers. And I had to write all that and all the transition pieces in about 2 months to create a 600-page book. It was an all-consuming undertaking.

We engaged the National Press Club and Sarah McClendon, the famed White House correspondent, was our official host.

When we launched this event at the National Press Club, all we could afford was a one-woman shop for a PR agent. I wrote all the press releases and she and I began to notify the press that this important event involving dozens of top-secret military witnesses to UFO events was about to happen. We lit up the system and everybody was waiting for this event to happen on May 9th, 2001.

"We'll get the little Holloman room for this event...It's all you'll need."

"Oh, no - we need the ballroom."

"But that room is never used — except for very large and important events."

"This *will* be a very large and important event!"

"You've got to be out of your mind."

"No, we need the entire ballroom!"

"Well, the last time they filled the ballroom was when President Reagan was there!"

"Just get it. Do it."

"Okay — you won't listen to me . . . but I'll get it."

The day of Disclosure, she was so glad we had the ballroom, because it was packed with 22 cameras at the back of the room and the entire media. About 20 of these military and government related witnesses were present.

Connect Live is the official web-cast and internet hosting entity for the National Press Club – and also for CNN and the Pentagon. They were engaged to webcast the entire event, live.

Well, the president of Connect Live told me after the event that as we went live, the first hour of the testimony was externally, electronically jammed! He had never seen this happen! Now, we knew there would be an attempt by the NSA to jam the webcast, and our security had seen activity to that effect the night before – logistics being set up. As it turned out, the webcast got back up after an hour and it ended up being the most watched web-cast in the history of the internet! The people at Connect Live later pulled me in and showed me the band width that was used: "This event used up every T-1 line – we have never seen this kind of volume for a news webcast!" The number of people viewing the event live was half a million people — and they do not know how many people tried to get on but were unable to connect.

Ultimately, the whole two-hour press conference was viewed by over three million people. It was covered briefly by various news agencies—

CNN and BBC and most other major news groups.

The general manager of the National Press Club was stunned at the number of news people present. News networks were canceling other programming and were heard saying, "This is the *real* X Files!" There was enormous excitement.

This event beta-tested the National Security shadow government control on this issue and over the media. It was interesting to see how they would handle it.

Well, word of this event got out. Ultimately, between the interviews on the BBC and the Voice of America and all the other media coverage, hundreds of millions heard about it.   The National Press Club staff thought we had a multi-million-dollar budget and a huge staff. But all we had was the incredible dedication of our volunteers!

When they found out that there wasn't a single paid person there except this one temporary PR woman, they couldn't believe it. The general manager of the National Press Club said, "Well, this is the most organized event that's ever been here!" They also told us that it was the best attended press event at the National Press Club since Ronald Reagan had been in the building.

The media was allowed to cover a certain amount of this event, or it would have been too obvious of a cover-up. But then they took it off the airwaves very quickly. So, it went up on CNN Headline News briefly, and CNN International actually had a very significant amount of coverage in Europe. Pravda and the Chinese news agency also covered it.

But what was interesting was to see the lack of follow-through with the big media organizations -- such as the "Wall Street Journal", who interviewed me, and the big news magazines and others. They would say, "This is really a significant event!"   And then later they would get back to me and they would say, "Well, 'they' won't let us run with this story…"

Ira Rosen, Executive Producer of ABC News, had been a key investigator for Mike Wallace at "60 Minutes" and had won an Emmy for his work. He had been involved for a year or so with what we were doing and had been at our home for meetings. He'd been through all the materials. We'd given him enormous amounts of documents, testimony, and information. He wanted to do a very strong "Prime Time Live" and "20/20" piece, if not a series, on this. But after this national press event, he called and said, "Well, it looks like I'm not going to be able to do this story." I asked, "Why not?" He says, "They won't let me put it on. They won't let me do this piece." I asked, "Who's 'they'?" He said, "Well, Dr. Greer, you know who they are…"

He told my wife and me, while he was at our home having lunch, that he had credible information that they couldn't 'go with' regarding shadowy FBI interests that had shot Martin Luther King. Rosen had been involved in getting to the bottom of that — but they also never ran that story. So it was interesting to see how ABC ultimately had to back off covering the UFO subject. There was enormous pressure brought to bear not to let this get too much traction.

The covert controllers knew that if the major news groups started pulling this yarn and unraveling it, the whole cover-up would come undone. We have enough assets and enough information to unravel the whole matrix. And certainly, the interests that want to keep this secret know this and brought pressure to bear to kill the in-depth follow-up stories.

Imagine what we could achieve if we had any real significant institutional support or funding! If we had had five or ten million dollars, we could have completely ended the secrecy.

A lot of this now is in the hands of the public; the information is there. People can put the testimony on cable access channels or show it in their communities. And this is happening all over the world.

The day after the National Press Club event, one of our military witnesses was outside the White House and had a Disclosure Project identification badge on. Andy Card, who is the Chief of Staff of the President, came out and saw it, and said, "Oh, the Disclosure Project. We've been watching this… Good luck with that!" This Disclosure military witness then gave Andy Card a briefing file, which Card then carried right into the White House! The "Washington Times" had a big half-page article about it, and that's the paper of record for the Republicans and certainly what they read at the White House.

The afternoon of the press conference, we began meeting with various members of Congress. I personally gave Senator Ted Kennedy the whole briefing document.

Congressman Kucinich, who is head of the progressive caucus in the Congress, invited us to his office for a sit-down briefing. There were nine of us who arrived immediately after the Disclosure Project National Press Club event. He sat with all of us and asked each witness to share a very short vignette of what they knew about the UFO matter.

After everyone had shared, he turned to me and looked me in the eyes and said, "I have to tell you that in all my years in Congress, I have never felt an energy and a spirit like I have today when you all walked through these doors." Then he said, "The fact that you are here tells me that time is short." He was the most perceptive government leader I have ever met— and certainly the most enlightened.

There are many people in the Congress who know what we're doing and are following it closely. We met with numerous members of Congress that week. John Cypher, the actor who introduced me at the National Press Club, and Carol Rosin, met with Daniel Golden, who at the time was the head of NASA. Golden came to NASA from Science Applications International Corporation. (Hmmmm — an interesting pattern develops....)

We continue to have meetings periodically with members of Congress about this. Congressman Virgil Goode, who is the Congressman for my home district, was on the House National Security Committee, and met with me for an hour, privately. He said, "I have been reading about what you've been doing, for some time— a lot of us have."

Then he said, "But, you know, there's another group that really runs the show. It's very shadowy, just as you've described. And we're [members of Congress] window dressing." He flat out told me: "Those of us in the Congress of the United States are window dressing." And I said, "Well, yes, sir, I know that. On the other hand, you have enough power to do something, if you collectively choose to do it." And we had a discussion about that. Towards the end of the meeting he said, "I really need to see the technologies. And that's what a lot of us are waiting for. What you need to do next is put together something that proves the technologies behind the phenomenon." I've heard this from a number of Congressmen.

Congressman Goode and I also discussed the extent to which the media is corrupt and controlled: If anyone did try to step out on this matter— just as Congressman Schiff had— he would be cut off, ridiculed, and attacked. So, it isn't that there are no people in the Congress who are supportive of Disclosure -- there really are. But they feel like they don't have the ability to do what they would like to, because of the structural obstacles that are in place to contain Disclosure, the worst of which is the corruption and control of the mass media.

The big media is completely corrupted, infiltrated by the worst elements of this control group and is no more free, here in the United States, than the Chinese News Agency. In fact, the Chinese News Agency and Pravda did a better job reporting what we're doing than the "Washington Post", "Newsweek", "Time", etc.

The only free press is the insignificant press. And this is something people never think about. People say, "Well, you can say anything." I say, "Yes, you can put it on the Internet, where it gets ignored and lost in all the digital flotsam, or you can put it in some insignificant journal. But when you're talking about the big media, big Hollywood, big publishing, big newspapers, big electronic media and TV -- they are completely corrupted and controlled by shills for the secret government.

The large media empires have been horizontally and vertically integrated into the corporate trans-national shadow entity that maintains secrecy. The fox is guarding the henhouse. Bob Schwartz, who had been on the board of Time-Life, flat out said that the media have become scribes sitting at the right hand of the king, taking dictation. He said this to me in the early '90s, in New York. So we have no 'Fourth Estate' that's meaningful. The checks and balances that the founding fathers of America envisioned have been gone for decades.

A few prestigious well placed people are also used to control the spin of this information. One of the people Y.H. introduced me to after the 2001 Disclosure event in San Francisco was a man who is a very wealthy European financier and hotelier. He had just been at the Bohemian Grove – a retreat in California near the Russian River where the world power elites gather for meetings and recreation - with about 2,500 of the world's most prominent people.

This meeting was happening at the same time the Disclosure Project was being rolled out, with a multi-city tour. This man told us very influential people were asking about the Disclosure Project at this Bohemian Grove gathering.

To quell this interest, the control group got a prestigious member of the gathering to go on stage and tell everyone that he had been on the inside of these investigations for the government, and that there was nothing to it! It was, in fact, all swamp gas and misapprehension of explainable meteorites and natural phenomena. And this wealthy man who had attended the meeting asked me, "Why would they have someone of that stature address us at the same time you're having this meeting with 1,000 people in San Francisco?" I said, "Because they operate by having a few 'respectable' people in every organization function as vectors of disinformation— whether it's the Bildebergers or CFR or the Tri-Lateral Commission or the Senate or the Vatican. Most of the people involved with these groups know nothing about these matters!" The conspiracy theorists are all wrong about how things are controlled. Masons -- virtually none of them know about this subject. Burl Ives knew little beyond what I told him. And he was a 32nd-degree Mason.

But there are always a few who *do* know, and it is their role to go to their peerage- because they have their trust and their respect-, and say, "None of this could be true, and you can trust me. I'm your buddy. I'm one of you." It's the country club mentality. They belong to the same peerage, and they're people of stature. But in reality such figures are on the payroll as assets of this shadowy group.

That is how the secrecy is maintained. It's actually very simple. And it's nowhere near as conspiratorial as many people would suppose. You don't need many of these control points if they're people of stature and have "high credibility and visibility". All they need to do is say, "None of this is true, and if it were true, you know I would tell you." Right.

29

Witness Testimony

Following is a tiny fraction of the testimony obtained from the military, government and corporate witnesses interviewed for The Disclosure Project. The entire testimony is in "Disclosure: Military and Government Witnesses Reveal the Greatest Secrets in Modern History" and may be obtained at www.disclosureproject.org.

<u>Testimony that explains the secrecy</u>

Merle Shane McDow:
US Navy Atlantic Command

"These two gentlemen began to question me about this event. They were being pretty rough about it, to be honest with you. I remember literally putting my hands up and saying, 'Wait a minute fellows. I am on your side. Just a minute.' Because they were not really nice. They were very intimidating and made it quite clear to the point that nothing that was seen, heard, or witnessed, that transpired was to leave this building. 'You are not to say a word about it to your co-workers. And off base, you just forget everything that you may have seen or heard concerning this. It didn't happen...'"

Lt. Col. Charles Brown:
US Air Force (Retired)

"It is sort of strange but we send people to prison, we send people to their death because of eyewitness accounts of crimes. Our legal system is based on that to a large degree. Yet in my following of unusual aerial phenomena for the past 50 years, there seems to be some reason to discredit very viable and very reputable witnesses when they say something is unidentified...

"I do know that there are agencies of our Government that can manipulate data. And you can create or recreate [whatever you want]. Craft, intelligently operated craft, have basically violated our laws of physics on this planet. And they have done that for a long time. The fact that the Government at this point — I know we have been investigating since 1947 — has not come up with an answer, to me indicates that there is something seriously wrong. Are we this incompetent in science? I don't think so. Are we this incompetent in intelligence? I know we are not this incompetent in intelligence. Now, Project Blue Book, when it was closed by Dr. Condon's group, I have every reason to believe that this was a total deliberate whitewash....

"UFO's have been investigated for an extended period of time and the general public is not being made aware, fully aware – but are given only bits and pieces, programmed responses and things like that."

Master Sgt. Dan Morris:
US Air Force, NRO Operative

"I became part of a group that would investigate, gather the information, and in the beginning it was still under the Blue Book, Snowbird and different covert programs. I would go interview people who claimed they had seen something and try to convince them they hadn't seen something or that they were hallucinating. Well, if that didn't work, another team would come in and give all the threats. And threaten them and their family and so on and so forth. And they would be in charge of discrediting them, making them look foolish and so on and so forth. Now if that didn't work, then there was another team that put an end to that problem, one way or another."

Dr. Robert Wood:
McDonnell Douglas Aerospace Engineer

"As you may know, when you get cleared for one of these classified programs you wear your special badge and you know you can talk to anybody who's in the room with a lot of candor and it feels like that's ones psychological group- there's a lot of camaraderie that builds up. And you had access to special libraries. So one of the things that we could do is go up to the library that the Air Force ran and sort of paw through top-secret material. Since I was interested in UFOs, when I had some usual business to take care of, I'd also look in their library to see what they had on UFOs. And for about a year I was getting quite a few hits on the subject about various reports. Then all of a sudden, the whole subject material vanished. The entire classification for the subject just vanished. The librarian in our group that I was working with said he'd been in that vault for twenty years and knew exactly how things were normally done. He said, this is remarkable. He said, I've never seen that before, you just don't have a whole subject vanish out from under you. He said, I think there is something there that you hit on...

"In the meantime, there was one other thing that came about as a result of my association with Jim McDonald. I liked the guy, he was really an energetic physicist and wouldn't let any grass grow under his feet. When he got a case he would dig his teeth into it and present an overwhelmingly convincing story to professional societies. He would talk to the American Institute of Aeronautics and Astronautics and the American Physical Society, and I happened to be members of both. So whenever he was in town I would pick him up, escort him, made sure he felt welcome.

"So once when I was traveling through Tucson, where he lived, I stopped- I had a two-hour layover to catch an airplane — and he came out to the airport to have a beer with me. I said, 'What's new, Jim?' He said, 'I think I've got it.' I said, 'What do you think you got?' He said, 'I think I got the answer.' I said, 'What is it?' He said, 'I can't tell you yet. I have got to be sure.' It was six weeks after that that he tried to shoot himself. A couple months after that he finally died.

"Knowing what I think I now suspect about the skills of our counterintelligence people, I think we had the capacity to convince him to do it himself. I think that's what happened...

"Clearly in order to have effective control of this subject, you have to control it at all levels and the most obvious level is the media. So you have to look at all the kinds of media there are, the movies, the magazines, and of course in the early days that's all it is, newspapers and movies and magazines. Now we have the Internet and video and all those other sorts of things. But as the technology has blossomed in these other avenues, the people worrying about this control have also just moved into those avenues right along with them. So every time a new avenue comes up they have a new counterpoint."

Dr. Paul Czysz:
McDonnell Douglas Career Engineer

"The black budget world is like trying to describe Casper the friendly ghost. You might see a cartoon of him but you don't know how big he is, you don't know where his funding comes from, you don't know how many there are because of the compartmentalization and the oath that people have to take. I know people today that worked on one of the things that I worked on, and if you asked them about it —even if it is being discussed on the Internet — they would say no, I have no idea what you're talking about. They're in their seventies now, but they still absolutely would never admit that they even know what you're talking about. You have no idea, but it's probably larger than you think."

John Callahan:
FAA Head of Accidents and Investigations

"...When they got done, they actually swore all these other guys in there that this (UFO event) never took place. We never had this meeting. And this was never recorded...

"This was one of the guys from the CIA. Okay? That they were never there and this never happened. At the time I said, well I don't know why you are saying this. I mean, there was something there and if it's not the stealth bomber, then you know, it's a UFO. And if it's a UFO, why wouldn't you want the people to know? Oh, they got all excited over that. You don't even want to say those words. He said this is the first time they ever had 30 minutes of radar data on a UFO. And they are all itching to get their hands onto the data and to find out what it is and what really goes on. He says if they come out and told the American public that they ran into a UFO out there, it would cause panic across the country. So therefore, you can't talk about it. And they are going to take all this data...

"When the CIA told us that this never happened and we never had this meeting, I believe it was because they didn't want the public to know that this was going on. Normally we would put out some type of a news release that such and such happened...

"Well, I've been involved in a lot of cover-ups with the FAA. When we gave the presentation to the Reagan staff I was behind the group that was there. And when they were speaking to the people in the room, they had all those people swear that this never happened."

Prof. Robert Jacobs:
US Air Force

"After an article [came out about the UFO incident], the shit hit the fan! I started being harassed at work. I started getting odd telephone calls that would come during the day. At night, at my house I would get telephone calls- all night long sometimes 3:00 in the morning, 4:00 in the morning, midnight, 10:00, people would call and start screaming at me. "You are going down mother fucker! You are going down mother fucker!" And that's all they would say. And they'd keep screaming that until I finally hung up the phone.

"One night somebody blew up my mail box by putting a big load of skyrockets in it. The mailbox went up in flames. And that night at 1:00 in the morning the phone rang. I picked it up and somebody said, "Skyrockets in your box at night, oh what a beautiful sight, motherfucker!"

"And things like that have happened on and off since 1982...

"I believe this nutty fringe around UFO's is part of a concerted effort to keep serious study of it down. Anytime anybody tries to study this subject seriously, we are subject to ridicule. I'm a full professor at a relatively major university. And I'm certain that my colleagues at the university laugh at me and hoot and holler behind my back when they hear that I have an interest in studying unidentified flying objects- and that's just one of the things that we have to live with...

"What happened to the (Air Force UFO) film is an interesting story in itself as Major Mansmann related to me and other people. Some time after I had gone, the guys in civilian clothes — I thought it was the CIA but he said no, it wasn't the CIA, it was somebody else- took the film and they spooled off the part that had the UFO on it and they took a pair of scissors and cut it off. They put that on a separate reel. They put it in their briefcase. They handed Major Mansmann back the rest of the film and said, "Here, I don't need to remind you, Major, of the severity of a security breach; we'll consider this incident closed." And they walked off with the film. Major Mansmann never saw it again."

Radar and Pilot Cases:

JC: Chief John Callahan   SG: Dr. Steven Greer

JC: ...Now in the 747 they have radar in the nose that picks up the weather outside there. So his radar is picking up a target. He sees this target with his eyes. And the target, the way he described it, was a huge ball with lights running around it. And I think he said it was like four times as big as a 747!

And the military man said something like, yeah, I see him 35 miles north of Anchorage…

The UFO was bouncing around the 747 here. And when he would say that, the military guy would cut in and say, he's now at 2:00 or 3:00 and he would confirm the position. The military controller has, what they call, height-finding radar, and they have long-range radar and short-range radar. So if they don't catch it on one of their systems they catch it on the other. And if you listen to the military man, at one time he said, I have it on the height radar, or my range radar, which indicated that they had a target on his system. Well they ran through for the best part of 31 minutes…

Then the next day I got a call from someone with the Scientific Study Group [for President Reagan], or the CIA, I'm not sure who it was, the first call. And they had some questions about the incident. And I had said, I don't know what you are talking about, you probably want to call the Admiral [FAA Administrator Engen].

Well a few minutes later the Admiral calls down and says, I have set up a briefing tomorrow morning at 9:00 am in the round room. Bring all the stuff you have. Bring everybody up there and give them whatever they want. We want to get out of it. Just let them do whatever they want. So I brought all the people from the Tech Center. We had all kinds of boxes of data that we had them print out; it filled up the room. They brought in three people from the FBI, three people from the CIA, and three people from Reagan's Scientific Study team—I don't know who the rest of the people were but they were all excited…

When they got done, they actually swore all these other guys in there that this never took place. We never had this meeting. And this was never recorded.

The only ones that see a UFO in the TV programs are the rednecks out in the country that are going coon hunting or alligator hunting at night. You don't find anybody with any kind of smarts or some professional individual saying hey, last night let me tell you what I saw. They don't display that in the United States. So if you talk about seeing a UFO, you are putting yourself in a funny kind of category. That's probably one of the reasons why you don't hear about it anymore. But as far as I'm concerned, I saw a UFO chase a Japanese 747 across the sky for over half an hour on radar. And it's faster than anything that I know of in our Government.

It still bothers me that I've seen all this, I know all this, and I'm walking around with the answer, and nobody wants to ask the question to get the answer. And it kind of irritates me a little bit. And I don't believe our

Government should be set up that way. I think when we have something like this, that you can probably find out more about what's going on in the world [by not covering it up]. If they [the UFOs] can travel that far, that distance with that type of machinery, who knows what they could do here for the health of the nation, the people, the food they could give them, the cancers we could cure. They have to know more than us to be able to travel at that speed.

For those people that say that if these UFOs existed, they would some day be on radar and that there'd be professionals who would see it, then I can tell them that back in 1986 there were enough professional people that saw it. It was brought down to headquarters, FAA headquarters, Washington D.C. The Administrator saw the tape of it. The people that we were debriefing, they've all seen. Reagan's Scientific Study team, three of those professors, doctors, they've seen it. As far as I was concerned they were the ones that verified my own thoughts about it. They were very, very excited about the data. They had said that this was the only time a UFO was ever recorded on radar for any length of time where it is 30 some minutes. And they have all this data to look at...

What I can tell you is what I've seen with my own eyes. I've got a videotape. I've got the voice tape. I've got the reports that were filed that will confirm what I've been telling you. And I'm one of those, what you would call the high Government officials in the FAA. I was a Division Chief. I was only three or four down from the Admiral...

SAC/ Nuke

Lieutenant Colonel Bob Salas:

... "The UFO incident happened on the morning of March 16, 1967. I was on duty along with my commander Fred Mywald. We were both on duty at Oscar Flight as part of the 490th strategic missile squad and there are five launch control facilities assigned to that particular squadron. We were at Oscar Flight.

It was still dark out and we're sixty feet underground [at the ICBM launch control facility]. It was early in the morning and I received a call from my topside security guard who's the flight security controller and he said that he and some of the guards had been observing some strange lights flying around the site around the launch control facility. He said they were acting very unusual just flying around, and I said, "You mean

UFO? He said, well, he didn't know what they were but they were lights and were flying around. They were not airplanes; they weren't making any noise. They were not helicopters; they were making some very strange maneuvers and he couldn't explain it…"

It wasn't more than a few minutes- maybe a half hour later- and he calls back and this time he's very frightened; I can tell by the tone of his voice he's very shook up. He says, "Sir, there's a glowing red object hovering right outside the front gate—I'm looking at it right now. I've got all the men out here with their weapons drawn…"

I immediately went over to my commander who was taking a nap—we have a little cot down there for rest periods—and I was telling him about the telephone call we just received. As I was relating this to him our missiles started shutting down one by one. By shutting down, I mean they went into a "no-go" condition meaning they could not be launched. So we get bells and whistles—a red light no-go condition…

These weapons were Minuteman One missiles and were of course nuclear-tipped warhead missiles.

As they started shutting down, immediately he gets up and we both start querying the status board. We've got the ability to query and determine what the cause of the shutdowns was. As I recall, most of them were guidance and control system failures. And then he started reporting to the command post. In the meantime I called upstairs to find out what the status was of this object and the guard said, well, the object has left—it just left at high speed…

The Air Force did an extensive investigation of the entire incident and was not able to come up with a probable cause for the shutdowns. And I've got quite a few witnesses that will testify to that—we've got a couple of people who worked on the investigative team—and I've got correspondence from the man who actually organized the investigative team. There was no viable explanation for this [shutdown of multiple ICBMs]. Each missile is basically self-supporting. Most of them are powered by commercial power but each missile has its own power generator…

At our site anywhere from six to eight went down but they went down in rapid succession which again is an extremely rare happening. We rarely had more than one missile go down for any reason at all…

After I talked to my guard upstairs, my commander talked to the command post. When he finished talking to the command post he turned to me and said, "The same thing occurred at ECHO Flight." ECHO Flight is another squadron, I'd say probably 50 - 60 miles away from our location but they had the same sort of thing happen. They had UFOs that were hovering, not at the launch control facility but at the actual launch facilities where the missiles are located. They had some maintenance and security people out there at the time and they observed the UFOs at those sites. Now they lost all ten of their weapons—all ten…

It was the same morning. So that morning we lost anywhere from between 16 to 18 ICBMs at the same time UFOs were in the area and were observed by airmen. Those missiles were down the entire day because we've got testimony from Colonel Don Crawford, who relieved the crew at ECHO Flight and he was there when the missiles were being brought up to alert status and he said it took the whole day. So I'm assuming it took our missiles all day to be brought back up also…

I wrote up a report about this incident; it was in my log and I turned it in. When we got to the base we had to report to our squadron commander right away. And in that room with my squadron commander was a fellow from AFOSI (we had an Air Force Office of Special Investigations on the base). He was there in the office with the commander. He asked for my logs and he wanted a quick briefing although it seemed to me he knew pretty much what had happened already. But we gave him a quick briefing and then he asked us both to sign a non-disclosure agreement saying this was classified information- we were not to release this to anybody, and that was it. We couldn't talk; he told us we could not talk about this to anyone, including any of the other crews, our spouses, our family, even amongst each other…

I've got a copy of a telex which we received under FOIA coming from SAC headquarters and coming to Malstrom and other bases right after the morning that happened saying that this incident was of extreme concern to SAC headquarters because they couldn't explain it. Nobody could explain what happened. And yet we never got de-briefed. And we were cleared for very high classification because these are nuclear weapons we're dealing with.

We did get the security incursion alarms at those sites when the missile went down. That is unusual because usually when a missile went down for something like guidance failure, we wouldn't get security incursion alarms, which means a perimeter is breached, an object crossed the fence, or something broke the security alarm system that we had on the perimeter of the launch facility. I did send out guards to a couple of those facilities to investigate that.

The reason I think this story is very significant is because, going back to August of 1966 at Minot, ND, a very similar thing happened at one of the launch control facilities at Minot Air Force Base. They had the same kind of weapon system that we had—they had M-1 missiles. This [UFO] was observed on radar, there was some communication failure and the object was observed over the launch control facility.

That happened in August 1966 and that's a well-documented incident. About a week prior to my incident, in March 1967, I've got a record of a call from one of the security guards who was out roaming looking at the launch facilities and saw an object very similar to what I just described over the launch facility...

Bob Kominski headed up the organization to look at all aspects of these shutdowns. Kominski relates to me in writing that at some point he was told by his boss that the Air Force said, "Stop the investigation; do no more on this and in addition do not write a final report." Again, this is very unusual especially in light of the fact that CINC-SAC headquarters was stating that this was of extreme importance to find out exactly what happened here. And yet, the head of the investigative team was told during the investigation to stop the investigation and not write a final report...

Professor Robert Jacobs:
Lt. US Air Force

We sent the (UFO) film back down to the base and- I don't know exactly how long it was after the event, it might have been a day or two— I was called into Major Mansmann's office at the First Strategic Aerospace Division Headquarters. I walked into his office and they had a screen and a 16mm projector set up. There was a couch and Major Mansmann said, "Sit down." And there were two guys in gray suits, civilian clothes, which was fairly unusual. Major Mansmann said, "Watch this" and turned on the film projector. I watched the screen and there was the launch from the day or two before...

We watched the third stage burnout. And then on that telescope we could see the dummy warhead. It's flying along and into the frame came something else. It flew into the frame like and it shot a beam of light at the warhead.

Now remember, all this stuff is flying at several thousand miles an hour. So this thing [UFO] fires a beam of light at the warhead, hits it and then it [the UFO] moves to the other side and fires another beam of light, then moves again and fires another beam of light, then goes down and fires another beam of light, and then flies out the way it came in. And the warhead tumbles out of space. The object, the points of light that we saw, the warhead and so forth, were traveling through subspace about 60 miles straight up. And they were going somewhere in the neighborhood of 11,000 to 14,000 miles an hour when this UFO caught up to them, flew in, flew around them, and flew back out.

Now, I saw that! I don't give a Goddamn what anybody else says about it. I saw that on film! I was there!

Now when the lights came on, Major Mansmann turned around looked at me and said, "Were you guys screwing around up there?" And I said, "No, sir." And he said, "What was that?" And I said, "It looks to me like we got a UFO." Now the thing that we saw, this object that flew in, was circular, was shaped like two saucers cupped together with a ping-pong ball on top. The beam of light came out of the ping-pong ball. That's what I saw on film.

Now Major Mansmann said to me after some discussion about it, you are never to speak of this again. As far as you are concerned, this never happened. And he said, "I don't need to emphasize the dire consequences of a security breach, do I?" I said, "No, sir." And he said, "Fine. This never happened." As I started for the door, he said, "Wait a minute." He said, "Years from now if you are ever forced by someone to talk about this, you are to tell them it was laser strikes, laser tracking strikes…"

It's not a secondhand story. This happened to me. And I was a part of a United States Air Force cover-up for 18 years.

Colonel Ross Dedrickson:
US Air Force/AEC (ret.)

Colonel Dedrickson is a retired Colonel from the USAF. He went to Stanford business school where he studied management. Back in the 1950's part of his responsibilities included maintaining the inventory of the nuclear weapon stockpile for the AEC and accompanying security teams checking out the security of the weapons. Many reports kept coming in that UFOs were seen at various nuclear storage facilities and some of the manufacturing plants. He has seen them himself many times and was present when the famous fly-over over the Capital happened in July of 1952. At that incident he recalls seeing nine illuminated disc-type craft. He also tells of at least two occasions where extraterrestrials destroyed nuclear weapons headed out to space, one heading to the moon to be detonated for tests. It was destroyed because "nuclear weapons in space … were not acceptable to the extraterrestrials…"

Government Insiders/ NASA/ Deep Insiders

Merle Shane McDow:
US Navy Atlantic Command

Mr. McDow entered the Navy in 1978 and gained a top-secret, Special Compartmented Intelligence (SCI) clearance with a Zebra Stripes. He was assigned to the Atlantic Operational Support Facility, Atlantic Command, then under Admiral Trane. Mr. McDow was present when a UFO was tracked by radar and seen by pilots visually moving at high speed up and down the Atlantic coast. The Command Center was put on Zebra alert and Admiral Trane gave the order to force down the UFO. Mr. McDow discusses the threats, intimidation and confiscation of logbooks that occurred after the event.

"…And the early warning system—I believe it came in from an Air Force base in Greenland or Nova Scotia at that time—said that we had contact with an unidentified flying object that had entered our air space.…

And within minutes Admiral Trane was rushed into the Command Center into his viewing booth that he had right under the Mezzanine there and the first thing that Admiral Trane wanted to know was how many contacts we had, where they were, which direction were they going and were the Soviets responding. Because we knew that it wasn't the Soviets that had entered our airspace. That was verified from the get go, from the start.

At that point, when Admiral Trane found out that it wasn't the Soviets and that he wanted to know were the Soviets responding to this threat also, that was the moment that he gave authorization to put two planes up to go see what this thing was. And that was when the chasing up and down the eastern seaboard began. We launched planes from as far north as Greenland to NAS (Naval Air Station), Oceania. This object, we had it on radar—this event lasted almost an hour. You could hear the pilots live voice transmissions being piped into the Command Center. And they had visual confirmation of the object and made descriptions of the object. Pilots were able to close a couple of times and were able to see that the object was not an aircraft that we were familiar with-it was nothing that we had and nothing that the Soviets had. That was determined very quickly. This vehicle or whatever it was that they were chasing showed very erratic flight up and down the coast, quick flight...

One minute it was here and the next minute bam, it was down several hundred miles down the coast, just playing tag...

The photographs that we did get back in the Command Center later on came from the first encounters that the planes had with it off of the northern North American coast. They did get close enough to get some photographs taken that were later brought over to the Command Center...

What was really bugging Admiral Trane, what was really driving him nuts, was this thing absolutely had complete control of the situation and could be anywhere that it wanted to be in a matter of seconds. One minute we were closing on it off the coast of Maine, and the next minute it is in Norfolk heading south towards Florida. And it is all that we can do to get the early warning radar up and down the coast to watch for this thing as it just had it's day with us.

Admiral Trane and his staff were quite concerned about it to say the least. They were quite concerned especially once they found out that it wasn't the Russians and it wasn't us and he wasn't aware of anyone else who had the technology to build such a craft that could move about so easily and so quickly. I remember distinctly looking over the rail of the mezzanine and just watching complete chaos break out because of their inability to keep an eye on this thing, whatever it was.

The UFO was moving around so erratically and so quickly up and down the coast... They were trying to notify as many commands as they could up and down the coast to track this thing or get a plane up. Admiral Trane was scrambling and authorizing planes just left and right, up and down the whole eastern seaboard to try and cut this thing off and to get some planes from the north and south to literally track it and to force it down. It was clear that they wanted to recover it, to force it down, by whatever means possible.

The order was given by Admiral Trane to try and get this object forced down out of the sky, if at all possible, by whatever means possible...

When this event, as I refer to it, ended, the object that we had been chasing up and down the seaboard headed out over the Atlantic, over the Azores. I do remember them saying that it had pulled up at a 66 degree angle as it approached the Azores like this, and it just pulled up at a 66 degree angle, without slowing down or anything, and left the atmosphere and was gone into space. It just took off into space and was gone like that [snaps fingers]. I mean it just absolutely left. You are talking about something that covered thousands of miles in a blink of an eye and it was just gone and it just left everyone sitting around scratching their heads. "Gee whiz, I wonder what that was."

It was comical in a way to see how the vast military might of the United States was put on its knees by something they had no idea what it was, where it came from, where it was going or anything. The only thing that they knew for sure was that it wasn't the Soviets and they were very adamant about finding that out...

... If this object had been hostile and wanted to drop weapons or shoot missiles at us or whatever, it would have been very easy for them to do that. There was no question about that. We didn't have anything at that time that could hold a candle to whatever this was. And it just had its own free run of our airspace and could do anything it wanted as far as traveling. We did not pose any threat to it whatsoever. That was painfully obvious; very much so. I do believe that Admiral Trane knew that too and was quite afraid. Just in a word I would say that that old boy was just plain scared...

I would say that the facilities that actually had this UFO on radar— there were five that I am sure of and that is from Greenland all the way to Florida, and there may be some others that I don't know. I know this because Admiral Trane was giving orders to NAS Oceania, "Let's get some planes up from there, scramble some fighters." He did make a call for them to alert Dover Air Force Base, Patuxent River, Maryland, Cecil Field down in Florida..."

Admiral Lord Hill-Norton:
Five-Star Admiral, Former Head of the British Ministry of Defense

Lord Hill-Norton is a five-star Admiral and the former Head of the British Ministry of Defense who was kept in the dark about the UFO subject during his official capacities. In this short interview, he states that this subject has great significance and should no longer be denied and kept secret. He emphatically states, "...that there is a serious possibility that we are being visited—and have been visited for many years—by people from outer space, from other civilizations; that it behooves us to find out who they are, where they come from, and what they want. This should be the subject of rigorous scientific investigation, and not the subject of rubbishing by tabloid newspapers."

Sergeant Clifford Stone:
United States Army

Sergeant Stone tells an amazing story about the history of UFOs and extraterrestrials dating back to the early 40's and probably before. General Douglas MacArthur organized a group called the Interplanetary Phenomena Research Unit back in 1943 to study this issue and it continues to this day. Their purpose is to recover objects of unknown origin particularly those that are of non-Earthly origin. They obtain field intelligence information and pass it on to those who are the "keepers of this information." Stone says that even Project Bluebook had an elite investigation unit, which was outside of Bluebook. This unit was thought to be working in conjunction with Bluebook but in fact was not. Stone has seen living and dead extraterrestrials in his official duties on an army team that retrieved crashed ET crafts. He thinks that the extraterrestrials will not permit us to explore the depths of outer space until we've learned to grow spiritually and that they will make themselves known soon if we don't first acknowledge their presence.

Mr. Don Phillips:
Lockheed Skunkworks, USAF, and CIA Contractor

Don Phillips was in the Air Force at Las Vegas Air Force Base during an event when UFOs were seen moving at enormous speeds near Mt. Charleston, northwest of Las Vegas. In addition, he worked with Kelly Johnson at the Lockheed Skunkworks—on design and construction of the U-2 and the SR-71 Blackbird. He testifies that we not only have these extraterrestrial devices, but have also achieved tremendous technological advances from their study. He states that in the 1950s and 1960s, NATO did research into the origin of ET races, and disseminated reports to the leaders of various countries. Mr. Phillips further states that there are records and filmed documentation of meetings in California in 1954 between ETs and leaders of the USA. He lists a few of the technologies we were able to develop because of the ETs: computer chips, lasers, night vision, bulletproof vests, and concludes, "Are these ET people hostile? Well, if they were hostile, with their weaponry they could have destroyed us a long time ago—or could have done some damage." Mr. Phillips now develops technologies that can help eliminate environmental pollutants and reduce the need for fossil fuels, such as energy generation systems that use natural energies from planet Earth.

Technology/Science

Mr. Fred Threlfell:
Royal Canadian Air Force

Mr. Threllfell was a communications instructor in the Royal Canadian Air Force at RCAF Station Toronto in 1953, when he witnessed an experiment involving the successful dematerialization and rematerialization of an object. Because of his top clearance, he was also able to check out from the base library, original films of gun camera footage from WWII planes. Many times, while watching these films, he noticed UFOs in the footage—different positions, different shapes, but, definitely UFOs. He has also himself seen UFOs maneuvering in the sky.

30

Monster of Unchecked Power

There is a relatively small group of people actually running the secret UFO programs. In terms of full knowledge and operational authority - executive authority - it has nothing to do with the President of the United States or the Congress.

In fact, I was told directly by an executive with E-Systems that E-Systems was heavily involved in these areas. He said, "But very few people who work with the corporation know it."

The monies that such corporations receive are passed through several shell operations and from various agencies and end up in these super-secret black projects.

There is an interlocking power structure of corporate, institutional, financial and religious entities. They do not operate according to anything resembling the rule of law or the Constitution of the United States, or any other country.

Within that shadowy world, there are rogue elements that have broken off of the main covert operation. There are some very powerful rogue elements in this country and elsewhere and within certain secret groups. They have shadowy ties to the main group — but can act independently and at times counter to the main group's agenda. So, it is very complex – it is like layers of an onion. You think you've gotten to the center, only to find there are 20 more layers to peel back. I've been peeling back these layers for about 15 years now and have a very good idea of who these people are and how it's structured and what the agenda is.

There are people in the central control group that have connections to government but who really don't know what the hell is going on inside FEMA or the Mormon corporate empire or bizarre, shadowy plans related to their eschatological solution to the human problem.

In the mid-1990s, I was invited to a 'salon' in San Francisco, in Pacific Heights. A socialite who is friends with Gordon Getty, Willy Brown and Steven Bechtel (of the Bechtel corporation) wanted me to brief her circle of friends on these issues. (By the way, Bechtel Corporation, is a big shadow government contractor, and George Schultz is associated with them. They are all part of this secret government apparatus... There is a very powerful cell involving a former Secretary of State, US President and former Secretary of Defense most now involved in global financial enterprises.)

The chairman of AT&T was there, and the former head of SRI, Stanford Research Institute, was present. I was there to present to them what we knew and to discuss our plans for the future. Sitting next to me was the former chairman of SRI. At one point he leaned into me and said, "You know, I never knew any of this, but I knew some of it had to be going on at SRI. What do you know about...."such and such. He explained that, like the CIA Director I briefed, he was an administrator, but did not have a need to know, and was left in the dark about such projects!

He said, "I was basically a bureaucrat, a bag man, trying to keep the money flowing into this huge operation. But if DARPA (Defense Advanced Research Projects Administration) had a project going on, I really didn't know any details! I might hear a whisper here and there, but these projects were tightly controlled, and it didn't matter that I was the chairman of SRI. And the way I got there was to know you don't ask too many questions! So now I want to ask you!"

During the Iran Contra hearings, Senator Inouye stated that there is a shadowy group that has its own air force, its own navy, its own funding mechanism, and is above the law. This is especially true in the areas of advanced covert technologies, UFO and extraterrestrial matters, and related weapons systems.

One of the most dangerous trends that has evolved between the 1960s and today is that this Shadow Government became so powerful because it was able to be self-funded. Now, let me explain. Dick D'Amato of the Senate Appropriations Committee was right when he said that there's upwards of $100 billion in the black, illegal budget. But the big action is in the corporate, private financial world. Let's say that you're Bell Labs at Murray Hill. I'm working with a witness who spent his entire career at Bell Labs. He was part of a cell that did a lot of super-secret covert contracting with military operations that had extraterrestrial communications devices and circuits. These corporate labs studied the technologies and uncovered how they worked and their possible uses. They came out with Widget A or X that then became something they patented, which in turn became a multi-hundred-billion-dollar industry. Think fiber optics, integrated circuits, lasers and the like.

This cancer of covert government funding metastasized into countless corporate, financial and technological assets. And now the covert private corporate world has technologies that can trump anything at DIA,

CIA or any of the other alphabet soup of government agencies.

Another corporate witness whom I have interviewed said that while at Bell Labs, he saw 28 or 29 of these free energy devices that they had acquired and 'black-shelved' or hidden. This witness had worked on these technologies. He's retired now.

General Motors and other large corporations are also sitting on earth-saving technologies but will not let them out to the public.

So these interlocking, multi-national corporate and financial interests are a multi-trillion-dollar operation that trumps any power of the Pentagon or the United States government or any nation on Earth. It is a monster of unchecked, corrupt corporate and covert power that is only partially governmental. So, unfortunately, even if you have a powerful person in what people call "the government" who may want the truth out, he feels overwhelmed by these other 'special interests'.

I spoke to a member of Congress in February of 2004 who was on the Congressional Energy Committee. When he was at a meeting with Cheney, he said, "Cheney ran the meeting and thinks exactly like an oil executive—he views everything as an oil executive, and that's it." What you have is the corporatization of the government - of all governments of the world - into a certain agenda.

One of the men that I've worked with for years is a covert corporate operative involved in these types of operations. When I asked him to come forward, he said, "There is no agency or government on Earth that can protect me from the wrath of this group, because it's outside these governments, and much more powerful."

Now, when you have something this large and complex, you have people involved with both joint interests and separate interests. And the more separate the interests become, the more likelihood there is of a break-away rogue group. The most violent rogue operations are the ones that are connected to *ideology*, as opposed to just money, and are rooted in a certain ideological and eschatological worldview.

These are the people who have a worldview of destruction and feel that the only way for Christ to come back is for the world to be destroyed and for billions of people to be killed. There is a very powerful group that holds to that belief system. But they really are looking in their rearview mirror. What they are awaiting has already come to pass. They don't know what cycle we are in already, never mind what century we're in.

So, they're completely off the timeline of the evolution of the human race but don't know it. They are driving the world in a certain direction, to fulfill their interpretation of a prophecy, which has already happened. Alas, it may be a self-fulfilling prophecy of Armageddon – one that they create through ignorance, superstition and hatred. So, ultimately, the problem is ignorance, and the solution is enlightenment, knowledge and genuine spirituality.

The problem seems complex, but it can be very simply fixed. Where there is darkness, you introduce light. So, what we need to do is shed light on this issue and some perspective that allows people to understand that they do not need to engage in global supremacy or global destruction, in order to have their dreams come true.

I remind people of the fact that no less a figure than Reagan's Interior Secretary, James Watt, after a meeting during the Reagan years, said something to the effect of, "All these environmentalists, they don't need to really worry about the environment, because the end of the world is coming soon and Christ is returning, and the world's going to be destroyed anyway! God wants us good Christians just to go ahead and use it up while we still have time." I am paraphrasing, but this is essentially what the man who was in charge of policy for the entire interior of America said!

People need to understand that these types of superstitious and retrograde belief systems actually drive decisions and policies. It's a tragedy. Now, it's not talked about. Watt's comment was a slip of tongue that he didn't know was being recorded or heard. But I have met with many people at that level of influence, and they really hold to that belief. At this point in time, the US government is fully infiltrated and run by people with this end-of-the-world belief system.

Think about it: If that is your belief, you don't really care if there's global warming or an $8 trillion debt, because if, indeed, these are the end days, and the world's going to come to an end and all life on Earth is going to end and the good Christians are going to float up into the sky to Jesus, who cares?

This may sound bizarre to the average person. But an eschatological worldview drives much of the world's covert decision-making- especially since the structure of that group is heavily dominated by covert Mormon, Vatican and other extremist religious interests. I have met directly with such interests.

Of course, there are others involved in the covert world who are only interested in conventional greed, power, money, and control. And still others who are concerned with homeostasis: Let's not rock the boat, even if the boat's getting ready to go over Niagara Falls! There are different agendas operating, but the ones that have the most power are the ones that are the most bizarre: those rooted in retrograde cult-like religiosity and superstition.

George Santayana was so right when he said, "Fanaticism consists of redoubling your efforts when you've forgotten your goal."

From a fanatical end-of-the-world perspective, it makes sense to add half a trillion dollars a year in debt to add to an $8 trillion debt to pass on to our children. It makes sense to hold up, for decades, technologies that could save the earth even though you know both polar ice caps are melting! And why not allow thousands of species of plants and animals to become extinct? The world is ending anyway! *No one* would stay on this course while also knowing the solution, unless they had clearly fixed in their mind this eschatological paradigm.

Once I discovered this covert agenda of global destruction, everything fell into place. I began to meet with people who were Satanic cultists -- who were involved in these rogue breakaway groups. They are addicted to destruction and love torture, suffering and sadism. And it turns out they are the other side of the mask of those who pray for the end-of-the-world. It is a very strange group of bedfellows. They think it's the literal end of the world, when in reality it is the end of one Divine Cycle and the opening of another!

This singular misinterpretation of Scripture and prophecy has enormous consequences.

The solution, as I see it, is to put out a different perspective: Yes, we can talk about the end of one cycle – it is the end of one world, the old world. But it doesn't mean we have to sit back while we literally destroy the Earth.

We may not necessarily be able to change them. But we can articulate an explanation that makes sense and hope that some of them see the solution before it's too late.

It doesn't make sense that we have fiber optics and integrated circuits and laptop computers that have the power of what once would fill a whole house—but we're still burning coal for over 50 percent of the electricity needs of the most advanced nation on Earth! Come on. To make sense of this, you have to understand what is in the hearts and minds of those people who have hijacked the human future.

These projects escaped the control of Eisenhower and others once corporate greed kicked in, and those projects broke away. People with very secret religious agendas then infiltrated agencies and corporations and now are calling the shots. I have been told that, because they identify and recruit their own, that very powerful, right-wing Mormon interests have been pulled into the senior echelons of the CIA, FBI, military, and a huge number of universities, laboratories, and corporations.

What most people don't realize is that we are already living in an *undeclared theocracy.* People just haven't been told they're living in a theocracy yet. It has happened very quietly- very covertly. What the Nazis, with their cult, the Thules, couldn't achieve overtly, they decided to do covertly. It is the continuation of World War II.

People don't want to know this, I know. It is disturbing and counter to the myth that we've been led to believe.

Among the people who have been sucked into this religiosity and worldview, are those who really could care less about that belief system or the existence of Christ. Rather, they have a Satanic world view, where they just enjoy destruction and suffering. They are in the very midst of the religious ones- but the religious ones do not know who is really leading the flock.

We are closing one chapter of human history, and we're going to open another. In the closing of one and the opening of another, much chaos is possible.

There are wonderful things happening on Earth and have been for 150 years. Wonderful new ideas, new institutions, new ways of living, the potential for new technology- -- there are many things that are extremely promising. On the one hand we have this carcass of an old world that is dying. It is going through the death throes. And yet, here is this new world that has already been born, and is growing and is going to continue for thousands of years. It isn't going to be the end of *the* world: it is the end of *an old world* and the simultaneous establishment of a new one. We are already in the early stages of the golden era of the human race- one that is going to go on for 500,000 years.

So, that's what's exciting and beautiful, and that's what has to be shared, even as we become aware of these very crazy and ignorant other dramas that are played out. We need to focus on the good and the positive that's coming, even though we're aware of what some of these other things are that are going on around us, because you need to know the lay of the land.

Spaceship Earth needs to be guided through this period and be firmly established as the civilization it's intended to be. There are extraterrestrial civilizations standing ready to assist, and at a certain point things will change very rapidly.

This transformation isn't going to happen by itself. We humans are going to have to guide it and facilitate it. But we're not going to be alone: The destiny of the human race and Earth has never been alone. It's never been without assistance, and it's never been in doubt. There's no doubt about what our future and our destiny is going to be. The only question is how we're going to extricate ourselves from the current situation and establish our world firmly on the path of peace and justice.

This is the planet of free will. Our free will has to be applied in order for this transformation to happen. This is the lesson we have to learn. And as soon as we all pull together and use our free will to make this happen, it will happen.

We are trained in our educational systems and our society to simply conform. But, you know what? If you're conforming to a system that is utterly insane, there's a problem. And the world that has crept around us has become very insane. Therefore, we need to see it for what it is, break from it, and manifest the good future that is sitting there, ripe like fruit ready to fall from a tree into our hands.

The Earth and humanity are ready to blossom. And it is not just the springtime of Earth. It is the springtime of the entire cosmos.

31

Separation Of Church And State – A Myth

I have always loved the exploration of consciousness and its manifestations. Once in Blanca Peak in Colorado, we were doing field work from our cars due to a thunder storm in the area. As we were sitting there, I did a technique where I entered unbounded Mind, and began to put enormous energy into the area by seeing two counter-rotating discs in my mind – like a Merkaba. Suddenly, our car just hopped up – in a moment of anti-gravity levitation. Other cars nearby did the same thing. Fellow field workers asked, "My God, what happened?!" And I smiled and said, "We were playing with what consciousness can really do…"

There is so much we can do. But the Earth is calling out for practical work: we still burn coal for most of our electricity, just like 100 years ago. Human evolution has been hijacked 100 years by the forces of ignorance and greed. So we must work for the Earth now.

I'm reminded of the story of the Buddha coming across a man who had spent 30 years practicing to levitate across a stream. Near him was a footbridge. This man was very proud of his accomplishment and said, "Look, oh Buddha, watch." And he floated across the stream to the other side. And the Buddha walked across the footbridge across the stream and said, "Yes, but you could have just walked across the bridge, instead of spending 30 years trying to levitate…"

It's not to say that some of these abilities aren't wonderful— they are. But one could spend a great deal of time and effort on such abilities. Meanwhile, we are destroying the Earth and our civilization is terminal. So when the most great task is at hand, even important things have to be set aside.

These abilities in consciousness can be developed just as soon as one understands the nature of mind and the nature of matter and the fact that there is no matter separate from its complete and perfect integration with consciousness. Nothing exists separate from mind. All matter and energy is simply awake-ness modulating and phasing and resonating in a different way.

This has been demonstrated through various tests that have been done by Dr. Bob Jahn at Princeton and others. It's all non-local: There is no barrier of time and space. And once you understand that, literally anything can be accomplished with enough training and focus.

One of the trips I took was to Italy, England and France. At the Vatican, Paola Harris set up a meeting between me and Monsignor Balducci. He is a senior theologian to the Pope. We went to his apartment overlooking St. Peter's for the interview. He's a very patrician, dignified and very sweet man, a wonderful person and genuinely spiritual.

I asked him, "Do you think these extraterrestrials are a threat or hostile in any way?" He said, "Oh, not at all! Besides, lower than humanity, there cannot be in this entire universe!"

Later he said, "You know, God cannot be so foolish as to entrust all of his hopes for intelligent beings just on this planet."

When we were out on his balcony overlooking St. Peter's and the Vatican, he said, "You know, I could not be saying these things unless I had the approval of Papa"—meaning the Pope had instructed him to speak on the reality of ET civilizations!

He told me point blank that he had the blessing of the Pope to talk about this and to acknowledge the fact that the UFOs are real and that the extraterrestrials are good beings. And there was nothing for us to be worried about. When I asked him about the issue of putting weapons in space to target ET spacecraft, he got very agitated and said this is an absolutely wrong thing to do.

I met also with the Vatican astronomer, who said the same thing and acknowledged that the UFOs were real and the ETs were real. And yet we know that there are cells within the Vatican, within the Opus Dei group, that have a very dark view of all this and have really taken the information away from the others at the Vatican. Like in the US, everything is very labyrinthine and compartmented at the Vatican; it is very secretive.

There have been Popes and senior people at the Vatican that are in the conventional religious structure who don't know what's going on within these black cells within their own bureaucracy. It's the same motif over and over again.

This motif repeats, whether you go to a religious entity, a political entity, a scientific entity, an agency of the government, or the military. Remember that motif. If you understand the motif of a rogue, compartmented, secretive operation within an institution, and multiply that process like a fractal -- it just propagates all over the world.

While in Rome, I also met with one of the Knights of Malta -- it does exist – and a representative of the Jesuit Secret Service and the Vatican Secret Service. These groups are intimately involved in global financial and technological issues related to this subject. They are some of the key people in the hierarchy.

They asked that I provide them with the materials that I was providing these other leaders in the "white world," that is the regular, conventional world of governments, senators, the President and what have you. And, of course, I did.

But I told them, "You know, there are traditions that have existed for many centuries, of secrecy and secret power. But this is the time for those operations to transform into another way of functioning– to openness and honesty, in a way that will benefit all of humanity." They listened very politely, and I could tell they were intensely interested, and more than a little shaken.

The Knights of Malta and the Vatican Secret Service and the Jesuit Secret Service have a very key role in maintaining the secrecy on the ET issue.

When President Carter wanted information on UFOs, he went to then-CIA Director Bush, George Bush, Sr. during the transition. He was told point blank, "No, you can't have that; go see if you can get it from the Congressional Research Service." Here you have a sitting CIA director who was knowledgeable of these matters– George Bush, Sr.- denying an incoming U.S. President information! This is true. And we have witnesses to this.

So Carter asked people associated with the Congressional Research Service to find out what was going on. They asked, in turn, a lawyer named Daniel Sheehan -- who was with the Christic Institute and was representing the Jesuits in Washington, to see if he could get this information from the Vatican. So, Sheehan contacted the Vatican on behalf of incoming President Carter.

Well, the Vatican came back and said, "No, we cannot give this to you." They specifically did not say, "We didn't have it," but said "We would not give it to you or the President." The covert Vatican library and files have extensive information on all of these matters. Remember, back in 1994, a secret government insider told me that, in terms of technology transfer and management, that I would be better off talking to certain groups of Jesuit priests than to the CIA Director or the U.S. President. He was completely correct.

We have a naval witness who was on a mission to go out into the Atlantic and search for what they were calling magnetic anomalies. Now, in those circles, 'magnetic anomalies' is a euphemism for underwater extraterrestrial vehicles. They used a specially equipped nuclear submarine to search for underwater UFOs.

As they were setting up to go out on this secret mission, a limousine pulled up, and out came a suit (an unnamed covert intelligence operative) and a priest in full clerical collar. They were the last ones on the submarine and gave all the instructions.

The submarine went to an area where they encountered enormous underwater extraterrestrial vehicles that were tracked at various times going 400 to 500 knots! These UFOs were zipping through the water at the speed of a jet but were not leaving any significant wake. Then suddenly, two of the UFOs came on either side of the submarine and took the entire nuclear drive system offline. The nuclear submarine couldn't move forward, backward or in any direction. They were just suspended there.

All this time, they have sophisticated electronic equipment collecting data. When the submarine returned to port, all this data was put together and was handed to this priest, who was not American. He was from the Vatican. He took all that data and left. It was a special operation directed by and for the Vatican, using a US Navy nuclear submarine!

Until this witness spoke to me, he could never figure out why a Catholic priest was the major-domo— the guy in charge—of such an operation.

We understand why. The myth of the separation of church and state is just that – a myth. Even people who understand that there's a shadow government can't believe the extent to which certain covert, rogue religious interests have infiltrated the organization. That's how the control is maintained.

The truth hides itself. In other words, if you can tell a version of the truth that is palatable, it can be accepted. But if you actually tell the truth, the whole truth, and pull the whole veil back, it hides itself because it seems not credible. But the strangest things really are true...

So, in an ironic way, because the actual truth of these matters is so far outside the matrix of conventional wisdom and belief, it's difficult to tell the whole truth. This has been a struggle for me for about 12 years. After I got into that level of covert knowledge, I thought, "Who the hell can I tell this to?"

Wisdom requires that you share the truth that can be comprehended by the person listening. What good does it do to teach calculus to someone in preschool who's just learning what two and two is?

And yet at the same time, I'm very troubled with knowing this information and not sharing it. So now I speak the truth, even if it discredits me…. We are getting to the end of the algorithm. We knew when 9/11 happened— after the Disclosure Project had tens of thousands of people demanding open hearings, and there were serious members of Congress looking into that possibility – that the agenda was being rolled out more quickly.

And what was the next thing on the algorithm after global terrorism? A hoaxed threat from outer space.

The final card the covert meta-government will play would be a hoaxed threat from outer space related to extraterrestrial intelligence. So, we are very close to the end of the algorithm. Time does not allow the luxury of staying quiet about the truth – even the Forbidden Truth.

32

Behind the Scenes

After 9/11, many mainstream people began to question what is really going on behind the scenes. A certain sinister manipulation is evident to many people. I don't have the luxury of putting all that information aside and thinking it's a conspiracy theory. I know it to be true. The only question I've ever had is: When do I put all these elements together and try to explain it so it makes sense to people? And sound the alarm: Wake up, and don't be deceived. People must not be stampeded into a fear of ETs and thus begin to openly support Star Wars against ET civilizations. These covert special interests want to unite and control the world through fear, rather than uniting the world through peace and hope. It is the antithesis of where we should be at this time in our evolution. Such efforts, therefore, are the antithesis of what would sustain life and a good future on Earth.

Most people can understand that there are secret projects. A smaller number of people comprehend that there are ultra-secret, black projects. Everyone in the government knows it. And then there are a certain number of people who can get their mind around the fact that some of them could be related to projects that have broken away and are rogue and illegal— that are centered in the corporate and military-industrial-laboratory complex that deal with advanced energy systems and UFOs.

But you then get into a smaller sub-set who understand that some of these rogue groups have fully operational devices that look like UFOs; have created artificial life forms that look like extraterrestrials; have been going around simulating contact events called "abductions;" have engaged in the mutilation of cattle for the fear factor that they can put out to the public and the sub-culture of UFOlogy, the pop media, the science fiction buffs, and others— because that's how they seed the consciousness with fear. And then there's even a smaller number who understand that the strings being pulled behind the scenes are from a trans-national, fascist-oriented group, not unlike the Thules that were behind the emergence of Hitler. What they couldn't do overtly during the Third Reich, they have done covertly. And through Operation Paperclip we brought them into the United States and seeded the aerospace industry and the CIA.

So, the global socialist fascist effort that did not take hold overtly in World War II has been going on, at a subterranean level, since then. We are about to see its unveiling in a larger way, as attempts to consolidate power in the world around such a philosophy and around such a structure become consummated. Meanwhile, they speak of democracy –but mean a pseudo-democracy of a centrally controlled society run covertly by an unidentified and unacknowledged power structure.

Now, if you find this disturbing, you should. And the only antidote to this that I can see is knowledge and truth and letting enough people know what's going on so that they won't be deceived. Because those running this covert agenda are counting on our collective ignorance. What they are banking on is a matrix of mis-education, dis-education and dis-information that has kept everyone consumer cows of belief systems and materialism. False belief systems, mixed with various material addictions, creates the poison of choice for the masses.

But by sharing from heart to heart, we can tell people the truth and explain another vision of the good future that awaits Earth and her children. We live in the time of these extremes: very dark and very bright. We live in the time of transformative change.

Most of the people who are at the Pentagon, in the White House, and in the CIA know nothing about these ultra-secret agendas. They are cogs in a machine, and are also victims of ignorance. Most are good people caught in a machine not of their making – and about which they have very little knowledge. It is our job to share this knowledge with everyone, including those in the government and military. For 12 years we have been moving this information into those circles, and many are realizing that they have been deceived. They then support Disclosure.

Just before 9/11, I was giving a lecture in Oregon. After the talk, a man came up to me who had been in the military for his whole career. He was there with a friend and they were acting very cautiously.

When most everyone had left, one of our Disclosure Project volunteers, Jordan Pease, said these men wanted a moment alone with me. One man, I'll call him R.J., had been involved in the military from an early age, and in the '60s had been pulled into these covert projects. One such project dealt with his ability to set up spy technologies from space that were so advanced that you could hear people talking from space and see everything they were doing. And this was in the '60s!

The technologies that are out there are far beyond anything ever reported in the news. This is why I laugh when they say, "Oh, we can't find Osama bin Laden." Right. That and other fairy tales. Please. I mean, how stupid do they think we are? But -- more on that later.

R.J. proceeded to tell me, because of his skills, he was pulled deeper and deeper into these projects and eventually was pulled into the projects dealing with UFOs. He said, "You know, I'm afraid you don't understand what these things are that you think are ETs." And I said, "Oh, you're referring to the man-made ones that are programmed life forms?" And he pushed back from the table; he asked, "How do you know about that?"

"Oh, I have around a dozen witnesses who've worked on these pseudo-ET creatures." I said, "But if I talk too much about it, people will think I've just absolutely lost my marbles." He said, "Let me tell you what I worked on." So, he proceeded to tell me about the projects he had participated in, both in the United States and Australia.

"We did have extraterrestrial materials that were being worked on and we developed very advanced technologies that were a type of anti-gravity craft. I saw trans-dimensional capabilities, things that involve the ability to go forward or backward in time— all kinds of things." He explained.

(We have another witness who was with Boeing and McDonnell Douglas who knew about Project Red Light and Operation Looking Glass that involve those capabilities.)

Then R.J. said, "You know, what most people don't realize is that I was involved in putting together the projects that were doing a lot of these things that people call abductions!"

"We were hoaxing a lot of these abduction events that people think are extraterrestrial contact. Well, this one place where I worked -- it was underground -- there were all these containers. And there were these creatures that we were growing in a culture medium that were at different stages of development. And these creatures looked like what people think are extraterrestrials."

R.J. proceeded to tell me that there were several generations of these artificial life forms. They were trying to perfect their man-made ETs; they had been doing these Nazi-like genetic experiments from the '40s, '50s, until he was out of those projects. These pseudo-ETs were all lined up, almost like an archive. He said the state-of-the-art ones were really quite good and believable.

"Of course, we had these creatures that were like automatons, being commanded by humans, on these things that people think are extraterrestrial ships." R.J. didn't know that I already knew that these hoaxes were going on and were very sophisticated. He thought that I had been deceived, like most UFO researchers.

"No, I've known about this for a very long time." I said. "Well, why don't you talk about it?" He asked.

"Because," I explained, I'm trying to get people to even acknowledge the fact that there's such a thing as a UFO."

"Yes, I understand your position;"

He said, "I'm very glad you know about this. But do you know something else? Much of this has been placed in facilities all over the world, in the jungle in the Amazon, in Australia, and other remote places. Eventually, I got assigned, to a deeper and deeper level, and before I was going to be deployed to this place in Australia, they took me into another level of my educational program."

He said, "You don't really know what's going on."

He explained that he witnessed a Satanic ritual initiation. Those present shared blood and there were sacrifices going on and torture. He was being acculturated to the programs of Satanic worship and Satanic sacrifice and the love of the bloodthirsty killing of innocents. He told us that once he got to that level, he had to take a vow to Lucifer. And he did.

This is not the first person who's told me about these programs. He was transferred to Pine Gap, Australia, and said it was the most unusual experience. He was flown in at night in a helicopter, to this facility. And as they approached this hill, what looked like a normal piece of land opened up. It was like it was a hologram and as they approached, the side of this hill opened and they flew right into the earth. They went deep inside, to where there were enormous, man-made UFOs. There were big triangular ones there, as well. He said, "We have facilities like these all over the world."

As he shared this with me, he would stop periodically and say, "I know you're going to think I'm making this up, and I know you can't believe this." At the end of his account, I said, "I want you to know that I have multiple witnesses like yourself -- who you don't know, because you were in your own compartmented project -- who have told me virtually the same story about different places at different times. And so I have no doubt in my mind that this has been going on."

He took a deep breath, then let it go; a huge sigh of relief.

One of the most sophisticated facilities of this type is in England. A lot of these so-called "reptilian"-looking creatures that people think are extraterrestrial are programmed life forms and bio-machines, and are being created there.

Now, most people would rather not hear this level of detail, quite frankly. But it's important for them to understand the kind of mindset we're dealing with. One of the gentlemen I'm working with, from a very well-connected family of centi-millionaires who are very involved in diplomatic and intelligence operations, had gone through the programming at a certain meditation institute. He got to Level 14 of the training. He said that unless they could do a profile on you and see that you were to the 'right of Genghis Khan', in terms of wanting to be aggressively violent and destructive, you couldn't get past that level. Since he wasn't wired to be extremely violent and hate-filled, they ended their involvement with him.

He said they talked a lot about Dr. Greer and the Disclosure Project, and they were really glad that I was getting information out that the UFOs and ETs were real. But they were furious to the point of deep hatred that I was exposing the false phenomenon and their false agenda. They are committed to this final battle of inter-planetary war, which is the chief agenda of the hard-core secrecy. They were livid that I would not go along with that agenda, and that I had discovered the plan for hoaxing an ET attack on earth- and was exposing it to people at the Pentagon and elsewhere. He said they wanted me dead. They do not want anyone of substance saying that the real extraterrestrial presence is not only very benign, but also extremely helpful and quite enlightened.

"Do you realize how much you are hated?" he asked. "Yes", I answered, "But that and their threats will never keep us from speaking the truth."

As The Disclosure Project picked up steam, I had been warned that if it went beyond what they could control through the mainstream big media, things would happen to shut it down. I was told this explicitly.

On 9/11, I was in Seattle, having just returned from Simon Frazier University in Vancouver for a lecture the night before. When I woke up on 9/11, I turned on the television and thought what I was seeing was a movie. After I realized this was real and not a movie, I called Emily, my wife, to see that everyone was okay. My next call was to my daughter in Washington, because I wanted her to get out of the city.

I couldn't get through to Washington, because all the phones were completely jammed. So, the next call was to my military adviser. The first words out of his mouth were, "Well, the conventional operations that people *think* are responsible for the security of the United States have no state-of-the-art equipment, inadequate personnel, and the people who can monitor these events in real time are a rogue black element, and never the twain shall meet."

I was 3,000 miles from home. This was a very emotional and diffi-cult time, not being with my family during all this chaos. But that night, I was scheduled for a lecture to the medical society of the area. I called one of the organizers and said, "What do we do? Do we cancel? This is a national emergency." And they said, "People are calling us saying they still want to hear what you're going to say."

I was hardly in the mood to give a lecture, to say the least, but I did.

It was standing room only— the best attended medical society meet-ing in memory.

I presented what we were doing, and put it into the framework of a manipulated agenda to move us from super-power conflict, to global ter-rorism, and eventually into a threat from outer space. There were ele-ments— not in the conventional military, not in the conventional intel-ligence services, not in the conventional quarters of power— but within rogue elements, that were manipulating these conditions. We had come to this point in history as no surprise to those of us who know this group and what the agenda and mindset is.

You could have heard a pin drop.

It was one of the first times I've ever said this in a gathering like this— these were all fellow physicians. This was not a new age UFO conference! But I said, "You have to understand, it's all about power— massive geo-political power." People running these programs have a 'Masters of the Universe' complex, a God complex. It is megalomania on steroids. And honestly, that is the mindset you have to get your own consciousness around, to comprehend what motivates this behavior.

I said, "Is it really that hard to figure out? Having lived personally in Israel for three years and almost having been killed twice by terrorist bombings, none of this is a surprise to me. For ten years, we have been in the Middle East after the first Gulf War, increasingly being resented by Osama bin Laden, and other fanatics. But he was an ally of ours in Afghanistan, in the fight against the USSR. But natives of the Middle East were furious that we were in their Holy Land of Saudi Arabia." And I asked, "Why are we there? We like the scenery? The culture? Or we like visiting Mecca? We like the 120-degree temperatures? We're there for one word: oil. We're still there for oil, and we're still using oil, because these other technologies have been kept secret. I will never defend terrorists; however, we have to understand why, all of a sudden, we're this big target. Well, it's not all of a sudden. This has been coming for a long time. And there are people who knew damned good and well it was coming for a long time. I've been working with people who have been talking about the chickens coming home to roost for a long time. Frankly, as the Chinese saying goes, ' Unless we change direction, we're likely to end up where we're going.' But no one's looking at where we're going. It's high time that we wake up and see where we're headed."

I said, "You know, now we're going to have to do some tactical things to contain this problem, because the conventional military and intelligence services are going to be scrambling around, trying to respond to this in a reactive way. But no one's looking at what the causative dynamic is behind it."

After 9/11, all the airports were closed, but I had a lecture tour already planned for the Pacific Northwest. So we decided to continue the Disclosure tour, in spite of the horror of 9/11.

The very last event that I did was in Washington state, in a rural area, with a group supported by Linda Evans, the actress. We had dinner together and a long talk about all these issues. Linda Evans is very supportive of what we're doing.

On the day that I was regularly scheduled to fly home, it turned out to be the first day of normal flights scheduled out of SEATAC! I never had to even change a ticket. I never had to miss a flight. It was as if we didn't skip a beat because of 9/11. And there's a deeper message in that: even as global chaos is occurring, we are able to speak the truth, reach thousands of people, and stay on our path in the midst of these extraordinary times.

If you're doing the right thing and you're speaking the truth, even the greatest barriers will part and move out of your way. You have to walk the mystical path with practical feet.

You know, Michael Moore said the only conspiracies he believes in are the ones that are true.

There is an almost Pavlovian response that's been programmed into the "mainstream" media and elites. If you use certain words -- "conspiracy" -- it immediately is associated with "kook."

And if you use the word "UFO," it immediately brings in "abduction" and "kook." So, there are certain automatic responses that have been programmed into our culture, especially by big media. A careful analysis of how the rogue national security state and psychological warfare people operate shows that they have programmed this response and reaction when those issues come up. This strategy has been very carefully cultured over many decades.

We have the responsibility of doing this in a credible way that makes sense, but one of the serious problems to doing this is: The closer you get to what the hidden truth is, the less believable it is, and you risk your credibility.

So, it's a Catch 22.

I have been asked a number of times what has been the most disappointing thing over the last 15 years. By far it's been the fact that there are people with whom I had spent significant time with, and who have accepted this information as true, and who have enormously powerful positions where they could do a great deal of good -- whether it's a senator or a President or a U.N. official or a general in the military or a senior scientist -- and basically when it gets to the point of following up the information with any productive, constructive action, they run with their tail between their legs and say, "I can't do this."

Henry Kissinger once said, "This is the hottest potato in the universe. I'm not going to deal too much more with it." So, he knew about it, but many of these people want to just take a pass on it. It's the ultimate buck to pass. Well, who are you going to pass it to, particularly if the President of the United States has taken a pass on it?

There are agendas within agendas within agendas within agendas. The question is: How do we get enough of the information out to enough of those with power, and to the public, to provide knowledge and shine a light into these dark corners? And we have to also clearly describe an alternative.

After 9/11, I immediately made the decision that we must quickly identify and get out to the public these new, earth saving technologies, while continuing Disclosure. We had to do something to create enough support and potential funding to be a countervailing force to this machine that's been going on for over 50 years. It was time for us to go from military witnesses and documents to the actual technologies. When 9/11 happened, we knew we were getting very late in the game.

In the fall of 2001, we formed Space Energy Access Systems, Inc (SEAS). A group of people put in a few hundred thousand dollars together so we could investigate what was available in the non-covert world. We have found some technologies at proof-of-principle stage, but none so far that are ready for release to the public as a free energy system. Those devices that are more advanced – and we have seen some – are held by scientists who have been extremely intimidated or brainwashed into secrecy.

For example, Dr. Loder and an engineer on our team went to visit one of these scientists who had been intercepted by a physicist who has been indoctrinating him with eschatological belief systems. This spook, who is masquerading as a scientist told the inventor, "Don't let any of your technology out until our society collapses. And then, Phoenix-like, you can be the science savior, and bring the technology out when everything has fallen apart."

So, basically, this man has been brainwashed with an eschatological timeline and is withholding the technology, pending these cataclysmic events. Of course, this is a self-fulfilling prophecy. If we don't have something to stave off the depletion of the oil reserves and the destruction of the biosphere, these terrible events will happen. So, it's circular thinking. But you can't really do anything once someone has been brainwashed with this belief system.

We have also identified an anti-gravity system that is in the early stages of development. With sufficient funding, it could be brought to maturity as a free energy and anti-gravity system. The world desperately needs these earth-saving technologies.

33

A New World – If You Can Take It

Now it is an order of magnitude to go from people with top-secret clearances, testimony and documents to an actual machine, because it is a material science. But we must convince some of the scientists who have the knowledge of these new energy technologies that a window is open, and if we are not going to walk through it now, what are we waiting for? We cannot force this on anyone. It is a voluntary association. And so all we can do is explain: Here are the security systems we have in place. And here is why now is the time to bring these wondrous new sciences into practical application.

Right now, in addition to behind-the-scenes tactical security, we have what I call "strategic security."

We have some very powerful people within this covert group who support what we are doing, and who will respond in kind to any threat against us.

And we have millions of people who know what you are doing. Remember what the National Security lawyer told me in 1990 when I was considering forming CSETI. He said "Don't walk, but run, and get this information out in front a lot of people."

And that is why I agreed to go on "Larry King Live", and why I agreed to go on a lot shows like "48 Hours", because whether the publicity is good or bad, having millions of people watching what we're doing provides enormous security.

Such exposure puts a billion-watt spotlight on you and everyone you're working with. And here's the good news about that: Secret power thrives in the darkness of secrecy.

If they step into the fray when there is a big spotlight shining on our efforts, they are going to have a lot people see their ugly actions happen in real-time.

All that we do, all that we find, all our evidence and so forth are duplicated and put into the hands of certain key prime movers who will get that information out to the public -- on the radio, on the internet, on the television— if anything were to happen to us.

If you do that with the plans for a new technology, it will not disappear, but rather be massively disclosed. And then killing us will not matter.

This is a counter-intuitive strategy that many scientists have a hard time understanding: Secrecy is impossible to maintain against the group we're dealing with. They have electronic systems that interface with consciousness. Forget the old NSA hooks in space. That was '60s technology.

They can monitor everything going on in real-time. And there is no way for us to keep what we're doing secret from that element. So we don't waste any time or effort or thought doing it. It is delusional to think you are going to do anything off the radar of this powerful covert machine.

Then what is your choice? Your choice is to do a type of Aikido. You take that energy and you flip it around to the opposite and you act in complete openness and transparency. So instead of being obscure and secretive and furtive, you do it in plain sight, and you get it out to the masses in real-time as quickly as you can.

That is why as soon as Dr. Loder, and a member of our board for SEAS, and I came back from an offshore location where we found an energy device in 2003, we went public and talked about it with millions of people listening.

The more that people know, the less likely it is these rogue interests can act, because there is a big spotlight on the effort. They're vampires, like Dracula. They don't want to step into the sun. When the sun comes up, they go running like cockroaches. You flip the light on and the cockroaches all go back into the crevices.

They do not want to be caught in a covert, murderous, disruptive action against a group with high profile. I have spoken to some people in the mainstream media, who have said: It would be very difficult for us to get the information out simply as a story about UFOs, but if you or anyone else gets a threat, and you can prove it, or anything happens to you, that is going to be a big story, because then it is going to be a scandal. And there will be millions of people wondering what the hell happened to you and your people.

We also have tapes, that are already duplicated and in the hands of people for sudden release, that disclose the key facilities and many names related to this covert group.

But, many of these scientists live in fear and trauma, a type of "new energy posttraumatic stress syndrome."

These scientists have been convinced through psychological warfare modalities, to be very paranoid and overly secretive - but that only works against them. They will never win the secrecy game. But we can succeed at Disclosure!

Because in speed and in openness, there is safety --contrary to what people think.

There is no way you're going to do it secretively. Your worst enemies are going to know everything you're doing in real-time; and the people who could be there supporting you, the masses who are concerned about the environment and oil, won't know what you're doing. This is the mistake that has been made for 100 years.

People want a solution to the environmental, oil and poverty issues of this planet. There is enormous support for any technology that helps resolve those problems.

Once mass support is in placc, you would have people rioting and burning down Washington before you could let the patent office issue a Section 181 to seize the technology!

When Ted Koppel invited me on "Nightline" if we finally identify a legitimate free energy device, I said, "I'll come on your show and tear any secrecy order up in front of millions of people if you'll let me."

He looked at me -- this is face-to-face with Ted Koppel and said "I will." No amount of money and no threat is going to stop us from doing what is right.

We cannot have the good future that awaits humanity without technologies that take us off fossil fuels and nuclear power. Therefore it is worth doing what we need to do to secure these technologies for peaceful applications and not allow them to be weaponized.

This is a completely achievable objective.

The secrecy and ruthless suppression of these technologies is related to power. If you are doing something where you are impacting a five- or six-trillion dollar part of the world economy, and it is the core operating paradigm of the world economy, it is a significant issue.

Many people don't know that one of the key areas of concern at the National Security Council of the United States is economic national security. One of the witnesses that I am working with worked under an admiral who was in charge of the Office of Naval Research. This admiral at a meeting said, point blank, "My chief job is maintaining the status quo of the world's energy supplies and grid."

Because imagine this: We come out with these technologies, and the billion people in Latin America or sub-Sahara Africa, or the 1.1 billion people in India or the billion and one-half or two billion in Asia would have the ability to have a device in every village that would generate all the energy they would need for clean water, electrification, refrigeration, transportation, light manufacturing - without pollution, and without any cost for the energy itself. The device would be no more expensive to produce than a generator.

You would have an enormous uplifting of the masses of the world's population that are now living in mind-boggling poverty.

We forget that there's only about 20 percent of the world's population that is living with anything resembling modern conveniences and modern technology. The other 80 percent are barely half a step out of the jungle, if that.

So in that setting, we have a world of increasing crises, increasing anger at the West, increasing likelihood of war and terrorism. But when these technologies come out, this is the tide that will lift all ships. It is really good news - unless you own a trillion-dollar oilfield.

What happens when billions of people in India, Sub-Sahara Africa, Latin American and Asia begin to have a level of economic activity that surpasses that of America and Europe?

Suddenly, you have the biggest geopolitical power shift in the history of the world, where the 'great white father' is no longer the only one on the plantation making decisions. And the truth is, this speaks to the heart of the fascist fears within some of the control elements: Once free energy is available to the world, these interests would have to actually share power with people who are from other continents, other races, other cultures. Geopolitical power doesn't flow from the size of your population-it flows from your economic clout!

If population alone determined world power, the most powerful countries in the world would be India and China, and they are not. Power flows from your technological and economic prowess, and resulting military power -- that and that alone.

The Soviet Union fell apart because its economic prowess was bankrupt. And now the lone superpower in the world is the United States.

And yet, humanity could have manufacturing, with no pollution, recycling 100 percent of all waste, energy for electrification and transportation without pollution—all with no cost for the energy itself. There would be no need for a multi-trillion dollar electric grid system that India and much of the world lacks, and which they do not have the financial resources to create.

These new free energy technologies would grow the world economy from a $30 trillion per year economy to a hundred or two hundred trillion dollar economy.

Hidden Truth – Forbidden Knowledge

However, most of that growth would be outside of America and Europe, which together only has 600 million people. The world has ten times that number: six billion.

This would cause the biggest shift in geopolitical power in the history of the human race. And it would be fairly sudden: 10-20 years - at the most 50 years.

This is one of the key reasons for the secrecy. Such secrecy is deeply rooted in power issues, and unfortunately also has a rather ugly racist undertone to it.

The old adage, "If you want peace, work for justice" is quite apt here. It is very hard to have justice in the world when a very small number of people are using up all the world's resources, while the vast majority live in mind-numbing poverty.

In order to change that dynamic, these technologies must come out. Once they do, the world will grow for all its peoples.

So this is the big question: Are we willing to create a world that's just and abundant for all of its citizens and really share power in the world? Are we willing to put a seat at the geopolitical table for all peoples?

So far the answer has been no to this good future. It is time we say yes.

Growth will be stunning and rapid in regions of the world long withheld from progress. It is similar to areas that have bypassed a hundred years of development of linear phone lines, and gone directly to satellite phones and cell phones.

On a much more fundamental and profound level, these regions of the world will skip over 150 years of smokestack industrial revolution, and go directly to point-of-site power generation without transmission wires, and without the need for fuels or expensive infrastructure.

So they will quickly become industrialized, but without pollution. And with that will come enormous economic activity, technological developments and geopolitical power.

Such a change in how we generate energy will cause a decentralization of power, literally and figuratively. Power generation will be decentralized, but so will power politics. Every village will begin to be self-sufficient, thus minimizing centralized control. Once you understand these technologies, you understand that they will be able to generate the energy needs of the local area and all transportation and manufacturing needs. And the more developed applications of these sciences allow for the manifestation of any material object needed in the local area.

So it will be an enormous revolution in the material fortunes of the earth.

We are coming out of an era where people have been clubbing each other over the head over a scrap of land or a piece of gold –this is a whole new paradigm.

But this new paradigm washes away the need for central, clandestine secret societies, centralized banking and excessive central control.

We will be unified and integrated as a world civilization, but there will be a concomitant increase in empowerment at the local level.

On the one hand, we will become increasingly integrated as a global village because of instant global communications and transportation. Travel from one continent to another will be extremely fast using these new anti-gravity propulsion systems.

And yet on the other hand, the level of self-sufficiency and empowerment will be centered primarily at the local, village, and neighborhood level.

These twin paradoxical processes of increasing empowerment at the village or local level, and increasing integration of the global community will occur simultaneously. It's a new world completely.

I'm reminded of the REM song: "It's the end of the world as we know it, but I feel fine!"

As wonderful as this global transformation is for the masses of humanity, and for the earth, it is a worst-case scenario for the very elite people who want to stay firmly in control of the world. Because when you decentralize power generation and economic activity, you also decentralize this top-heavy kleptocracy currently running the planet.

I am reminded of a story that Colonel Corso told a mutual friend about an experience he had at Holloman Air Force Base in 1956.

At that time, many extraterrestrial vehicles were zipping around over the base and were being tracked on radar. Of course it was a very sensitive area, near the Trinity site, where we detonated the first atomic weapon.

On this one particular day, an object was tracked on radar during daytime. This ET craft descended and landed out on the Holloman range.

Col. Corso jumped in a jeep by himself to go out to that area. When he arrived, he saw a seamless, silvery egg-shaped craft, hovering just above the ground, silently. It would become fully materialized, shining in the sun, and then disappear -- and all he would see was a mirage- a heat wave- over the sand. The ET craft would dematerialize into this energy field in the shape of the craft, and then it would flash back and be materialized again.

Suddenly, an extraterrestrial being appeared outside the craft with some sort of a communication device, to communicate telepathically.

Col. Corso asked, "Who goes there friend or foe?"

And the ET said, "Neither."

The ET then proceeded to say, "We would like for you to stop using some of these radar systems that are interfering with our craft…". (Remember that the Roswell crash had happened because there were high-powered radar system set up on a certain frequency that would disrupt ET craft propulsion and navigation systems.)

Col. Corso, being a rather brash military guy, said, "Well, what's in it for me?"

The ET turned to him, and said, "A new world, if you can take it!"

Now 50 years later, we must learn to take it — to accept the new world being offered to us. We need to learn to accept the new world that has been delayed for decades -- and initiate what will be thousands of years of a sustainable, enlightened civilization.

That is what the ET civilizations are waiting for us to do, and we are the generation that must achieve it.

34

Solving our Own Dysfunction

It was once said to me by an oil man, that using oil for fuel is like burning your Picasso in the fireplace for heat: Oil is too precious to use for energy. When we look at the needs of a civilization that will be here for hundreds of thousands of years, we should save oil as something that can be held in reserve for essential purposes like synthetics, lubricants, plastics and the like. Used wisely, the Earth has adequate resources for an advanced civilization for thousands and maybe millions of years. But used foolishly, as we do today, Earth cannot sustain us.

That makes sense to anyone who is logical. But if your decision-making is based on insane fear and greed, or some kind of end-of-the-world eschatological belief system, then you don't care about thousands of years from now. You don't even care about 20 years from now.

These technologies that have been withheld have caused us to literally burn through resources that should have been held in reserve for more appropriate uses long-term by our children's children's children's children's children's children.

My father was half Cherokee, and the Cherokee believed that everything we do should be looking at many generations not yet born. But at this time in history, we are beginning a cycle that is half a million years in duration.

So everything we are doing today should be looking at 20,000 generations not yet born. A man that I worked with in the 1990s, who was on Ronald Reagan's National Security Council staff, said long-term planning for the National Security Council was six months! It was just reactionary -- going from crisis to crisis.

It has been argued that these new energy and propulsion technologies can be weaponized, which is true. *Anything* can be weaponized: As an ER doctor, I have seen people killed with beer bottles! But does that mean we shouldn't have these technologies, and just let the world be cannibalized and destroyed out of foolishness?

Or instead, should we create international cooperative and collective security, so that we insure, guarantee, and enforce the safe use of such technologies? Under such a system, anyone or any group or nation who would even plan to use such technologies for war, violence or harm would be immediately stopped. We cannot release these technologies and then pretend that there is not going to be another Hitler or Saddam Hussein or Pol Pot.

It *does* mean that today we have the means to monitor such matters and the means to enforce a stable peace. Technologies now exist in the covert world that, used by those ardent for peace, could monitor and stop any harmful application of these new energy systems *in real time*.

We must be realistic: Everyone isn't going to go instantly into samadhi and enlightenment and become non-violent and peaceful. We are humans.

But, there are enough good people in the world and enough good leaders in the world to provide the leadership we need. When there is an abusive or potentially dangerous character who arrives on the scene, the policy should be the following: Every civilized country on earth should rise up and stop him before it becomes a problem.

If this policy had really been followed, World War I would have never happened, nor would World War II. Today, the means of communication and monitoring exist, but the question is: Is the will power and the intent there to enforce the peace?

Take for example Saddam Hussein and his chemical weapons. Who provided him with the technology and chemicals? The Germans and Americans and French did, with some help from the Russians. Rumsfeld himself was involved in this technology transfer to Saddam.

And how did such figures acquire the wealth to secure these weapons programs? Oil.

It has nothing to do about whether or not we can do it, and the sooner people learn this lesson, the better. The state of the world is manipulated by those who benefit most from conflict.

We certainly didn't learn this lesson after World War I, and we didn't learn it after World War II. And here we are now.

So the question is: Just exactly what has to happen before the body politic learns this lesson?

We have already hit peak oil production, and we are going to become like "Mad Max", the movie, fighting over the last barrel of oil. The time has come to do the right thing, and move our civilization to its next level of development.

Are we willing to live with the rule of law, like a civilized world, or are we going to be cowardly and look the other way when rogue and illegal operations and 'Murder Incorporated' run roughshod over the interests of the people?

Once we disclose effectively the existence of these technologies, the public will say, "We want them"! Billy Bob, with his eight-cylinder pick-up, doesn't want to pay ten dollars a gallon to run his truck down the road. There are forces that will bring these concerns to a head, and they are inevitable. And inevitably we will come out on the other side of this, and the world will embrace this vision.

But the question is: How much chaos and stupidity will transpire before we come out on the other side? That is the only question. Humans are, as a group, survivors, and when push comes to shove, we will survive.

I welcome the fact that releasing these technologies would *require* us to create an enforceable, sustainable, peaceful civilization just to survive. We're at the point now where every one knows we can't put off much longer dealing with these large structural and environmental issues. So when a solution comes along, it will focus people's attention and finally require us to do what we should have done decades ago.

Without peace there can be no further progress on earth. The simple truth is this: We have reached the point in human evolution where the only possible future is a peaceful one.

Now, there are many people who argue: "Oh, we're never peaceful and we'll always try to kill each other."

The truth is most people don't want to go around murdering each other. Out of six billion people, most are actually very nice peaceful people.

Unfortunately we have not been willing to restrain the few rabid dogs that routinely like to attack the flock.

In super-secret projects, there are people who fantasize about using these technologies to go into space, like 'Star Wars', with guns blazing. But technologies that go beyond the crossing point of light cannot be applied for a weapon system and have a people survive its use, any more than we could have survived a thermonuclear launch.

Some in these covert projects have misinterpreted certain ET actions: For example, when we tried to detonate a nuclear weapon on the moon, to show the USSR how powerful America was, an extraterrestrial vehicle came in and intercepted it and destroyed it. Now, you could take that to be evidence that these ETs were hostile towards us, when in reality they were trying to protect facilities on the moon, and also the sanctity of space as a peaceful place free from weapons of mass destruction.

But from the shoes of those humans who wanted to see that moon detonation happen, their frustration could lead to the assumption that this ET action was proof of their hostility!

A number of such events have happened, where humans have misinterpreted ET actions as evidence of hostility, when in reality it was evidence of enlightenment. These extraterrestrial civilizations are simply trying to contain an immature and out-of-control militarized civilization on earth from escaping the biosphere and going out into space.

But depending on your perspective, you can view it as one way or another. I am quite certain that the ET intent is peaceful. But if you *wanted to spin such an event* to, say, President Reagan, or to someone else inclined to support Star Wars, you could cite that event and say, "See, there is a threat we're facing. We need to build up weapons in space and hit them hard!"

I am not speaking theoretically as I give you these examples. These are things that have actually happened and have led to justifications for targeting extraterrestrial vehicles and weaponizing space.

We have Disclosure Project witnesses to ET events where 16 to 18 intercontinental ballistic missiles were taken offline completely, instantly. (see Bob Salas' testimony in Chapter 29.)

And when I asked them, "What do you think the ETs were saying?"

They say, "We think they were trying to tell us, please don't blow up this beautiful planet."

Now, you could take that same event and come to a different assessment, and say, "Well they are interfering with our national security preparedness. They were making us vulnerable to the Soviets".

The same action can be interpreted different ways, depending on whether you are in a paranoid mindset and are motivated by aggrandizing your military-industrial budget.

ET actions have shown us on many occasions, that if we were to engage in acts that would jeopardize the survivability of life on earth, they would intervene and stop it— and they could do it very quickly.

This was demonstrated over and over again -- the launch at Vandenburg AFB which was intercepted and destroyed, the moon intercept, taking these 16 intercontinental ballistic missiles offline. I am certain the extraterrestrial civilizations were trying to tell us, "Don't go down the path of mutually assured destruction, but if you do, we can stop it."

Now, what a lot of people don't know is that similar events were happening in Russia *at exactly the same time*. ET actions were trying to say to all these parties on earth: "Make peace, and don't go down this path of mass destruction—and if you try, we're going to stop you anyway."

They weren't trying to give the Soviets an advantage over us, if they were doing the same things in the Soviet Union at the same time!

ET civilizations certainly are not going to let us send these weapons into space. And if we try, they will be tossed back like a bad penny.

When covert shadow government operations have tried to go out in space with ARVs and other super-advanced spacecraft, they have been shut down.

A Defense Intelligence Agency witness told me that we had a number of sophisticated satellite systems that were pointed out into space -- not down to the Soviet Union. They were being used to track and target extraterrestrial vehicles out in space. He said the ET s were routinely shutting these systems down, out of self-defense. But such actions angered the 'Masters of the Universe' types who are not accustomed to having their plans frustrated.

So, if you wanted to spin such events to people inclined towards paranoia and militarism, it would be easy to do. And that is what's happened over the last 50 years.

A president or other high official is vulnerable to this "cherry-picking of intelligence," and a xenophobic spin being placed on events. And who else is available to such officials to provide another perspective? This is one of the real risks of closed, secret systems.

But ETs want us to solve our own dysfunction; they will intervene significantly and openly only in the case of global thermonuclear war, a massive geophysical collapse, or in the event that humans take actions that would upset the order of peace in the universe.

This is not the route of first choice, because if one culture moves into another culture and tries to artificially impose something, it is almost universally a failure.

The idea that extraterrestrial civilizations will come to earth, and impose some new order is a fantasy. These are lessons that we have to learn as a people who are stumbling out of childhood's end and into maturity and adulthood.

Extraterrestrial civilizations have been observing our development for many, many, years -- maybe thousands and perhaps millions. They will not let one perverse generation destroy a biosphere that has been in development for billions of years, or a world that is intended to be here for hundreds of thousands to millions of years to come as a place for the development of intelligent life and enlightenment.

There have always been two space programs. There is the conventional space program that my uncle worked in. He was the senior project engineer with Grumman designing the lunar module, using jet thrusters etc.

A parallel space program exists using more advanced technologies, including early anti-gravity spacecraft capable of going faster than the speed of light.

But Earth is under a type of cosmic quarantine. It is known that we are not yet socially and spiritually evolved enough to go into space with such advanced technologies – and so our wings are clipped for now. The key to our being welcome in the cosmos is peace.

There are entire worlds that don't even have a concept of war that are highly developed and are at or beyond our level of technological achievement. So a world like ours would be enormously risky to turn loose on the cosmos; we are just still too violent and primitive.

Our ability to utilize all the technologies we have developed covertly has been truncated by extraterrestrial enforcement of a type of quarantine. They are charged with protecting the universe from a species whose technologies have way outstripped their social and spiritual development. This is manifest universal justice. It would be the height of insanity and folly to turn militaristic humans loose on the cosmos!

Neil Armstrong was over-heard saying as we landed on the moon, there were numerous extraterrestrial vehicles on the crater, watching us and that we were essentially warned off the moon.

Now think about it. During the height of the cold war, the space program was really a military asset: It was a race to the moon *competitively* with the Soviets, and plans were in place to put military assets on the moon. The extraterrestrial people do not want us carving up other worlds into "us versus them," territories, thus exporting human conflict into space. It will not be allowed.

Now, again, if you wanted to spin that in a certain way, you could say, "See! There is a threat." When in reality what they are doing is protecting space from conflict and warfare.

But, if we go out into space, united and in peace, the universe is an open book for us.

There are artificial structures on the moon that predate the 1969 lunar landing. Some of them are very old while others look newer and functional.

There are extraterrestrial assets that are out in space on a fairly permanent basis, and underneath the surface of Mars there are extensive extraterrestrial facilities.

These ancient ET facilities on the moon and Mars, as well as ancient evidence of ET visitation to Earth, have led some to suggest that humans have been partly assisted in our evolution by ET genetic augmentation. I believe this is likely and logical. There certainly is a missing link in the time line of our evolution, and it is likely that advanced civilizations assisted and augmented our species.

Now, when I say that, I am very careful not to, at the same time, say that we are " created" by ETs. I believe that there is an infinite God that creates all of us. But that doesn't mean that as a physician I can't assist or fix a problem. These are not mutually exclusive dynamics, except to scientific and religious fundamentalists. People may ask, "Well, if that is the case, does it mean that there is a God?"

Well, of course. There can be a divine Creator who also moves and operates through the relative world, and through channels and through means. And we are those channels and means. And so are peoples from other planets.

I have contacts at JPL (Jet Propulsion Labs) who have told me that they know the structures on the moon and Mars are ancient, and that for theological and religious reasons, this information is being suppressed. The orthodoxy of conventional religious dogma would be up-ended by such a revelation.

The existence of an infinite Creator and the likelihood that there have been developments that have assisted the evolution of humans as part of a divine plan are not mutually exclusive concepts. In fact, I find them to be quite complementary -- advanced theological ideas perhaps, but not inconsistent with the fundamental reality of the existence of an intelligent supreme Being.

Because if we can apprehend, however dimly, the intent of God or a divine plan, why can't others— including extraterrestrials? And then why can't they act within that knowledge?

There is a universal form of intelligent species. It appears that the non-local morphogenic propagation of an upright being with a head, bimorphism with two arms and two legs is a universal constant.

In Sheldrake's morphogenic fields, there is the concept that once a pattern develops that works, it tends to then replicate, and not only replicate through known and local means, but through non-local connections in remote places at the same time.

It's like the hundredth monkey phenomenon where you have one island with a population of monkeys learning a skill, and all of a sudden, at a distant place, with no direct contact, the other monkeys begin to do the same thing.

So there is a non-local transfer of patterns of evolution and knowledge that takes place. If you understand the power of consciousness, and the fact that *mind* is always omnipresent, and is the ultimate non-local integrator, it becomes clear that our thoughts and our prayers and vision can have a non-local effect all over the earth, and throughout the universe.

One of the central purposes of the CSETI expeditions is for the entire group to be in that state of unity consciousness and see and co-create a universe that is at peace.

The state of unity consciousness has material effects as well. You have heard accounts of remote healing. Well, how does that happen? You have two people removed in space and yet a healing is effected. This happens because everything is non-local. We don't recognize it, but in reality even matter is awake-ness, mind-stuff, phasing in a different resonance frequency.

And so space, matter, and time are intimately and at all times connected to consciousness. But consciousness is a singularity. It is indivisible. We divide it in our intellectual mind, but this is an artificial construct: the reality is that consciousness is perfectly integrated and omnipresent, and that's why there can be remote healing. That is why there can be telepathy. That is why you can break outside the bounds of space and time and see a distant point in space or time or effect a remote change. The nature of mind itself is always non-local. It is always in a state where it is in its fullness, everywhere, at every time, in an omnipresent manner.

This is why even physical systems, engineering systems or genetic systems can be evolving in one place, and if it is very successful, begin to propagate non-locally elsewhere in another part of the universe. This is non-local nodal propagation through the perfect integrating quality of consciousness.

35

A Guided Meditation: The Structure of the Universe

You can experience everything, from the Unbounded to the manifest, to distant places in time and space, through the perfectly integrating, connecting effect of pure mind or consciousness.

You can do this guided meditation with a friend or in a group with one person reading; or you can go to the www.cseti.org and get the CD.

Now let's close our eyes. Be in a relaxed state. Allow yourself to hear and understand, but also see and experience as we share the unfolding of the order and structure of the cosmos from the infinite to the most manifest creation.

And as we sit here in silence, at this beautiful spot on earth, let us begin to center within ourselves, and sense that we are awake.

Now take some deep breaths of this pure, life-filled air, and allow your diaphragm to expand as you inhale through your nose, and then exhale fully through your mouth.

And as you inhale, see your entire mind and body being filled with the life and light and energy around us, and as you exhale, see yourself becoming completely relaxed, and all stresses and all negativity leaving your mind and your body, and being swept away in the wind and cleansed by the infinite wisdom of Mother Earth.

With each breath, bring in a new and higher level of energy and awake-ness, and with each expiration, dive deeper in a state of complete silence and relaxation and release yourself of any limitations or negativity; let them be swept away in the vastness and the purifying influence of earth.

Feel yourself breathing with Mother Earth as she gives us this air and as she takes from us the breath as we exhale, and breathe in the conscious life and light of this infinitely wise mother, and release into the earth, all of your worries and concerns, all of your pain and suffering, and find yourself in a state of perfect equanimity and peace.

Now, very gently, without straining the mind, allow yourself to observe your own breath as it goes in and out, as you are in a perfect state of quiet and peace. And as you are observing your breath, gently see the awake mind that is watching the breath; see it is steady and ever present.

What is watching the breath? See that there is an awake-ness within yourself that is steady and unchanging, observing all things. Peaceful. And as you see your breath rising and falling, going in and out, in this beautiful peaceful state, you also see that the mind that is watching quietly, is an infinite ocean of awake-ness.

Now we dive into this vast ocean and allow ourselves to go very very deeply into quiet and peaceful conscious mind that observes all things. And we behold that the breath of our life, the sounds around us, the thoughts that rise and fall and come and go within the mind— all that we hear and see and feel and touch and know is submerged in this vast ocean of awake-ness.

And very gently we go ever more deeply into that awake mind. And we see that even our individuality, that which we call "I," ourselves, is but a window -- a very clear and pure window -- through which this infinite light of awareness is shining. And in this moment we see, as we dive now more deeply into this ocean of consciousness, that it is an infinite single omnipresent field of awake-ness, as it shines through our own individuality, and it is this awake-ness which enables us to watch our breath, to hear the sounds, to see the sights, to observe the thoughts, and to even apprehend our own selves.

Leaving then, this small self behind, let us dive completely in freedom as we would into an infinite ocean, this beautiful and infinite conscious mind, and we see then that we are awake and that this awake-ness is a singularity, always indivisible, shining within all beings, and that every one of us sitting here together, and every being on earth, and every being in the cosmos is awake by this same unbroken indivisible light of consciousness -- the mind in its unbounded and infinite true nature.

Then, soaring on the wings of this infinite mind, as we would through the vastness of a fathomless ocean, we see that each of us is one, and that this silent, absolute, infinite and eternal awake Being is standing within all things, shining within each atom, moving every photon, illuminating every soul, shining from every star.

And we see in this instant that the entirety of creation and all that exists, is this same awake-ness, shining, moving, phasing, in unique shapes and forms. But it is all one. It is indivisible. It is eternal.

Within the field of this absolute awake-ness, we see that because it is beyond space, it is infinite, and because it is not bound by any point in time, it is infinite and eternal.

And yet in its fullness, without division, it is present at every point in space and every point in time, and in this we see the state of divine perfection, perfect harmony. And being thus centered, in this awake-ness, which is infinite, we now begin to explore the structure of the cosmos. And we see that this omnipresent awake-ness, and the infinite manifest creation, are perfectly one, and yet within the sphere of that which is relative, there are distinctions.

Being then established in this infinite cosmic Mind, let us gaze into the finest level of its manifestation as this infinite Being, and this eternal Mind, through the operation of its own will, takes on the form of the Creator. Moving then within the realm of infinity, the Creator aspect of this infinite Mind and Being exists as the primal source that manifests and maintains the entire universe and the entire creation.

And the first emanation from this infinite and absolute Mind is a sound, a thought, the sound vibration of which has within it the seed sound and idea of all that has been, all that is, and all that will be.

And from this primal thought issuing forth from the infinite and divine Oneness of the conscious being of the Divine Mind, we see the cosmos becoming manifest and differentiated. And from this primal thought issuing forth from the morn of eternity, we see within this primal thought and sound, the thought and seed idea for all things, all places, all ideas, all structures, all forms, all sounds— all that can be and will ever be and ever was in the entirety of creation.

And so we perceive this primal thought and this primal sound— which are one— differentiating into an infinite number of realities. And within one we can see a star. And within another we see an apple. And within another, we see our own individuality and self, and within another we see our friends, and within another we see the grass, and within another we see the wolf, and within another we see the earth, and within another we see other worlds...

Thus in infinite progression, the seed idea forms, each with their own primal thought and sound issuing forth from this most great thought, through the operation of will of the Creator, rises forth from the silent eternal Being.

And as we perceive this becoming more manifest, we see within this great Being, the most great Light. And from this primal thought, and this most elemental sound, issues forth the form of the perfect light, the perfect form, which has within it all of the creation, and the infinite cosmic creation suffused in light, emerges and unfolds within our vision.

And in this most great Light, we see then the form of all that there can be. And within this world of light— an ocean of infinite light— we see that every form is manifest and corresponding to the sound and thought vibration for an apple, issuing from the primal thought and tone, we behold the astral *light form* of an apple. And so too, with each created thing, whether it be a wolf, or a tree, or a star, or a world. And all of it is there, both in perfect oneness with the awake mind of the Creator, who created it, and in its own fullness as a perfect creation, first in thought, then in form, and then light.

And so we see this infinite light expanding and becoming differentiated, and the vast celestial worlds unfold before our vision and worlds infinite and divine are stretched out around us, in all directions, infinitely extending through space and time.

And so we behold the structure and the light of the celestial blueprint for the entirety of creation and the universe and all that exists within the world of change and expression and time and space.

And as this begins to become more differentiated, we see that within this world of light, exists the perfect sound and seed idea of each thing, and within each sound is the primal sound, and as we dive more deeply, we see the Creator Itself manifesting the entire creation, pouring within it, this unbroken awake mind, whereby we are conscious at this moment, in this time, in this space.

And seeing this firmly within us, we now behold the material creation being supported through the fine crystalline form of the world of astral light, and emanating from the blueprints of the form within the astral worlds of light, emerge the baseline form of energy which supports every atom, which supports every electron, which supports all the forces of creation and of the material cosmos.

And so we see, emerging, manifesting and expressing from this vast celestial creation, the differentiated and perfect worlds of light, and then the physical reality of the expressed universe.

And so we see our own star, the sun, emerging from this perfect astral sun, which has emerged from the most great Light, and which has within it the perfect idea form from the sun, emerging from the primal sound and primal thought, issuing forth from the sovereign will of the infinite Creator.

And with each thing we contemplate, we see it unfolding before us, whether it be a blade of grass, an animal, our own individualities and bodies, worlds far from here with peoples who are conscious as we are— all of it, emerging from this perfect template of the astral worlds of light which are unfolding from the most great Light, and the finest level of celestial light which are issuing forth from the most great thought, and the primal thought, which has within it the first emanation of sound coming forth from the morn of eternity.

And as we dive even further, we are left on the edge of the infinite, the timeless, and the eternal.

And so we see this perfect unity between the infinite Mind, whereby we are conscious and awake, and our own existence.

And the awake-ness whereby each of us is conscious, can never be divided from this single awake Being, standing within all things; we are never divided, and never separate from anything.

And then as we gaze in all directions around us, we behold a perfect divine order and that this great Being, from time to time has sent to earth and to other worlds Avatars or Manifestations of divinity, who enliven entire worlds and refresh in a new springtime the entire creation.

And we are filled with happiness as we see that the time of a new springtime has arrived and an era of a thousand years of unbroken peace and enlightenment are dawning upon the earth and upon every world in creation, within the entire cosmos.

Seeing then, in perfection the creation, the Creator and the Infinite Mind, we are now aware that it is true that every created thing is a door-way to the Infinite, and that the unbounded and infinite Being is truly omnipresent, omniscient, ever-abiding at every point in space and time and at every level of creation. And that indeed folded within us and within all things, is a perfect quantum hologram of all that there is.

And thus the entire universe is folded within us, and that our own individualities, which are part of the creation, have issued forth from the Creator— and our highest state of realization is to be as nothing and to be still.

And we see that we are clear windows through which the infinite light of the great Being is shining.

And the awake Mind whereby we are conscious at this instant, is the eternal Being, the infinite Self, the cosmic Mind, from which all things, all time, all space is emanating.

Now, let our minds rest at that point of the first emanation where awake-ness begins to become relative existence, where the absolute phases into the relative existence of the cosmos and of creation. We see that within this most great thought is the seed idea of all knowledge. And at this level, every thing may be known. All knowledge exists; every science, every art, every fact, every truth. And that is folded within the reality of man and is a fountain that can give forth all knowledge, all science, and all truth. And we may learn to go to this spot, this place of the place-less within us, and to see the truth, and to unravel the sciences and to know the facts and to perceive reality.

On the wings of this infinite awake Mind within us we realize that we are integrated in perfect harmony, indivisibly, with every point in space and time. Through gently, subtly using the free will given to us by the Creator, in accordance with the divine will, all things are possible and all life is benefited. Humbly turning to this unbounded Being, we may then awaken to a distant point in space or time and perceive what is happening in that place and in that time.

And so it is, that perchance we may fall asleep one night and perceive what will happen the next day or the next year or the next century, because folded within us is all time and all space. The nature of the mind within us is omnipresent, and is present within every point of creation— at every point in time and space.

Thus we see the entirety of the universe is open to us because the most great Mind, the single awake Being, is standing within all of us. And this infinite ocean of awake-ness, which can never be divided, is that whereby we are awake. It is that whereby we are always conscious. And if we become silent and still, we may perceive this silent Mind, and we may meditate upon the truth, and we may see any point in space and we may ask any question and find the answer.

And so it is that we — meaning all advanced intelligent beings— have the capacity to be at one with the unbounded Being, and to use our free will to discern the divine will, and to put ourselves at service to the divine plan.

And this is the apex of the achievement of our being. As we sit upon the earth, we are called to answer the needs of this time and place, even though we see that we are established in this eternal home and this infinite space.

And from this deep and abiding conscious Being, on the wings of this infinite Awareness, we rise into the sky above us, and we are all one in spirit and this spirit is indivisible. And in this infinite Mind, we see the Earth herself, a beautiful blue planet submerged in the infinity of space.

And Earth is an awake being herself. We see this awake being, and we feel at one with her, as her children, and yet in perfect oneness with the awake-ness whereby she has her own existence. And as we gaze around the Earth, we see the space of our solar system, and we see the Earth's sisters and brothers, the other planets, and Father Sun. And we see the space around us is filled with infinite light and infinite energy, and that it is not empty but full, and it is not dead space, but it is awake mind.

We see that the entirety of space is conscious. And on the wings of that awake-ness, the same awake-ness folded within us, we soar through the infinity of space and we behold myriad worlds and we see the entire spiral galaxy of the Milky Way, and expanding further, we go into intergalactic space, and we see billions of galaxies, infinite worlds stretching out beyond us, within us, and the fullness of that unbounded space is that vast ocean of mind within us.

We are always one with this cosmic Being, and we are always awake through the cosmic Mind. And at will we may then travel throughout the cosmos, and gaze upon every world and see every star system.

Being in this state of cosmic consciousness, we see beyond the infinite conscious material universe, and see the infinite astral worlds of light within them, and beyond we see the perfect idea form and sound sustaining the forms of light and the infinite material cosmos. And we are one with the Creator and we are one with creation.

We see that the Creator and the creation are one. And that within us, we are always one with it. Being in this state of unity we ask the celestial realm, the angelic beings, the Manifestations of God, and every conscious and enlightened being in the cosmos, to join us as we gaze upon the earth and we invite them here. As we see the earth at this time, we see that it is emerging into a time of enlightenment. And we ask the infinite God, as all of us focus on the earth, to transform every dark thought into enlightenment, and to send into every selfish heart, the infinite love of the divine, and that wherever there is hatred, that it be replaced with affection and love, and wherever there is greed and selfishness, that it be replaced with altruism and generosity.

Those forces on earth that we see wandering in the ignorance of hatred and greed, we see being illumined with the light of knowledge and love and peace.

Within the heart of the reality of earth and her people, we see a beautiful golden light dawning, and we see the earth transformed into a rose garden of peace. As she goes forward from this point onward, Earth becomes one of the diadems of creation, one of the genuine repositories of peace and knowledge in the cosmos.

In this state of peace, all peoples turn to the earth and are filled with joy because the time of the fulfillment of the promise of humanity has arrived, and we are here to witness that time and to usher in that reality.

We see ourselves joined by beings celestial, astral, and extraterrestrial, and all the good people on earth joining with us in the exercise of our will, wedded to the divine Being as we manifest that time of enlighten-ment and an unbroken period of thousands of years of peace.

Sitting quietly now, we see that we are joined by the angelic realm, the celestial beings, the astral worlds filled with our ancestors and with the beings from diverse worlds. And we see that there are extraterrestri-al peoples joining us, and that there are people on this planet who are joining us in conscious thought and prayer. And we hold within us this thought, and this vision of suffusing the earth in this golden light as it is brought in to this time of peace, and all the wars will be silenced and all the suffering will end.

Injustice will give way to justice, and poverty to abundance, and from destruction we will go into a time of beautiful and perfect architecture and a perfect and enlightened social order.

As we see this within us, we now are certain that it will come to pass. We see that we are joined by worlds infinite and divine, as well as mate-rial and extraterrestrial. The time has arrived for the old and corrupt ways to end and for the old order to be rolled up and for a new world to be unfurled, the hallmark of which will be oneness, peace, and unbroken enlightenment for thousands of generations of children on the earth.

36

Boundless Mind

Know that every stable star system has planets. And every one of those solar systems has life forms, beings capable of knowing the Divine Mind. So as we gaze into the space around us, we see that this enlightened awake Being, this Mind whereby we are conscious, which is always omnipresent, is shared by those beings, and that this is the foundation of inter-planetary peace. The requirement for world peace, and the first point of enlightenment for every being – is that they recognize that within them exists this cosmic mind, which gives them the light of awareness, the one spirit within them.

And so we are always one in spirit, and the great Spirit is always one and indivisible.

We welcome these beings here, in whatever form they may appear -- whether they be a materialized ship, or a message or a tone, or a light, or an etheric craft, shimmering in the field around us. But whatever is seen and heard, that is always less important than what is known within us. And we see that we are awake, and that these beings who are similarly enlightened and conscious are seeing us through their mind's eye, even as we are seeing them. And this divine eye of oneness is shared by all intelligent life.

As an ambassador from Earth to their people, with humility, we invite them here, always letting them know that they may appear in any form or shape or manner that is safe and appropriate for this time, recognizing that Earth is very dangerous right now, and that safety is paramount. We know that they may see us and we may see them effortlessly through this inner sight which all of us possess, because all of us are awake. And that awake-ness is omnipresent.

As time goes on, there will be no distinction between the spiritually enlightened ones, and those who we consider for political or leadership positions. You won't be allowed to be a leader if you are not enlightened. It will be like the time of the philosopher kings.

Keep in mind also that there are ETs underground and under bodies of water that are increasingly staying in this etheric form, but ready to respond, if there is a need. And so frequently you'll see a craft or an etheric aspect of the craft emerging from underneath the earth rather than come in from outer space.

Once in Colorado, while on an expedition, we felt the earth move and lift right under our feet. And then we could see all around us a craft, and the temperature rose 10 or 15 degrees. We were in an etheric craft that was translucent, but you could see the shape of it and the dimensions of it and the beings moving within it.

Since the electronics of these technologies allow matter to transform through the crossing point of the speed of light and solid matter into this etheric, near-astral form, it means they can go straight through solid matter, straight through mountains, as if it is not there.

Even classified human projects have technologies that do that. They can be in a state where they are not detected at all and yet are present.

The fact is, then, most people won't know that they're there. Some will, but most will not. And the more they fully come into the material three-dimensional space-time dimension, the more their craft is vulnerable to current human technologies and being targeted.

These are very powerful propulsion systems and electronics. If they do fully materialize, we let them approach us. We don't go running towards them. It is not safe, and it is unwise.

When you're in a small group and you do this protocol, often people will just stretch out and fall asleep, and then go into a dream state.

And in that state, often people will be able to let go of their internal blocks and see the ETs even better. Remember, they are frequently in the etheric or near astral form, and very easily can interact with our astral bodies, which are what is activated during the lucid dream state.

In that state, or when we are awake and centered in cosmic awareness, the ETs will draw more closely. Why? Because it is safer for them when we're not connected just to our small selves, our fearful selves, and our egos.

As Krishna said to Arjuna on the battlefield, "A little of This" -- capital "T" -- "eliminates all fear." The 'This' is boundless Mind.

In that state, there is no reason to be afraid. And therefore they are more comfortable with us because we can connect to them as awake beings. It is a beautiful experience.

And they can relate to us because we're connecting to that universal aspect of ourselves— the only aspect of us that is universal. But it's also the core of our beings. So by connecting to that we are ready and receptive and able to connect to them.

The single greatest determinative factor for contact is the state of consciousness that you're in.

What is most important about the contact protocol is taking the time to settle and center into consciousness quietly. It is done in the following phases: First, sit quietly, and do some meditative technique that enables you to be in touch with just being awake -- whatever works for you. Second, once you're aware of that awake-ness, go through the process of expanding it, sensing and seeing that it isn't just bound to your individual space right here, that it is really a universal awareness.

Third, on the wings of that universal awake-ness, allow yourself to awaken to or see -- "remotely view,"— space. You can literally just scan space freely, or let your mind be drawn to an extraterrestrial craft. Be careful not to just imagine it; let it actually unfold and come into your vision, where you actually perceive it. Fourth, once you see an ET or an ET ship, connect to the extraterrestrial being, by reconnecting to your own inner awake-ness, and see in the inner awake-ness shining from their eyes.

And in that state of oneness, invite them to be with you here, in whatever way that is safe and appropriate.

An advanced version is also to connect to the interplanetary center or council, to check and get permission and say, "Please allow them to come or bring them here," or be with them.

Fifth, you then guide them to your precise location. Show them. It is almost like you're zooming in from space, and you show them visually your exact location, connecting to their mind or to their guidance system or both— because their technologies are connected to their consciousness. Remember -- that's how they are traveling through space. That is how their guidance systems work and how they fly the craft. It is all with mind connecting; their mind, body and the craft are all perfectly integrated. The spaceship itself is a bio-machine that is awake and has conscious intelligence associated with it.

You can sit in a small group and use this protocol for an hour or two. It is very powerful when a group of people practice this together.

Once when an etheric ET was at one of these expeditions, we offered a crystal to this being. As I extended my hand to give this beautiful crystal to the ET, we all looked at my hand, and it morphed in front us and changed; it elongated, and then had only three fingers- and looked just like the ET's hand!

All of us saw that. It was like his hand and my hand became one. All of us saw my hand completely change.

So the way that these ETs can appear is really amazing. And it can be shocking because it seems so bizarre. It would be hard to even create a

The

science fiction movie that would contain as much high strangeness as we have actually seen and experienced on these expeditions.

As we gather here under the stars, remember this wonderful time together, and see that we are always connected in this state of oneness, and that we're going to work together to make it through this time into the time that we have seen.

37

The Drop and the Ocean Are One

There is a wonderful saying, "Knowledge is a single point, but the foolish have multiplied it."

The direct perception of mind is very simple, but there is a lot of detail about how it all is expressed that we can discuss. We are sitting at this point in space and yet, at the same time, folded within this point, is that which is beyond time and space. This activity is emanating from infinity and the relativity itself is infinite and the creation itself is not limited. The cosmos itself has no end in time or space, any more than the unbounded Mind has ending in time or space. The creation is the infinite outer garb of the inner unbounded Mind, and all of it together is the great Being.

Can you see that?

It is very easy to sit quietly and experience mind in its subtle, unbounded nature, and see the reality around us. We have to go from being awake *and* lightly focused, to simply being, and reflecting and seeing within ourselves the awake-ness.

We identify consciousness with our egos, because it's shining within us— but it is also beyond self at the same time. Look into the eyes of those around you. See they are awake. And even though they're different, the consciousness itself is the same - the awake mind-stuff within them is one: We are all one in Spirit.

That whereby they are conscious is the same awake-ness whereby you're awake. Their individualities are different, their intellects are different, their bodies are different, but the awake-ness itself is a singularity. And so we are all one and we have always been one. And we have never been separate.

And if you acknowledge and experience this unity, then you can be one with anyone else, and you can be one with the animals and the trees and the stars and the extraterrestrials, and those within the covert government and the White House and everywhere.

No place is barred from you. No being is a stranger and no place is strange. The entire cosmos is your home.

And this is not an intellectual realization alone. It is experienced.

And all those worlds that we were traveling through, and all those inner states, to each and every one of them you will no doubt attain...

Our individualities are windows through which infinity is expressing itself. At some point, we learn at will to take this drop and let it go back into the ocean, and then, at will, reconstitute the drop and be individual again.

This is what we learn to do through the course of our spiritual journey. 'Be as nothing, and then walk upon the water.'

So the drop of our individuality can become one with the ocean, and then we are the ocean. At the same instant we can realize that we are still that individual drop— in a state of unity consciousness.

We can perceive this not only within ourselves, but we see that all things and all beings and the earth beneath our feet is all awake, infinite Being.

We realize it is all sacred— the entirety of creation is sacred and every being is sacred, because spirit, the awake Being, is the very fabric of all that there is. And it is always perfectly one, even if it's playing and displaying upon itself as if it is different.

The challenge is to see the oneness within the difference, and also enjoy the difference.

We have been in places all over the world that have just the most horrible weather, and we will sit and do this meditation and prayer, and within minutes, the whole sky will clear-- it is an opening that happens above this state of consciousness. And this has happened hundreds of times -- almost inexplicably, no matter how bad or stormy the weather.

The question is: Is there interplay between oneness and duality?

They co-exist. They are not mutually exclusive. In other words, the relative and the changing, time and space and matter and the infinite silent absolute are the same. There's no separation, and therefore there's no duality.

Now, that which is relative has differentiation. We have individual bodies, there is male and there is female, there are different energies, there are different elements. But at the same time, there is this perfect divine unity and awake-ness that co-exists with it, suffuses all of it, and permeates all of it.

There is a balance in being able to see the differentiation and the duality of things, and at the same time see the oneness that is permeating all the duality.

So it isn't an either-or question.

Everything is established and emanating from unbounded, absolute, undifferentiated, pure Mind. But it is perceived as one or the other. Our task is to evolve to a point where we see it not as either-or, but all as one, even while we see the distinctions.

Even experiments that have been done with mechanical systems or devices, such as those done by Dr. Robert Jahn of Princeton, show that mind is connected to matter.

How does that happen? It is because the material object itself *is* mind, *is* awake-ness — phasing, resonating as that thing.

It takes practice, but the perception of Oneness begins to come back and forth, back and forth, back and forth— until you see that there is no back and forth. It is all one. The drop and the ocean are one, even when the drop can be distinguished.

It is useful sometimes to simply look and sit quietly and be with other people, and then become aware of the fact that they're awake and you're awake.

Now, subtract all the differences and be left with the awake-ness itself, and go into that state of being awake within yourself, and then see that you are freed from self and individuality so that you can connect to the awake-ness of others, and be one.

And in this sense, we are all one being. We are truly all one in spirit, and therefore we can relate to and find within ourselves genuine compassion.

Expanding that idea, consider the fact that every person on earth, every sentient being in the cosmos, whether angelic or astral or deceased humans, or extraterrestrial people with bodies and material existences on other planets -- all of those awake beings are capable of being aware of awareness, and therefore can enter into a state of oneness -- intentional oneness that is transcendental and perfect.

Now, that state is beyond the peace of a political peace, which has been called at times, "the lesser peace."

What I am describing now is the most great peace— the perfect peace that is inner and spiritual. Because in that state you see indeed that we are all one in Spirit.

Thus, any source of conflict ceases to exist, because instead of being centered in difference, people will be centered in oneness -- and not just as an intellectualization or philosophical perspective, but a genuine experience in enlightenment, and that is an enlightened state of being.

Oh, my God, it is beautiful.

All that you need has been given to you. It is all within you. All I am doing is trying to unfold an understanding and then you can do it yourself.

At the same time there is oneness, there is relativity. We are sitting here. We do have distinct bodies. There is space and time and stars and distance. Those co-exist. They are not mutually exclusive concepts at all -- in fact, they are perfectly integrated.

And so, understanding the nuance between the absolute and the relative is really important, because that is the journey our souls are traversing. And becoming proficient in that understanding and experience enables you to manifest from this state of infinite awareness into this existence.

Without the fundamental experience and understanding of silent infinite awareness and how that absolute Unbounded-ness becomes manifest into the relative, you cannot reach your fulfillment as a being.

Wherever there is form within it is astral light. And there is the pure idea form and awareness, that is the causal -- the level of the cosmology that is in that idea seed-form. The infinite Awareness manifests this seed idea. It's the idea form and thought vibration of lets say an apple -- without the form and shape of an apple. Can you consider an apple without its form- just its thought essence?

It is rather abstract, I agree. But then from that idea thought vibration, see emerging the light and form and shape and color of an apple. See that astral template becoming more and more differentiated and more manifest, emerging into the subtle sub-electro-magnetic energies -- zero point energies, magnetic forces and other forces that then recruit and form the atoms and the molecules etcetera of the apple.

This process, this divine architecture, exists with every thing -- whether it be a galaxy or a star or a person. And this is how conscious mind creates the thought-causative level of an object, and then manifests the astral and then manifests the physical object.

What is essential is pure consciousness. Through deep silent, non-local mind, we can connect to an object and dematerialize it or rematerialize or move it across points in space and time. This is how certain Yogi adepts have been able to take an object and make it dematerialize and rematerialize like a teleportation device. You can connect to any object through awareness, and if you understand how awareness and mind-stuff becomes matter, you can affect that object. There is no separation whatsoever except the intellectual constructs that we have made. We build our own cages and only we can open them.

And so we have to unlearn those habituated intellectualizations, and quietly experience the 'unitive state'— the state of oneness. And empowered with the subtle operation of will and an active faith, 'this will be', almost anything is possible. Do you see what I'm saying? This will be. This is and it will be ... Without any doubt of it whatsoever.

Our lives have been created this way. The fact that we are still connected to our bodies is because of this. Think about it. You build a house. You had an idea of it that emanated from your conscious mind, and then you saw it and then you drew it, and then you built it.

This is the creative process and the Creator -- the divine Being --has created the entire cosmos this way. And within us is folded the same ability.

This is why it has often been said, "He who has known his true self has verily known God."

The question is: Are there different gradations within the astral realm?

And the answer is absolutely yes -- just like there are different gradations within the material.

You can be in the sewers of Manhattan or you can be in a beautiful garden. We choose.

Within the worlds of light, there are lesser and greater worlds, and there are different stations, and different levels. And when someone passes out of this world, and is in their astral body, remember that "like seeketh like and taketh pleasure in the company of its kind."

That means that those of a certain level of consciousness and proclivity will gravitate to those of like mind. And they may not necessarily be pleased with their company. Do you see?

When people speak of hell, it is a state of mind on the other side. It is because of your own state of mind that you are with people who are a lot like you. Those worlds are created through thought forms, and if those beings or people are thinking terrible things, they are creating terrible manifestations around then.

You can sit and visualize a rose garden or a torture chamber. Do you see? That is the reality of that.

Now, there are finer and finer levels of the astral that create the "fine celestial realm," and the really high angelic realm. This refinement in mind, thought and energy continues until you get to the level of the station of the Avatar -- the station of the Godhead -- the Creator state.

There are countless degrees of refinement -- without cessation. And that is just the astral. Beyond that, there is the so-called idea/causal -- the essence of what relative existence is. At a certain level, you may evolve to where you don't even need to be in the astral body form, and you are in this point of thought/consciousness. It is very expansive, beautiful, and divine.

For example, when I had my near-death experience, I didn't have a body shape. I was in this point of pure conscious light that was individuality and awake – it was causal. I went straight to causal and then went into infinite Mind.

The emotional texture of the astral worlds is very full and the light and the color are very beautiful - celestial.

But the existence that is beyond that -- the causative state — is a finer frequency. It is more essential, less differentiated and directly connected to the pureness of mind and spirit.

The question is: Where does reincarnation come into this cosmology?

This is an often asked question. 'The truth will set you free, but first it will piss you off'. So now I am going to piss off everybody.

The fact is this: The mass retail teachings of reincarnation are no more true than the mass retail teaching of other orthodoxies.

The truth about reincarnation is that it is true and it is absolutely false. Remember what we just experienced. Every individuality is a unique creation. And once it is in creation, it exists forever as a unique thing. That individuality is here, and it will continue forever.

And yet the awake mind within each of us is the same mind that is within all of us.

Every individual, by connecting to this non-local aspect of awareness, can experience the individual life of any individual now on earth or who has ever been on earth or who will ever be on earth or who has ever been in existence anywhere in the universe.

The description of reincarnation is therefore a misnomer. In reality, it is the realization of the oneness between individuality and infinity. That aspect of each of us that is the infinite Self, is also experiencing each of us. Thus, an individual's awareness can connect to this expanded non-local awareness and then experience the life of another. *Because in reality, we are always all one Being.*

Now, I have met probably five people who swear to God they were Cleopatra! And in a sense they were: Because the awake-ness within us is universal. In this way, an archetype person— or someone who has had an important impact as an icon within society or history like Cleopatra — can be experienced by certain other related souls in her fullness.

But does one die and kind of dissolve into nothingness and then reincarnate as Joe Cohen in Brooklyn, New York in the year 2030?   No. What is understood about reincarnation is completely false, and yet within it is a profound truth that doesn't get taught because it's more abstract and non-local and higher ordered in complexity.

It is possible that people with individual souls will resonate with beings of a similar nature, or overarching resonant frequency. It isn't as if one ends life in this body, dissolves into some nothingness of the matrix of awareness, and then becomes another being or person. That isn't it at all. It is something much more profound. And the profound truth is *we are all beings at all times*. And if we choose to, we can experience an individual being and life in the past, in the now, or in the future — in its *complete fullness*.

Do you know who you are? Do you know that the entire universe is folded within you, and therefore the awake Mind within you is omnipresent and that it transcends space and time? And you can resonate with, and experience in its complete fullness, all the soul experience of any being, with complete compassion?

Within ourselves is an infinite and eternal conscious Being. So if you understand the nature of mind and consciousness within ourselves, it is very understandable how we may go to sleep at night and within that relaxed state, break the bonds of space and time and see what will happen next week, or see what happened a thousand years ago or even experience fully the life of someone who lived a million years ago...

We are coming into the maturity of the human race and need to have a more profound understanding of these things, so we don't fall into superstition and silliness, where people have to do certain rituals so they don't come back as an ant!

Of course, if you want to experience what it is like to be an oak tree or an ant or a dog, you can. You do not have to wait for another life!

When I swim with the dolphins, the reason they accept me is that they see me as one of them. They literally experience me as a dolphin. I *become* a dolphin.

When you drop the body and go to the next level, you will have all your memories, you will remember every one you were with on earth, you will evolve as this individuality through all the worlds of creation and through all the states of consciousness. At some point, if you wish, you will be the drop returning to the ocean.

Remember, from the infinite ocean of God have we emerged, and to that infinite ocean we will all return. And this is the purpose and journey of our soul.

The experience of being an individual is to learn the bliss of becoming nothing and becoming infinite again, and yet to be able to enjoy the existence and the fullness of creation.

38

Celestial Perception

Through the intercession of the divine beings, through the prayers of those on earth, and through their own efforts, a soul can advance from one level to the next level; it is an infinite progression.

Now, one may have to go through a lot of suffering to do that, because one must let go of all attachments. Suffering and attachments are synonyms.

So a firmly attached belief or idea or grief is suffering.

Someone wisely described hell as being in that state of remorse because you have realized what you have done, and more importantly realized what you *didn't* do. True regret isn't so much about what you have *done* (unless you're an axe murderer or something) but is related more to what you haven't done -- the effort you didn't expend, the kindness you didn't extend, the times you were selfish when you should have been giving -- that is where regret comes from.

We have a weird way of focusing on what we have done and worrying about that, when in reality, we should be more concerned about what we are neglecting to do, that is positive and helpful to the world.

These sins of omission almost always trump the sins of commission. So do not miss an opportunity to do good, to love, to share, to sacrifice, and to take an opportunity to create a better world or to love people or to extend a kindness.

Every individual created being has a certain optimal point of service and optimal role to play, that is consonant with their own unique self.

Now, what I have just described is what is called Dharma— your right work and path. It can be something very modest to something very great within each person, depending on the extent to which we exercise free will to discover our full potential and apply it.

The state of cosmic awareness I am referring to has always existed, eternally, and will always exist eternally, and it is always infinite. And the universe has always existed, will always exist, and is infinite. So the idea that the universe is limited or had a beginning or an end, is actually not correct.

The eternity of the plane of the Absolute, the awake cosmic Mind, has as its expressed corollary, an infinite eternal creation.

So even in terms of space, as we think of it materially, there is no end
to it. It's infinite. Because even if you got to the edge of what we think
would be the universe by definition, then what's beyond that edge? It is
infinite.

As a young child, I used to contemplate these things all the time. I
would walk around thinking of these things and looking at the stars and
sensing that, feeling that, seeing that.

Even when I saw the cosmic egg, the celestial form of creation as a
discreet shape and form, it was also eternal and infinite. It is a paradox...

If you're looking at the night sky with celestial vision you will see an
enormous amount of light! Everything is paradoxical, and perfectly so...

With astral/celestial perception, we directly see that even the depths
of 'empty, dark space' is illumined with a light glowing from within. Can
you see it?

We can see the discrete planets and stars, spinning in an infinite ocean
of celestial light. So it's light upon light, worlds of light all radiating from
within -- just as the light of a star is actually coming from within.

The question is: Do all possible realities exist concurrently or on a
parallel basis, and is there communication between them?

The answer to this is wholly dependent on the state of awareness of
the perceiver.

In other words, the answer is yes, from the perspective of a highly
integrated quantum holographic view of the universe, where everything
is folded within each other. And just like a hologram, you can take one
part of the universe and the entirety of the universe is present. Nothing
is ever separate; Divine Unity permeates all things.

So all the possible realities of the universe are going on simultaneously, and the connection is via this non-local mind-stuff, the conscious
intelligent integrating aspect of all things. Conscious intelligence is the
ultimate integrator of these various realms. On one level of intellectual
understanding, we may speak of various dimensions or parallel univers-
es, but in reality, they are all folded within each other. Looking with the
"eye of oneness," we see this perfect integration via the non-locality of
mind.

At another level of perception, you could say that there is no connection at all. For example, you could certainly say there is no connection
between us sitting here right now in Virginia and someone sitting in
India. Since we're not touching them and they are not hearing us, you
could say that's correct.

On another level, you could say, "Well, we are all in the biosphere of earth. So we are touching the earth, and we're breathing the same air, and we are connected."

These are all intellectual constructs, as opposed to how they are *actually operating*. The way they're actually operating is that the finer resonance fields eventually give rise to the coarser ones, and there is a seamless connection between them. There is a non-local connection and resonance that takes place through conscious intelligence.

When something is teleported and goes from point A to point B in space, it is possible because there is perfect integration between any point in space or any two points— or any infinite number of points in space. Due to the non-local integration of energy, matter, space, time and dimensions via mind-stuff, every point in space and time has access to every other point in space and time. And the finer aspects of the cosmos – the astral, thought, causal, etc, are *increasingly non-local*.

So there is "relative non-locality."

Everyone thinks of non-locality as being either non-local or local. It is either fixed and linear, or it is non-local.

In reality, there is relativity within non-locality. The architecture of the cosmos is exquisitely beautiful; at once complex and yet simple, once a few principles are realized.

To go from point A to B by, 'dematerializing' something and having it reappear at another point in space, you are accessing relative non-locality. The material object is being altered so that its spin and frequency are actually shifting into something approximating what the mystics would call astral or etheric energy.

And because that realm is *less* fixed and linear than linear material space-time, the object can appear there virtually instantaneously. This is accomplished through non-local nodal resonance – where point A and point B in space are accessed through resonance and spin via a level of the universe that is more non-local than fixed time/space.

Thus, the more you cross over into fields of resonance and frequency that are beyond the speed of light— this crossing point of light— you access realms that are closer and closer to the so-called etheric or astral fields of energy, which are increasingly non-local.

Now, the most perfect non-locality is pure undifferentiated Mind. And the least non-local is the fixed material space-time matter universe, but they are all integrated and they are always one, and therefore if you move a material object and alter its state electronically, it can be in an increasingly non-local form. Thus, it can be teleported from one point in space to another.

It is possible to do this at the level of causation: the point of thought/sound/vibration, and that is even faster than etheric teleportation.

So there is relative speed and relative non-locality, depending on how much finer you're going to take any given object and put it into either the etheric, astral, or causal state *that is folded within that object.*

An extraterrestrial vehicle, for example- or a man-made craft that actually goes faster than the speed of light- does not speed up like you go down the highway from 50 miles an hour to 60 to 70.

It shifts in a quantum leap, a quantum jump, from a resonance field in what we call, "Stable, space-time matter material form", to a frequency and resonance beyond that, in one resonance jump.

At that point, the spacecraft can move outside of linear vectors of space and go from one point in space to another, almost instantaneously— and certainly faster than the speed of light. But it is still not at *infinite* velocity.

So to go from Earth to, say, many thousands of light years from here, may actually take a few days, because you're in a form that is *relatively* non-local— but not *perfectly non-local,* such as pure consciousness.

Now, a civilization that would be able to reduce the craft and everything in it to a frequency form that would be purely causal, or on a very refined astral frequency, would be able to make that same journey in a much shorter time interval.

A pure thought form connected to mind can go from one point in the universe to the other truly instantaneously -- no matter how many light years. It is connected very intimately to that perfect non-locality of infinite awareness.

And so there is relativity within non-locality.

We can also experience this non-technologically, in the lucid dream. In the lucid dream, we are moving, flying non-locally in our spirit or astral body, which is as real (or more so...) than our physical bodies. That is why you can easily slip off the linear space-time coordinate and be at another point on the earth, even while you are in bed sleeping. In that state you can see what is going on in real-time somewhere else on Earth or in space — or slip off the time coordinate into the future, and see something that is going to happen tomorrow, or a year from now. This is called a pre-cognitive lucid dream.

So pre-cognition, or seeing something that happened in the past, or seeing remotely something happening right now, is possible because consciousness is omnipresent and we can learn to experience a finer and more subtle level of mind, while still being in our body and individual consciousness.

In a similar way, technological communication by an advanced extraterrestrial civilization involves this paradigm. They have communication devices that interface with thought, and can go from a point here to a point in space a million light years from here, instantaneously. Such a technological device is interfacing with the pure thought itself, dropping out of the normal electromagnetic realm into a sub-electromagnetic or finer energy realm.

But when an entire huge spacecraft is moving through the cosmos there is what I call a co-efficient of drag from the spacecraft as it is adhering to the underbelly of the material linear space-time universe. As it skips on the underside of linear space-time, in the *gap* between finer astral and material frequencies, there is some drag, preventing instantaneous transport.

It has to maintain a certain amount of connectivity to the material universe in order to reemerge into it. Hence velocity is not infinite. Over short distances, such transfer through space/time would appear instantaneous, but over vast cosmic distances, there is a time and space domain involved.

There are some *very* advanced extraterrestrial technologies that actually do not require this— and those are truly celestial ships. They can reside and be in a very fine celestial form, and then emerge through various levels of astral energy and then fully materialize. Not all extraterrestrial civilization are at the same level of integrating this cosmology into operational technologies.

You know, a nickname for one of the areas out at Area 51 is "Dreamland."

The reason it is called Dreamland is because when they started doing experiments moving faster than the speed of light, and you are actually on a craft, and in that form for any length of time, it is like a lucid dream. It's like you're awake but it has a dream-like quality and the energy forms are somewhat plasma-like or etheric, and time is different and space are different.

39

Gradations of Energy

A man who worked for many years at Lockheed Skunk Works described to me an experience related to an astral interface with ETs. He is also one of our witnesses. He surfaced because he wanted me to explain something that made no sense to him and had been bothering him for years.

In the 1960s, he learned how to do what's commonly called "astral projection" -- leaving the physical body with the astral body and traveling around -- which almost everyone has experienced if they have ever had a flying dream. He was learning to do this consciously, in a relaxed meditative state.

One night while he was practicing his technique, his teacher said, "You're ready to do this now, and you'll be able to do it."

So he laid down, relaxed and then suddenly left his body. He went up through the ceiling of his house, out into space, and slammed into the side of an extraterrestrial vehicle that was high in the atmosphere of Earth.

Now, he said that he actually rocked the spacecraft, and that the occupants could see him.

And he said, they looked at him and said telepathically, "My God, why don't you watch where you're going?!!" He was embarrassed at this celestial faux pas, and later went back into his body!

He said the thing that he could never understand was that he wasn't in his physical body, he was in his subtle astral body—but the craft that he encountered was of the same sort of density as his astral form, and he could interact with it. The occupants saw him, and he saw them, but it wasn't like he was interacting with just other souls flying around. This was a spacecraft!

I said, "Well, you may not like this answer, but since you're an aerospace engineer, I think you will understand this."

Extraterrestrial vehicles, particularly being around earth where we're trying to target and hit them with weapon systems, spend most of their time in a dematerialized form, resonating faster than the speed of light.

This means that they are not materialized -- they are not solid matter— but are a physical material spacecraft from another planet with flesh-and-blood beings on board. If you encounter one in the dream state, they will see you, because they are in a form of energy where they see that level of frequency of energy very easily, and you will see them, and you can interact with them and the spacecraft.

It doesn't mean that they are angelic or non-extraterrestrial. It does mean that they are extraterrestrial *and* inter-dimensional -- if you want to use "dimension," although that is not an accurate term. In reality, we are talking about an entire spectrum of energy and reality that is a continuum, although there are certain phases to the continuum, which some would call a distinct dimension. Just like the separation of different chemicals or different densities of water and soil, there are striations at different frequencies.

While there are gradations, they exist within a spectrum that is continuous just like the electromagnetic spectrum from ultraviolet to infrared.

This man had an out-of-body experience and he was conscious and awake in it. It wasn't a fantasy at all. And when he had this uncontrolled launch and encountered the extraterrestrial vehicle, the craft was of a similar density as his astral body. And yet it was still extraterrestrial, just not fully materialized.

A human being looking with these material eyes would have neither seen him nor the space ship nor the ETs— unless they had trained themselves to see the subtle energy of what scientists call "neutrino light" that is emitted from the astral realm.

There are technological sensors that have been developed by scientists to pick up that kind of light, but that technology was stolen from them by the NRO and put out into space so they could detect ET craft when they are not materialized, to more easily target and destroy them.

That is another whole discussion.

When something is dematerialized for even a brief period, the resonance frequency of that object has shifted into an etheric quasi-plasma form of energy that closely *approximates* astral energy.

Now, there are different gradations within the astral realm, from a coarser astral that is interfacing with the material existence of atoms and electromagnetic energy, all the way to the finest astral, which is called the "high celestial,". Every level of the astral can be interfaced technologically, if your sciences are refined enough.

Entry to the finer aspects of the astral is very tightly guarded, because it requires great enlightenment to function at that level. Such realms are guarded by evolved extraterrestrials and celestial beings, by the Godhead and by forces way beyond anything on earth.

There are extraterrestrial civilizations that are in the several hundred thousand to several million years or more technologically evolved beyond us, who are in a state of consciousness where the entire civilization is in cosmic consciousness, God consciousness, or unity consciousness or beyond. Their technologies are commensurate with their level of consciousness and enable them to understand and interface with the material universe and these finer astral and causal levels of the cosmos.

They can appear and manifest like an extremely enlightened master who can materialize, dematerialize, alter form, shape, and have a presence that would feel extremely enlightened.

Now, not all extraterrestrial civilizations capable of inter-stellar travel are at that level of development and evolution. Some are just a little beyond what we have. They're peaceful and they have established global peace, or they wouldn't have been allowed to leave their planet. They would still be under quarantine.

There is an order in the universe that would prevent them from leaving, just like there is one that is preventing us from going to other star systems. But once you have established a peaceful existence, you begin to have more and more freedom of movement. The technologies, and the material sciences, become increasingly rooted in understanding the science of consciousness.

Extremely evolved extraterrestrial civilizations manifest all of their spacecraft and material needs through the vibratory aspect of sound, as it relates to thought— the sound vibration of thought. In other words, the component of thought that is a sound vibration. That is how you get these truly celestial ships— they emerge from that level through the finest levels of astral energy. The components, by the time they emerge into the material plane, are extraordinarily pure, and have within them the fullness of the light of the celestial shining from within them.

This is why some of the ships that I have been close to and seen fully materialized have a light not of this world. It is so pure and celestial, and yet it is fully materialized and 'solid'.

I have been told by people who have studied the very advanced extraterrestrial vehicles that they are extraordinarily sophisticated -- even the crude ones are seamless. There is never a seam. How are they made?

Well, they are not made by taking a chunk of iron ore or alloy and banging it crudely into a shape! They are actually made through what I call "infra ultrasound". The object is made by assembling and maneuver-

ing the astral matrix to build the template of the craft at that subtle level
—and it then emerges as a perfect molded form into material physical
molecules.

As they emerge, using this infra ultrasonic way of manufacturing, the
"etheric" and "astral" energy level imbues the spaceship with intelligence. They can be so structured technologically at a sub- atomic level,
that there is organizing intelligence associated with it, and life. So they
are actually intelligent bio-machines. They are so sophisticated that they
take on a level of self-integration and intelligence.

People who I have interviewed who were actually present where
these ET craft were downed described these craft as acting like they
were injured and were trying to heal themselves. They had what
appeared to be a circulatory system, and an immune system, and were
conscious. And we are talking about the ship now!

One of the craft that crashed in New Mexico had a gash in it, and the
craft was trying to heal itself. This witness said it was like when you cut
yourself and the wound heals shut --but it was a time lapsed version,
healing and trying to close right in front of his eyes.

So you're dealing with a level of ultra-nano-technology. At this level,
astral and etheric energy emerges into this realm and organizes atoms and
molecules. Such craft have a type of artificial intelligence associated with
it, and a life force associated with it, like a bio-machine.

This is not your grandfather's Oldsmobile.

The question is: Why would they need technology and ships at all.

They don't need them any more than we do. Astrally, we can go
anywhere we want to! But if they want to interface with the material universe in a way that is material, they need a material aspect. So they
choose to keep it, and they utilize it.

It becomes a matter of choice.

They can appear at any point without a ship, without a spacecraft.
But so can humans. Humans even at this point have teleportation capabilities -- unfortunately they are being used by people who shouldn't
have them -- to go from one point or another all over the planet, without a jet, or without a ship or a car, or even an alien reproduction vehicle. This has been done with technologies that are being developed in
classified projects.

Throughout recorded history, there are reports of humans who
would be in some country far away and would, through the operation of
their own will, bilocate their body and materialize to visit a friend some-

where else. There are accounts even in the 20th century of this happening that are credible accounts.

So if humans can do that, why can't extraterrestrials?

But technological means and spacecraft are necessary if you are going to exist materially in difficult environments – say underwater, in deep space, etc. So even very advanced ET peoples do have craft.

Remember the story of the ET that came to the bay window in England in 1997, when Shari Adamiak found out her cancer was metastatic and I had metastatic cancer? It came out of the sky. It was lit like a star and came from a point of light, which was a craft. The ET arrived in a nearly astral form, but it was physically visible with the eyes of everyone. It was not a celestial perception. It was material light – and it came through the window, over to the fireplace and then, whish, manifested as a scintillating luminous extraterrestrial being.

These ETs are from material worlds like earth and they have biological people on them, who are evolved enough in consciousness to develop their material sciences so that they involve these other finer levels of the cosmology, including consciousness, the astral realm and the causal/thought vibration realm.

They have material sciences for creating objects utilizing the understanding of causal thought vibration, sound vibration, and other celestial sciences. But if they want to be here materially, they will be here with a material craft and a material body. They will utilize that, even though they are in a state of consciousness where they can also be here in a spiritual state—even as a human can be someplace out in space spiritually today.

Humans do have the ability to be in a spiritual state and see remote places, but it is still nice to get in a car and see the Smithsonian in one's material body!

Also, however, keep in mind that many of the craft that are extraterrestrial that have beings on board have robotic bio-machine humanoids rather than actual extraterrestrial beings, for security reasons.

So there is relative non-locality, and the technologies associated with these relative states and gradations are distinct, even though they are on a continuum of reality. It is like the difference between a Model-T and nice seven series BMW. There is commonality and yet there are distinctions— and there are some really marked distinctions.

The exploration of the cosmos is virtually endless – and not just the three dimensional material cosmos. As civilizations evolve, they discover

the astral and then finer levels that then cross over into the causal—
which *also* have coarser and finer levels. The numbers of degrees of gradations are virtually infinite – and each has its own applications, technologies, sciences and the like.

My experience is that there is a highly organized inter-planetary and
inter-species group that directs and plans anything that would have to do
with extraterrestrial civilizations inter-facing with an emerging world
such as our own. It is highly ordered; it is not space anarchy!

Even at our stage of evolution, we have at least a semblance of international cooperation and organization for international air travel and
things of this sort.

There is a highly functional inter-planetary diplomatic operation that
controls and coordinates interaction with Earth, and it has been operative
for a very long time -- certainly since before recorded human history.

Humans have attained, in individual instances, the highest level of
evolution possible-- as high as any in creation.

But collectively, there is a great deal to be desired. The potential within humanity is equal to the potential within any species in the universe.
Our capacity to evolve into very highly conscious enlightened individuals with a concomitant social structure is equal to any civilization that has
ever existed or will ever exist in the universe. That we are not there yet
only means that our journey is not complete.

This is why I think life on earth— and humanity specifically— is very
cherished and greatly loved and is being nurtured, observed and protected. There is great anticipation that we will soon grow up and quit clubbing ourselves in the head, like a bunch of crazy cavemen, and begin to
live in a civilized fashion.

And indeed this is the time when that will happen, and peace will be
firmly established permanently. And by permanently, I mean for hundreds of thousand of years, in an unbroken period of peace and growing
enlightenment.

This era is a universal cycle. And this universal cycle has ramifications for earth and other planets as well. Indeed, there may be planets
that are at a similar level of development as ours or even less technologically developed than ours.

But know this: The cycle we are in is one of universal peace on earth
and in heaven—on earth and throughout the cosmos. We live in the time
of the greatest potential – and the greatest challenges...

Humans should not be down on ourselves— in terms of our capacity. We are not inferior, nor are we superior, to any other intelligent

species in the universe. We are absolutely equal, because within us, as within them, the universe is folded. The universal concept, "man," has equal potential for complete enlightenment and the realization of the existence of the Infinite and all of its applications and wondrous sciences, within each intelligent being.

Extraterrestrial civilizations that are here, I am sure, have very specific purposes and functions. One of them is to be able to interact with humans that are peaceful towards them and are willing to interact openly with them. This is why the CE-5 initiative has met with so much success. Any effort to contact ETs peacefully is greatly respected. Because let's face it, out of the six billion people on earth, there aren't that many people who know about this, and of those, there are a very few number who are actually willing to do anything proactive and positive to contact them. It is time for humanity to make peaceful contact.

40

Inter-Stellar Community

You really can't understand the nature of the future unless you understand the nature of reality. As we talk about the future, we can only talk about *probable* futures. The details may shift and time lines may shift, but the meta-themes are known. This is most important.

If we understand the blueprint of the new world that has already been created in the Empyrean realm, we can see the patterns of the next several millennia on Earth. The oak tree is always within the seed. And if you can perceive what's in the seed and understand it, you can then see all the stages of the maturation of the oak tree as it grows for hundreds of years.

And yet all of this is tempered by the existence of "probable futures," — because of the operation of free will by humans on earth in intersecting the larger Plan that exists. Everything that everyone collectively is doing is affecting the timing and the specific expression of this era. We are over a hundred years into a time when we could have already had universal peace, the elimination of poverty, free energy, anti-gravity travel and even been out in space, peacefully, amongst the stars. But we are not there because of the misapplication of free will, and ignorance.

People who say that they are psychics and firmly say, "X, Y and Z are going to happen on this date," they are almost always wrong. They are either self-deluded or just charlatans: there are just too many variables because of the interaction between the overarching divine plan and its descent and manifestation, which has to occur *through people*. This process can be either assisted or obstructed through the operation of free will.

There is a specific plan that has already been laid out -- a blueprint or architecture of the future. What I want to do now is describe the blueprint of this beautiful structure that is being built.

Perhaps right now only some of the foundation and cornerstones are being laid, but if we can understand what the divine Architect has laid down in this blueprint, we can get a very good sense of what the overall will look like.

The big theme is one of increasing levels of oneness and integration on every level of existence. An era of at least 500,000 years of human peace and fulfillment has opened – and we are witnesses to its early light.

We will see the complete agreement between the spiritual realm and science.

The full elucidation of these wondrous sciences and their applications to benefit the entire planet will assure a time of unbroken abundance and peace.

These sciences, used for peaceful purposes, will create a civilization that will witness an end to material poverty— and with that will come a permanent foundation for a just and lasting peace.

Only then will we be suitable members of an inter-stellar community of people.

The current state of affairs will change because it must. But it won't be easy. Easy would have been 100 to 150 years ago. But we have missed that window. Through our own perversity and rebellion, and our refusal to do what was right, we have now reached this millennium without yet having established peace, without having turned the swords into plowshares.

Hence, the transition is going to be either difficult or genuinely catastrophic. I say this very frankly. I have no illusions about it, nor should you.

And yet, no effort in this regard is wasted, even though at times we may be demoralized, and even at times we may see nothing but despair and despondency. In reality, everything is still possible, and everything is in play.

While it is important not to ignore the risks of the present era, what is essential is that we have our sights clearly fixed on that far horizon— the inevitable civilization that will be established on earth, and that we are here to help create. We must keep moving forward, and doing the right thing and speaking the truth. Even though some people may not like the truth they hear, it needs to be told.

In one of my lucid dreams as a teen, I was up in the sky floating, as if in a UFO. I found myself in a part of the world where I had never been, and it was the west coast of America. I was hovering over the LA basin, and I saw the buildings of downtown Los Angeles. The buildings that I saw weren't there at that time but all of them are there now. The Bonaventure Center was the big one— it wasn't there then but it is there now.

It looked like daytime and there were enormous changes occurring on the earth. Suddenly, there was a tsunami coming in from the Pacific.

If you can visualize the Bonaventure Center being about an inch in height, this tsunami was two to three inches high -- so two to three times the height of the tallest buildings in LA.

This tsunami came in and completely swept across the LA basin. And yet, as this was happening, I felt a strange calmness. I felt no fear at all. I was just looking as if a movie was being shown of events that could happen if we didn't change our course.

Now, this dream happened around 1970 -- there wasn't a lot of talk about global warming and the fact that we could have a sudden environmental collapse.

In the dream, I could see that there were enormous geophysical changes and environmental changes that were happening. And they led to some event that was sudden and catastrophic.

Then, as the dream proceeded, I looked around and as far as I could see, the sky was filled with thousands of extraterrestrial vehicles. They were involved in some kind of assistance effort.

We are in a time now where the chance of serious and sudden environmental events is growing.

There exist within covert programs 'scalar' weapon systems that could trigger enormous earthquakes and earth changes like this.

There is no question that these projects are deliberately, with malice aforethought, withholding those earth-saving energy technologies that could prevent the melting of the polar ice caps, and other catastrophic changes in the environment.

So whether it is through an extraordinary and covert technology or through the consequences of our social and industrial stupidity, we are now at a time where even mainstream science and the Pentagon are putting out warnings of sudden climatic and environmental changes.

I am not saying this at all to cause any panic— that is why up until now I've never spoken publicly about these things. But we are at the point where we need to know that this is one possible future that is unfortunately becoming more probable,.

Subsequently, I had a recurring dream where I am shown a color-coded global map, and the colors went from blue to yellow to orange to red. And blue areas were regions that had less catastrophic geophysical effect, with yellow, more, orange quite a bit of damage and red catastrophic. The red areas were regions of massive destruction or loss of entire landmasses.

The entire continent of Australia was red, as were many other areas in Asia. The area that was most blue was an area that was in the upper mid west, and high plains of the United States, extending into Canada. The most orange and red were all coastal areas, and particularly the

Pacific ring of fire.

In parts of Europe, particularly going up through the Pyrenees and parts of the Alps, I saw all the gas pipelines exploding, and with them all the villages, as the earth changed, and the earth's crust was cracking.

Entire land masses were gone, and others emerged or came up from the oceans. This happened not over thousands of years, but pretty much overnight.

In another lucid dream, I saw the earth spin and tilt out of its normal axis so that the sun seemed to stay in one place, , and the stars were moving in a very strange way, once night came. The climatic changes were enormous, and there were phalanxes of tornadic storms sweeping across from the Rockies to the Appalachians across the central part of the United States.

Most of the major cities were either in utter chaos or destroyed.

In the event of a significant change -- and this has evolved since the nuclear era – the government has a system, called the Continuity of Government plan, or COG. There are underground facilities here in Virginia, for example, where there is a continuously operating parallel government.

I have a very close friend, who served in one of those positions, so that if the government of the United States had been wiped out by some event- nuclear or massive environmental- he would have stepped into the position of one of the cabinet secretaries, and he was operating in this facility. There is actually more than one facility. There is the old one, at Mt. Weather, VA and there's actually another state of the art one that is not far from our home.

The idea is that there would be people left to govern, but it would be very difficult, and there would be mass chaos.

In another lucid dream, I saw that an asteroid was coming from space; it had made its way through because we had forced the ETs to shrink behind the crossing point of light.

One of the asteroids hit, and then there was another one that was coming, and we knew it was going to be much bigger. We were talking to people via short wave radio and learned that there was no electrification in all of North America or Europe.

The first one that hit was so strong that every piece of infrastructure— meaning every bridge and every roadway— had collapsed west of the Mississippi. CONUS -- the continental United States command— was mobilizing the military, moving west, trying to build temporary bridges and setting up operations to assist people.

But the one that was still coming was going to be several orders of magnitude stronger than that one, and we were just sitting waiting for it.

In some areas the atmosphere appeared to be ignited, and everything underneath the area was burned.

After this had happened, there were still people on the earth who were living in a brief dark age. I couldn't tell if it was for months or years, but I got the feeling it was between a few months and seven years.

Then, I was out in space again, looking at the earth and saw a light emerge -- it was both a spiritual light and an electrical light, and it was emanating from the area of Norway or Scandinavia. It was very specific. The time frame was towards the end of the last century and the early part of the 21st century. There was nothing more specific.

I also remember back in the early '70s, seeing headlines of papers written in huge letters describing events that had happened— some of which have actually come to pass, like 9/11, but others that have not yet happened. And it was almost like a newsreel. It sounds ridiculous, but it was in living color, very realistic, and these headlines were marching through time, over a period of many years.

Now, time is not fixed. Time is relative and so is space. And all these things can happen or not happen *depending on what we do.*

There are some things that we have already avoided, and other things we haven't. Everything is in play.

We have to understand the nature of the interplay between what individual humans do, what large powerful institutions are doing, what the collective actions of humans create, and what the divine plan is. There are certain inevitable things that are going to happen because we are not going to be allowed to destroy Mother Earth in one feckless, blind generation. Earth is intended to be here for the evolution of intelligent life for hundreds of thousands of years.

She loves us and is very patient, but that patience has limits -- and if we do not change, the earth will cast off her burden.

Well, cast off how? Like a dog shaking fleas off if need be. Literally shaking. It all depends on whether we're willing to consciously and willingly use our free will to lift the burden and change the way we're doing things.

So none of these things are absolutely inevitable. They may be likely. And it is becoming more likely, because we have refused to do the things that common sense and wisdom would require.

Unfortunately, the current status quo of increasing warfare, covert actions, and ruthlessness in enforcing secrecy is the antithesis of the direction we should be going in, and therefore does not augur well for an easy resolution of the current conundrum.

There are things that humans are doing that can help or harm, and there are things that extraterrestrials will do to help. They're certainly not here to harm. If they wanted to harm, it would be all over by now. Every individual has some role to play in how this is all going to end up. And this is why it is so complex.

The Chernobyl event actually could have been much worse. Recently, people have surfaced with photographs of ET craft above Chernobyl that are thought to have helped stabilize and prevent some of the worst sequela from happening.

I am sharing these things with some trepidation, because people are going to take them and say, "Dr. Greer said this is absolutely going to happen."

That is not what I am saying. I am saying these are possible to probable – some are very likely events. And yet, collectively, as people, we can affect that outcome if we so choose to. It is never too late.

The question is: Has this happened before?

Yes. We have passed this way before. You know, there are the legends of Atlantis, and there are the stories of Lemuria, and Mu, in the Pacific. It is true there have been entire continents and civilizations at or beyond the level of where we are technologically for which there are virtually no traces. What traces there are have been suppressed, because it flies in the face of orthodox science, orthodox archeology, orthodox anthropology and orthodox religion.

Remember, fanaticism consists of redoubling your efforts when you have forgotten your goal. The goal of truth has been forgotten by many people, whether scientific or religious. Therefore information does not make it out to the public because those in control are guided by lust for power, control dramas, false belief systems and corruption.

The difference is that during the last cycle, which was 400-and-some thousand years, civilizations disappeared and long periods of time transpired before human society regrouped. In this new cycle, no matter how dark it may get, the dawn has already occurred. The new day has already been established. And the next half a million years will be marked by the fact that there will be no loss of continuity of civilization once we make this transition. I am qualifying: *Once we make this transition.*

There will be an unbroken progressive civilization for hundreds of thousands of years. There will not be a rise and fall of various civilizations that become somewhat enlightened and then sink back into igno-rance and warfare and another stone age.

Since Earth has been in her orbit, there is nothing in the past history of Earth that equates to this time. That is how incredibly beautiful it is.

So don't be overwhelmed by the chaos and the madness that is around us. I am only sharing these things to indicate that there are some possible futures that are rather worrisome and that may be imminent— the exact timing of which could be anywhere from this moment to the next decade or two.

If we are wise, we may avoid the worst of these things.

In one of my experiences, I was on board an extraterrestrial vehicle, looking down into Mexico. I saw a massive volcano, Popo, which is the fourth largest volcano in the world, and a severely dangerous one.

When I first started going there, I told people, "This is going to get more and more active," and shortly after that, it started erupting more frequently.

And people asked, "How did you know that?"

I explained that all these ET craft are going in and out of it, trying to stabilize it, and are investigating it, because it is a very unstable part of the Pacific ring of fire. During these Earth changing events, I saw thousands and thousands of luminous oval-shaped objects that were glowing from within, coming out from under the ground, all over that part of Mexico and around the volcano. They were floating upwards, like bubbles coming up from the bottom of the ocean, going up to the surface. Envision thousands of them going up, in columns, into the sky and fanning out. It was beautiful.

The population of the earth, as I saw it, was greatly reduced. It was a fraction of what it is today -- how small a fraction, I don't know. And those who were left here had learned an extraordinary lesson.

The lesson will be learned. The question is how serious must events get for people on this planet to learn that lesson.

Up to now, neither World War I nor World War II nor Hiroshima nor 9/11 nor the specter of environmental collapse have changed the perver-sity of our collective behavior.

But no matter what happens, on the far side of these changes, whether they are this severe or something less severe, those left will have learned a serious lesson, and quite frankly will be chastened and will vow to put down the means of war, and will use these wondrous new sciences and technologies, permanently, only for peaceful purposes. That lesson will be learned never to have to be learned again; so deeply will the lesson be ingrained in the psyche of all the inhabitants of the earth.

Now, we could learn that lesson without going through such a traumatic change, except humans tend to be very stubborn and very refractory to enlightened change unless we are compelled to make that change.

We have chosen so far not to take the lesser events to heart and make the changes, and therefore as the native American peoples would say, "We are in the time of changes," and the time of what they call "the great purification.".

These events I am describing will be not only manmade chaos and catastrophe, but natural catastrophic events. They will purify the minds and hearts of men through the fire of these tests so that they will vow never to do the destructive things we have been doing. We will learn not to blow each other up because of a difference in religion or a difference in race or a difference in ideology or what have you -- all the silly nonsense that have been the bane of human civilizations for thousands of years. We will retire that thinking, and it will be a permanent change.

Then, Phoenix-like, out of the ashes, we will quickly reconstitute an advanced civilization on this planet that will be permanently peaceful. We will have the ability to apply all these wondrous technologies that are already on the planet. Everything that is needed has been vouchsafed to the human race and is *here*. Everything that's needed for the next half a million years is actually already here. That is the really good news.

41

Phase Transition

An analogy from quantum physics — a concept called phase transition—is useful here.

If you take a container of helium and cool it down to absolute zero, it begins to boil and agitate very violently. Chaos and disorder increase even as some of the molecules begin to align coherently. At the point that only about one percent -- not 99 percent, but about 1 percent— of the molecules within the container become coherently aligned, the entire field, all of the molecules reach a state of coherence -- super-fluidity is actually what it is called.

Helium then takes on these magical properties; it behaves very differently and the entire field of molecules is coherent. But just prior to that moment of extraordinary coherence is the point when it is most chaotic and most violent.

We are right now at that phase transition moment in the history of the human race. It is going to get more chaotic and seemingly more disordered. But what we need to see are those islands of coherence that are developing. We must become these islands of coherence and vision. And when enough of humanity has, a phase transition will happen and the field of human society will quickly transform.

So what is that good future going to look like? Luckily, the Architect has left us a beautiful blueprint, and all of us have that folded within us, and we can see it, if we choose to gaze with a steady vision.

We must learn to be seers, because to the extent we see it and understand , we will be vehicles for manifesting and creating this vision.

Humans are still going to be humans, but the excesses of violence and wars will have ended.

The great wars and the tremendous difficulties will be a thing of the past. Initially there will be a period of peace that is tenuous—with certain rabid dogs firmly chained. This political peace will precede widespread higher states of consciousness and enlightenment amongst the majority of the population. Ultimately, the only way to insure behavior that is not damaging to others is enlightenment. That is why peace and enlightenment go together.

In the early decades after the phase transition, civilization on earth will be reformed, rebuilt, and transformed around peaceful, non-violent pursuits. Mind numbing and debasing poverty and illness is not a milieu in which significant numbers of people can grow and become enlightened.

As we reestablish civilization with these new technologies, over the next hundred years or so, there will be a permanent peace, the elimination of poverty and growing abundance on Earth. As these technologies are applied for peaceful purposes, and every nation and people on Earth have vowed to absolutely crush any attempt to weaponize them, we will see a flowering of humanity unlike anytime in Earth's history.

Every village and every community will have the means to create pollution-free energy that is unlimited for manufacturing, clean water, transportation, the ability to grow organic natural food, etc.

Imagine: You can be anywhere in the world, and have all you need, at very little cost. With no cost for energy, you could have all the light and controlled temperature you want in any climate, and grow any type of food needed, under computerized, automated conditions. This technology exists today. There will be abundant food of the highest quality without petrochemicals, fertilizers and pesticides for everyone. If you look at foods today, their growth, and their delivery, is an enormously petrochemical heavy process. So free energy is the key.

The earth, being two-thirds covered with water, has plenty of water, if you can desalinate it. Well, you can't desalinate it unless you have the energy systems to do it. When energy is free and abundant, this will be possible.

Manufacturing will be abundant, clean, and very inexpensive. The biggest expense related to the total cost of manufacturing anything we have is the energy that goes into acquiring the raw material, transporting it, fabricating it, packaging it and shipping it to you.

It is mostly energy related. What happens when the energy component of that becomes zero? It is a whole new world of abundance and pollution-free sustainability in harmony with nature.

Because of these advances technologically, the work week will shrink to between 15 and 25 hours, mostly out of choice, and the rest of people's time will be spent in the pursuit of creativity, recreation, learning and other positive pursuits.

The economics of the transformative effect of these technologies will be such that there will be no need to work 40-60 hours a week; in fact, doing so would be socially harmful. People will then be able to discover their Dharma, their calling, for what they can contribute that is most consonant with their God-given skills and their innate capabilities and talent, as opposed to a survival level of subsistence out of necessity.

Thus, a civilization where people can pursue higher states of consciousness and enlightenment, will at last be possible.

The era of big urban-suburban areas will be over. Earth will be a globe of villages.

Why?

Because if you can go from Phoenix to Paris in three or four minutes, there will be no need to aggregate in these very dense, sprawling cities. Some people will choose to live in larger communities, but there will be no economic necessity for huge metropolises. Transport will be rapid, above ground and efficient, using ARV technologies.

Such travel above ground with anti-gravity systems will allow for the most remote places on earth to be fully inhabitable, with little environmental impact.

In one lucid dream, I saw that the latitude of where Chicago is now will be subtropical with palm trees. What is now the Arctic and Canada, will be very livable and a comfortable climate.

The climate of the earth will be much warmer overall. But remember, it is likely large-scale geophysical changes will have occurred.

With these new free energy technologies, 100 percent recycling will be feasible, including for water. Water can be trapped and recycled, rather than being spoiled and just dumped into waterways and the ground.

I am speaking now of technologies which are extant, not ones that have to be invented.

I remember Archibald MacLeish saying back in the '70s that we already had the technologies to scrub to zero effluent every bit of manufacturing pollution. But the amount of energy that it would take to scrub all pollution out, given the fact that we're using fossil fuels to create the energy, quickly reaches a point of diminishing returns.

Now, I am talking about the early decades of the first hundred or couple of hundred years. Looking beyond that, the sciences I alluded to in the cosmology will allow for the manifestation of any item or any commodity out of the fabric of space around us.

That technology actually exists already. So what material need would there be that couldn't be met?

There isn't one. And this is the big message. There would be no material need unmet. And in that state, the human condition can begin to blossom from one of need and fear to a state of repose, and move on to higher spiritual pursuits.

Also, shelter will be altered tremendously. Think about the fact that if you have anti-gravity capabilities, building materials can be moved into place just like the pyramids were built. You can have buildings that are made out of whatever materials are least harmful to the earth. Technologies would exist so that many of the chemicals that are used now won't be necessary. Heating and cooling, since the energy is free, would not require structures that are chemically toxic and sealed up in unhealthy ways.

Housing will actually be much less expensive and the means to build them will be radically altered because of these technologies.

The architecture of these buildings will be very different. One of the things I want to do as soon as we acquire an operational over-unity, free energy device is to build a demonstration house in the high desert of Colorado in Crestone, where it gets 20 below in the winter, but gets 80-90 degrees with blazing sun in the summer.

When you look at the ancient peoples, you see they lived together closely in villages, preserving the surrounding land for agriculture, recreation or just being natural. Humans, being social animals, will choose to live in such villages in the future, in a way that is high-tech self-sufficient.

Today, we live in a way that is like a metastatic cancer: an urban city, with a hideous sprawl of McMansions and cookie cutter suburbs.

Psychologically, people are happier if they are living in a more intensive village setting, with neighbors and friends and the ability to walk or bike to commercial and social venues.

Right now, we are gobbling up all the natural beauty and paving it over, turning it into strip malls, McMansions and suburbs.

Right now we have to build so that the house or building is wired. But the future of manufacturing will be that everything that needs power will have a free energy source within it. There will be no need to have wiring in a house; everything will be wireless.

Thus, the cost and complexity of building will be greatly reduced. Construction will be simpler, cleaner, and more natural -- less expensive, and more beautiful.

So this is how we will rebuild the earth, with this consciousness and these new technologies. On that foundation, a civilization that is at peace and abundant, and where humans are freed to pursue more enlightened activity will thrive. It will be a totally altered economic order, manufacturing structure, and industrial structure. In the aftermath of all this change, there will be a single global currency; there will be national boundaries, but they will be less and less important.

In medicine, most of the problems that we're struggling with now are lifestyle related. How one eats, lives and exercises determines at least 90 percent of your health. Genetics are important, but even given those parameters, how one lives is very determinative.

Having a physical body, there will always be things that happen -- whether it is from genetics or from accident, or choosing a bad diet.

These advanced electromagnetic technologies can be configured as sophisticated electromagnetic healing and diagnostic systems.

In classified projects, technologies exist that would enable people to completely regenerate limbs or an injured spinal cord. *Those exist now*. But if they let them out, they would also let out the secret of these free energy systems, because it is the same basic area of physics. But in the future, when this new physics is known, we will also have a new medicine.

Diseases that appear now to be incurable, ranging from cancer to AIDS to other infectious diseases— even severe injuries— will be curable.

Right now, we live in a very corrupt world where the decision as to whether or not something is told to the public is part of a large medi-business system. It has more to do with whether a 100-million dollar drug company investment will get an adequate pay-off or not. It has very little to do with health – or the truth.

It has to do with money and the abuse of power.

Scientific healing will be vastly more evolved than what we have today, because we will add to it the knowledge of these new electromagnetic systems and sciences that have been kept secret.

Right now, in the United States we spend an enormous amount of money on a medical system that is very ineffective for many of the conditions and diseases that people confront. That will change. In the future, medicine will be both high-tech and more holistic- at the same time.

The natural genetic encoded life span of a human being is around 120 years. In the future, people will be living very healthy lives up to 110, 115, 120 years.

There is a time to be born, there is a time to live, and there is a time to let go, and drop the body.

There is no need to live forever in a physical body. Life on Earth is precious – but so is life in the astral worlds of light.

Once we understand the beauty of the afterlife, we will be less anxious about leaving this one.

Even in this regard, I think medicine will change. We spend an enormous percentage of our health care funding on the last 60 days of life, often doing inhumane things to stave off the inevitable. In the future, more emphasis will be on having a good life- and a good death, at home, in peace, surrounded by loved ones, not machines.

There is a certain spiritual grace and wisdom to knowing when to let go and move on.

I believe this spiritual wisdom, will parallel the medical sciences.

So we will optimize the natural lifespan of humans, meaning a high quality of life will exist into old age.

Right now, we compartmentalize science and spirituality, when really a skilled physician should also be a very spiritual being. We will have people who are skilled in the healing arts, who are also spiritually aware and will be able to help people make this transition when it is inevitable.

The passage from this material plain into the worlds of light and consciousness will be very much like what Shari had. It is beautiful. Each person who passes to the other side should have the spiritual assistance so that he or she ascends to the highest level possible- according to their own state of consciousness and life-path.

As genuine spirituality grows, the desperate clinging to the last few seconds of life, at enormous expense and suffering, will change to a more compassionate transition. The more we become materialistic and less spiritual, the more we become neurotically unable to enjoy either life or its passing.

In the future, this level of abundance will allow us to optimize not only medicine and healing but also the education of every child. We will learn how to truly educate, and it will begin at an early age. Certain meditative and spiritual techniques unlock enormous potential and will be taught at 4-6 years of age.

Over time, there will be an enormous growth in the mean IQ, which is now not optimized at all.

In the undeveloped world, poverty and malnutrition greatly stunts the mental and physical growth of children. With the elimination of poverty – impossible without these new technologies- the minds of these children will also blossom.

In the developed and developing world, there is much chemical and toxic poisoning -- heavy metals, lead paint, air pollution. These will also be eliminated.

We live in a time of probably the worst family integrity ever known. Divorce rates are over 50 percent. The majority of children in some minority groups have no fathers in the home.

This is truly a spiritual problem in my opinion. I think that people will begin to view family differently, as an *eternal commitment*. (People may say that I sound like a very conservative person in this regard. It is not a conservative vs liberal issue. It is looking at it from a spiritual point of view).

When people decide to bring children into this world, that should be a permanent commitment. Every child should be a planned and wanted child. So we will have universally available birth control, and couples will have children when they are ready for the spiritual, material and social responsibility to care for another human soul. I think this will become an increasingly common value. Now, I will also say that I think it will be increasingly common that people are loving and tolerant of situations that don't work out so there will be an extended sense of support around people and their children when bad things do happen -- if they are orphaned, or if they split up.

And while I don't think it should be forbidden to divorce, it will be very rare. The selfishness involved will diminish, because selfishness is usually what drives these problems. The focus should be on the welfare, love and rearing of the children.

People will learn to find mates that they are maturely connected to and then really commit- and then have children. Children should have the parents and extended family to support them and provide the love and the discipline needed. Every child will be seen as a sacred trust, to protect, nurture and raise towards enlightenment.

Right now, we do not have a culture that values that—and we certainly don't have a social and economic order that even facilitates it, because of the mind-numbing poverty and the disintegration of families.

Once you have joined and brought a child into this world, whether you know it (or like it!) or not, an eternal bond is created. Even after you pass on to the other world, you are with your family and you will have your children near you, and grandchildren and great grandchildren. There is an unbroken line and those individual souls -- they are part of creation -- go on eternally, through all the states of evolution and enlightenment. People will grow in their understanding of what an extraordinary event it is to bring a soul into this world, to create a conscious life.

Once people understand that, they will also understand the sacred obligation of it, and have the patience to work through life's difficulties.

I am a big advocate of people acknowledging and being tolerant of people who are gay and lesbian, because I'm quite certain it is a natural variant of human existence which is present at the time of birth. The kind of wholesale bigotry that is attached to gender and sexuality will be a thing of the past. It is already, unless you are part of the immoral minority who really do believe gays, lesbians and feminists caused 9/11! The moral questions of our day have nothing to do with those issues whatsoever; it is a distraction from the real moral questions that should concern us.

42

Universal Spirituality

Even if you forget about the question of global warming, the environment, and the geopolitical consequences of having oil wars, the suffering that takes place in the world today because of artificial poverty resulting from the withholding of these technologies has caused hundreds of millions of deaths. This covert policy has forced billions of people to live in desperation and ignorance, without education or the basic means of a dignified life.

That suffering alone would justify a change in the current order and a disclosure of these technologies and wonderful new sciences. Because while most people worry about what kind of terrible cataclysms might befall us environmentally, economically and geo-politically if we continue on our course, most of the world's population is already living in the hell of poverty and desperation. For them, it is already a catastrophe -- right now.

Consider this: Since before we started the Eisenhower Interstate System, we have not needed an interstate system. In the future, all transportation between cities will be above ground, through anti-gravity magnetic systems, and the hundreds of billions of dollars spent on maintaining and building surface roads will be freed for education, health and other useful purposes.

Moreover, the enormous amount of prime real estate and arable land that is now sitting underneath all of that concrete will be available for agriculture or recreation.

The resources that we now spend on energy, fuel systems, transportation, and surface roads will be used for real progress for human civilization. We also spend over a trillion dollars a year on military-industrial operations --an enormous part of world economic activity. Most of those resources will become available for other purposes.

So it is not as if the resources or the money isn't there to create an extraordinary planet. It has just all been misdirected and squandered.

Once that dynamic changes, whatever you can imagine will be possible!

All the technologies are here already. We have the knowledge to do it. And there are enough wise people on this planet to do it. So why hasn't it happened?

The structures and institutions around religion today are going to be greatly transformed and for the most part, swept away. Remember that the evolution of a priesthood -- rabbis, priests, reverends, mullahs, etc— occurred because very few people could read.

But in a time of universal education, there will be no illiteracy. Even today, most of the people can read and write. Thus, the need to have a centralized priesthood will end. This need is actually over already— we haven't needed it for 150 years.

In the near future, every person will arise to the responsibility of independently seeking the truth, reading, studying, meditating and praying for their own spiritual development. There will be spiritual teachers, but not people who are elevated to the point of being "the reverend," or "the rabbi" or "the Imam," of for that matter "the Dalai Lama."

These religious structures have served a good purpose in the past, at times, but have been co-opted by men for the abuse of power and to amass power and control. This dynamic has nothing to do with the purpose of any religion on earth -- any religion -- or any of the founders of any religion on earth.

If one wants to identify as a Christian or Jew or Buddhist or what have you, that will be fine. But the clergy will be replaced by lay-people, sharing. Societies will evolve around seeking spiritual truth and experiencing spiritual reality, and looking to the teachings of the entire knowledge of spiritual teachers -- of all the spiritual teachers. They will assemble in counsels and assemblies where there will be no central priest or reverend in that community, but they will rotate or take turns and share as a group.

Certainly people of greater capacity or experience might teach or share with others. This will always be the case. We will always have teachers. But the idea that there will be a paid professional priesthood: The time for that is over. It is over because it has been abused, and because humans have the capacity now to read, and to investigate truth on their own. It is actually very corrupting to have some other person interpret for you the meaning of truth; we can share our truth with one another, but ultimately we make the truth our own, in our own way. It is spiritually infantilizing to have a priest do those things for you -- there is an abdication of our spiritual responsibility for ourselves that goes along with that kind of relationship. People need to take spiritual responsibility for their own evolution.

Now, this doesn't mean that there won't be spiritual communities or spiritual organizations or religions. But they will be greatly changed, because if they are genuinely pursuing enlightenment and spirituality -as opposed to amassing power and controlling people- they will be looking to empower everyone spiritually.

This area of human life will focus on the experience of spiritual evolution and the genuine understanding of the divine and the sacred.

The things that today pass as big "religious issues," will be changed and refocused to the actual purpose that all of the great prophets, Avatars and spiritual teachers came here to give us: the knowledge of the existence of a divine Being, and the ability for people to pray to and meditate within this divinity and realize that in their lives.

The corruption of religion is intimately related to both the masses giving up their spiritual power and a priesthood that is prone to abusing power.

And no matter how many fine people there may be in the priesthood, there are always those who go into a demagogic mode— who can then affect weaker minds and bring them under their control, whether it is Jim Jones or someone who is trying to induce a jihad or inquisition.

This kind of fanaticism and thinking will be exposed for what it is, and retired, just like the thinking about nationalities or ideologies requiring massive warfare and destruction will be retired. And it will be retired permanently.

Transformed, truth-seeking religious groups will have a deep and abiding respect for others. People will discover as time goes on that truth is one – and the religious differences are unimportant or based on falsehood, misinterpretations or perversions of the original spiritual teachings.

We will eventually evolve a universal spirituality. People are simply not going to be able to hold on to the chauvinism of this sect versus that sect if they are awake. Because if they are awake, they are going to realize that there is really no difference at all -- that the Light is the same in every lantern no matter what the lantern may have been externally: whether it was Buddha or Krishna or Christ or Mohammed or any other Manifestation of Divinity. People will start searching for that *Light,* and they are not going to be separated by hatred and divisions due to the *form* of the lantern.

My understanding of what happens at the time of the separation of the spirit body and soul from the physical body, what people call death, is that there is a seamless continuity of awareness. This is what I experienced and this is what I also know from other people who have had a near-death experience. There is a continuity of your individuality— you have all your memories, all your knowledge. But you are suddenly freed. It is like a bird leaving a cage. The vast cosmos that is the astral realm, the worlds of lights and beyond, is your new home. You ascend to a level that is commensurate with the state of your evolution and consciousness reached on earth. And you openly consort with loved ones and friends that you have connected with on earth.

In that spirit form, you continue to grow and evolve through every level of the cosmology, into greater and greater realization of the astral worlds. One can say it is heaven, these beautiful worlds of knowledge and light. You continue on that path forever, until you choose, from enlightenment, to merge with the Ocean. And yet 'you' always exist: time is an illusion. The drop of your individuality can merge with the ocean of the unbounded Divine Mind, and yet you can also continue as an individual, with work in that realm.

The individuality that is this unique creation, that is you, does not get destroyed. The awake Being within every thing is a singularity, and always has been, and always will be. But your individual soul exists eternally as well. We are all part of what God created. Our individual awareness will continue until such time as the drop is joined with the ocean— and you choose, by choice, to remain there, or not.

There is a beautiful continuity that takes place. Your children, your loved ones, your ancestors, your parents -- you will see them. You will know them. And they will welcome you.

You will see others and will associate with those souls that are at a level of capacity and knowledge and consciousness that you have reached.

One of the key things to remember at the moment of passing: "Forget all that you have known. Let go, and go into that most great Light."

We don't have any idea how high a station we may reach at that moment, but I can tell you this: The best possible outcome requires being as detached as possible from everything you know, everything you have done, everything you think you are, and allow yourself to just completely be immersed in that most great light, that divine light.

What holds people back as they transition from this plane to the next, are their attachments, whether it be material, egotistical or what they think they know. So the condition of detachment and purity, and the willingness to completely put one's self into that divine light, takes you to the highest possible state of existence.

What is the difference between achieving those states after death and achieving God consciousness, unity consciousness, in a meditative state in this life?

It depends on the level of consciousness you attain here. It is possible to have experiences and be in a state even on earth that is as high and as extraordinary as anything that can be attained through billions of years of evolution after you leave your body.

On the other hand, for most people, being freed from the body, there is enormous joy, freedom, bliss and new abilities that appear. Within one's own mind, one can manifest everything -- just as you can now visualize a castle -- that castle is real in that realm.

There are no limitations whatsoever.

Now, of course, there are people who have been on this planet who can see something and actually manifest it. While this is unusual, it has happened. But in the astral and causal realm of thought, this is easily done.

Now, the flip side of that is because of the condition of having the physical body, and the suffering that's attached to it, one is propelled to more quickly attain states of spiritual freedom and enlightenment. Being on earth creates opportunities for rapid evolution. This is why life on earth is precious. The ability to reach enlightenment and to attain very high states of consciousness, and to grow as a soul, is much more concentrated on earth than any other phase of existence.

That is the mystery of the material universe. That is why there is the material universe. That is why there is the physical body. And that is why there is the suffering attendant thereto.

Being in the body creates an enormous opportunity to evolve into extraordinary states fairly quickly.

Now, "quickly" means time and time is relative, and when you get into the astral world, time is totally different.

When you are on the other side and you are in that state, it is so beautiful and peaceful, that the search for the infinite home, and the need to find that solace, is not nearly as great as it is in a physical body. Here, there is a daily opportunity for suffering. In a sense, being in a physical body opens to us the superhighway of spiritual evolution – if we chose it!

So the mystery of suffering and sacrifice is very intimately related to spiritual development and the ability to go to great heights of enlightenment while on earth. Now, one can go through an entire life of being in a body and never take that opportunity. But still there are lessons to be learned.

Earth is one great big schoolhouse, and there are lessons to be learned and different levels of those lessons. We can avail ourselves of them only if we chose to.

This means that we can go from being in a state of the physical body, and if we have the knowledge and spiritual experience, go to extraordinarily high astral or finer celestial astral levels of existence, or even directly beyond that into the causal realms of pure knowledge—or even completely to the unbounded Being.

Most people choose to be in phases that are in the next step beyond where we are -- from the material world into the astral and etheric -- just because there's more familiarity: there is *form*. They are more comfortable. It is beautiful. There's tremendous freedom. But eventually, we all pass into a knowledge even beyond that level.

But, if one understands the cosmology and has experienced them on this plane, it is possible to experience the full range of evolution at the time of one's passing.

This is why taking the opportunity to learn about and experience the finer levels of spiritual development is very important – because then, when you leave your body, your ability to advance through the divine worlds is greatly facilitated.

One might ask, "Well then, what is a ghost?"

A ghost is someone who has left his body, but still has such strong attachments to this plane, that they are 'adhering' closely to some place or person on earth.

Once, while in the emergency department, we had a terrible trauma case with an intoxicated person who died a violent death. Later that night, when the ER was empty, I was sitting at the center station with the nurses. All of a sudden, in the trauma room where this person had expired, the EKG machine turned on by itself, and the cabinets at the back of the room opened and IV bags and supplies begin to fly out!

It was a classic poltergeist. We all knew it was this person, who was able to effect these events through the astral/mental/emotional interface with the material plane. If you understand the cosmology described earlier, you will understand the physics of poltergeist.

This angry, confused person was obviously upset and in a rage. So I turned to the divine presence, saw that soul and connected him to Godhead; asked him to leave and ushered him out with some of his cohorts on the other side. And he left.

Now, people ask, "Well, what would be the state of that soul?"

You can't predict that. The evolution of someone who passes from this life to the next is assisted by the intervention of those in a more enlightened state on the other side as well as those still on earth.

This is why praying for the spiritual advancement and enlightenment of those who have passed away is very important.

It is said that there are three primary ways to evolve in these other states after death: First, through the prayer of others here on earth, second, through the intercession of the enlightened ones on the other side, and third, through doing good deeds here on earth in the name of those who have passed away.

In the future, as I have seen it, this will be routine knowledge, and when people pass to the other side, they will have gathered around them people who will be completely devoted to God and to connecting them to this other state, enabling them to reach the highest possible gradations of the celestial world and enlightenment.

The hell that people speak of are those lower aspects of the astral realm, lower meaning coarser. People of similar proclivities and behaviors, of common energies, coalesce together. Of course, if they leave behind all that they have done, ask forgiveness and let go of everything they have done, turning to the pure, divine Being, such beings can advance.

All can be transcended in an instant, if any given soul truly submits to divinity, and let's go of what he has done, asks for absolution and forgiveness and turns to that most great Light.

Ultimately, you cannot judge the station of anyone else. Thus, "Judge not, lest you be judged."

We should see every soul as educable, as capable of enlightenment.

At the moment of death, with one's last breath, someone who has lived a rather difficult and at times destructive life could let go of all that they have done and all that they have seen and turn to that most great Light, and ascend to a very high state.

Therefore, one should not judge.

At the same time, people who have regarded themselves, or been regarded by others, as having been very righteous and spiritual, at the moment of death have been filled with so much pride and egotism that they create a huge veil between them and the most great Light. So at the time of death we need humility, a certain grace and the spiritual assistance of others.

43

Accessing Consciousness

We confuse the map for the place.

I can give you a map of Washington D.C., but it is not the place that is Washington D.C. Everything is folded within us. Now, we are looking outside with our physical bodies, but in reality, the nature of mind, the consciousness within us, that whereby we are awake, is omnipresent, and crosses through space and time, and every gradation of the cosmology. This means that you are not 'going anywhere' when you astrally project, because you are already everywhere. You are already omnipresent – it is the nature of mind. But your individuality, playing on itself, can perceive it as a gateway or journey.

Now, in a very powerful experience, the body can be altered to the extent that it dematerializes. It can shift and disappear and be etheric or at the astral level of existence— and then reappear. We have seen entire ET craft shift into the astral form of energy. Remember on Blanca Peak, as I went into this area of light, my body became somewhat rarefied, and I thought at one point I might actually lift up. Other people could see that I partly disappeared from certain angles, and could see right through me.

The physical body and the physical world has very close, intimate connections to the consciousness that is within us. The holographic quantum universe, through the integrating function of conscious intelligence, connects every point in space and time, and every level and dimension and gradation of the cosmology, with every other point.

The perception of distance and separation on *one* level of perception is accurate. On another, it fades away into non-locality.

So you can access what people call other "realms," by virtue of accessing consciousness in a more non-local manner. Sometimes peoples have achieved this through chanting, singing, meditating, etc. Such exercises may allow the mind to become steady, and transcend the limitations of the fixed perception of the material three-dimensional world to see what is beyond.

Certain people are able to see spirit beings or the auras of people, or to look at a plant and sense what it might be used for in healing.

These are all gifts that are folded within us, depending on the degree to which we develop them.

Within the drop, the entire ocean can be discerned. So within each of us- this drop- the totality of the ocean is teeming.

Creation never ends. At the time that two people join, and the unique reality of the genetics of two people form a new person -- encoded within the new genetics is the potential for this new being, this new soul.

Creation is always being created within itself. The unbounded being is always creating more conscious intelligent life.

There is no lack of space! The universe is infinite. So there is no limitation to the number of beings and souls that can exist. And each one has the totality of conscious mind within it, and each will eventually realize this divinity, and become a drop returning to the ocean.

From this primal soul and primal, most great light, all that could be created is present. And so the potential for all that can be created, has been created, and will be created, has *always been present, at that level of the cosmology*.

When a new person is created, it is realized from that divine matrix *that has always been there*.

There is a state of consciousness you can reach where you can be gathered with the divine Being in the presence of all who have ever been, all who are, and all who will ever be.

I experienced this state seven days before Shari passed away. I heard a trillion, trillion, trillion beautiful voices singing, "We are all one in spirit". Every being in its perfect causal idea form emanating from the creator was present. It was stunningly beautiful. It was one of the most beautiful experiences of my life.

So from God have we come and unto God will we return... Each life brought into this world— or any other world— has always been part of creation.

The unbounded Mind emanating through the operation of its own will, manifests the pure causal thought in its sound form, from which the entire universe then emanates.

Sound is more elemental than form or light, and precedes it. This is why humming, chanting, mantras, prayer, thought -- repeated thoughts— are so powerful as vehicles for transcendence.

Each and every created thing has its own tone, has its own sound vibration within it, that then gives shape to the astral form of it, which serves as the template for the material object itself.

Can you see that? If you experience that on a certain level of consciousness then, using the sound component of thought, you can move things, manifest things, and affect the material world.

In the future, we will learn to manufacture by assembling elements from these deeper or finer levels. By operating on the level of sound and thought, we can assemble the astral form and bring it into the full material three-dimensional world.

Sanskrit is an ancient language which is the root of all Indo-European languages. In that tradition, the Vedas, they talk about name and form.

What they are referring to is the sound vibration of objects, which gives rise to its form. People trained in certain techniques can, in fact, go into a state of consciousness and through sound and thought vibration, bring into reality an item -- whether it is an apple or a ring or any other object.

There is a level of the cosmology where the seed form of all knowledge is located. You can receive knowledge from this level of consciousness, depending on your own proclivity and interest.

A very close military confidante told me that a technology was invented a long time ago, apparently in the '60s or '70s, that allows them to extract intelligence, events or conversations from what they call the "white noise" of space. Using an advanced electronic system developed at White Oaks Naval facility in Maryland, everything that had ever been said or done at a given place could be extracted. The technologies that have been developed in the ultra-black world are truly astounding.

Every point in space and time is an entry point to any other point in space and time. Encoded within any given point in space, everything that's ever happened there leaves a signature, an essence, that can be seen. The true Akashic record is within the structure of conscious intelligence, and therefore is everywhere and can be accessed anywhere.

In the American west, I have actually heard and seen the ancient native peoples who lived there. I have heard the drums and something like a tambourine sound, and chanting. It is like a movie that is always running there, once you tune into that frequency.

Everything we are saying and doing throughout our whole lives is always, permanently encoded -- like crystalline rock, but it's on the level of consciousness and spirit.

44

A Celestial Quality

Within this great cycle that has opened, we find that there are hundreds of smaller cycles. After around another thousand years, there will be another augmentation of the larger cycle, with another Avatar. And after that, another in a thousand years or so.

These Manifestations of Divinity will potentiate the capabilities within mankind to fully realize our destiny and establish the golden era on earth. This time of peace reaches far beyond a political peace or a material peace. This will be the time of genuine enlightenment and the establishment of God consciousness in greater and greater numbers of people. Even as we live on earth in bodies, we will have the fullness of the realization of divinity within us.

The major theme for the next several hundred thousand years will be the establishment of a divine civilization— a civilization that is on earth in a state of spiritual enlightenment. Whereas in this day, there may be a few people at any given time in a society that are enlightened, by the end of this cycle, every man, woman, and child on earth -- and every child that comes into this world— will be in that state.

In fact, the children being born in this world, will already be born in a high state of consciousness. But now I am speaking many thousands of years from now.

It will not take long for humanity to reach the peace of the 'chained dogs' — a political peace. Abundance, the end of poverty and the reforming of the earth into a sustainable civilization will quickly follow.

But the process of humans living on this planet in a state of enlightenment— where that is the common experience and the great aspiration—is the major theme of the next half a million years.

Everyone asks, "Well, after that, what else would there be to accomplish?"

There is so much. All the wondrous worlds -- all the fine celestial realms—will be opened up to the knowledge of people, even as they dwell on the earth.

And the earth will become one of the great jewels in the crown of the entire cosmos. This is the destiny of earth and the destiny of humanity.

Imagine for a moment: eventually we will have technology-assisted consciousness, and consciousness-assisted technologies. The sciences that we now see as material, will be understood as sciences that are fully integrated into the knowledge of consciousness. This includes healing, transportation, energy generation, manufacturing, biology, agriculture— all of these areas will have a component involving the science of consciousness.

These sciences of consciousness will potentiate material technologies and sciences. We will see that every endeavor is an opening for practicing the knowledge of conscious awareness. And in that there will be great joy and wonderful discoveries.

The early stages of peace on earth will be paralleled by early, open contact with extraterrestrial civilizations. It will be commonly known that we're not alone and that we have never been alone. The true history of humanity, including the cycles and millennia where there had been advanced civilizations on Earth that have vanished, will become openly known.

This early relationship with extraterrestrial civilization will be based in peace, not conflict in space. We will openly exchange ambassadors with other peoples in the universe.

The sciences that are extraterrestrial in origin, that deal with bio-machines, artificial intelligence, non-locality of matter and mind, communication using consciousness-assisted technologies across vast distances of space— these will begin to be accepted and understood by more and more scientists and leaders.

The masses of humanity will realize that these extraterrestrial people and humanity share a common oneness in spirit, in pure Mind, and that the sciences emanating from the knowledge of consciousness will begin to be shared openly with humans. We will begin to go into space and explore other worlds with other extraterrestrial civilizations -- first with those with whom we can relate most easily. We will evolve organically as a space-faring people; it will not be all at once.

There is a threshold we must first cross: universal peace.

There will be hundreds of milestones and gradations of relationship that are wholly dependent on the level of evolution of consciousness on earth. To the extent that there is a greater and greater level of the evolution of consciousness and the establishment of enlightenment, to that extent we will be able to interface with civilizations at that level.

There will always be people on every planet that are pioneers who lead in those states of consciousness. Eventually, the whole of society evolves in that direction. Humanity will evolve as an entire species into higher states of consciousness; we will then interface with other worlds that are in the state of cosmic awareness.

And there will be interplanetary cultural and technological exchange.

The earth will develop as an extraordinary and beautiful culture, and will become a cosmic culture. While the first thousand years of this new era have the hallmark of peace and a highly abundant world civilization, the later millennia to follow will have as their hallmark a growing cosmic culture. Eventually, we will evolve adequately to share the benefit of our wisdom with other worlds. They will learn that we have passed that way before, even as these older ET civilizations have who are visiting us today. And just as we are being visited today by civilizations that have established peaceful worlds, we will be emissaries and guardians of civilizations that are also crossing into maturity.

Even the material objects made by our society will be of such high quality that they will have their own consciousness associated with it. It will be like looking at a beautiful piece of art or a beautiful sunset: Everything will have a celestial quality to it, even if it is a material item, so beautiful will be the craftsmanship and design.

We will develop technologies that have their own life and consciousness. An intelligent, conscious quality will exist in almost everything that we make -- even if it is something that today we view as 'inanimate'.

We will see that nothing is really inanimate -- that there is no such thing as anything that isn't living, that is devoid of a life-force and conscious intelligence within it. Everything has life, everything *is* life, and everything is awake -- every rock, every mineral, every atom, every photon.

This will be realized and not just an intellectualization, and will have profound implications for the material sciences.

Cities will evolve into celestial appearing structures, with a light of their own. Everything will have a special life-energy and consciousness within it. And as we go thousands of years into the future, the earth will become a beautiful biosphere with human civilization manifesting a divine, celestial quality in every aspect of life.

The human body will reflect the inner state we are achieving. We will attain a level of perfection where diseases and illnesses simply do not exist through the course of one's life span. Illness will be very rare. And then when the time has come for one to move on to the next stage, that will be a choice, and we will leave the body consciously.

At the end of this 500,000 year cycle, every aspect of life on earth becomes divine. Extraterrestrial peoples, angelic and celestial beings, humans— all will be perceived and interacting together.

The world we live in today, where a very heavy veil blocks humans from the perception of these other worlds, will be transformed to a world of celestial perception and knowledge.

In the future, we will not need to cling to ignorance to feel safe. We will not hide in our ignorance. We will not find comfort any longer in being blind, but we will be free and rejoice in seeing. We will welcome not only the extraterrestrial beings, and travel amongst the stars, but will also see the celestial beings, and commune with them openly.

We see an era where every being on earth has attained this state of celestial perception and consciousness, and a moment will come when the entirety of our civilization will choose to create a world. We will create a spacecraft that will be of such a form and celestial texture that the craft and everyone on board will be in a state of God consciousness.

And being in that state, we will travel throughout the cosmos as a civilization, teaching other civilizations in an unbroken chain of God-conscious, evolved people.

Some of what we are witnessing today is showing us our future. Those who have seen the extremely evolved extraterrestrial civilizations that, while material, are firmly established in divine consciousness have caught a glimmer of the human future.

As we move from earth into the cosmos as a people, completely established in this divine state of God consciousness, we will become a dynamic force of an example where they will be some day— even as today there are civilizations showing us where we will be in the future.

And so this beautiful cycle continues, and is never broken.

Can you see that time? That is the destiny of the human race. It is celestial. It is divine. We will become "extraterrestrials", in a state of cosmic consciousness.

45

The Generation of Transformation

Half a million years is actually not very long. It seems like an enormous amount of time. But time will be perceived rather differently once people understand that life is eternal. As we gaze through this time and reflect on the current situation, we see a poignant sweetness to how primitive we are. And yet, we see within us the potential for a future where the earth will be inhabited by enlightened beings that are our descendants.

All of us, by then, will have passed on to the other world. But we will be the leaven that raises up this world, and all the generations after us. We are eternally connected to earth and her people and her children. We will continue to guide and nurture this vision and this knowledge amongst the people of the earth until the earth reaches the culmination of its development in its golden age.

Never be discouraged by this transient time of chaos. Keep your sight fixed on that far horizon—knowing the far horizon is not really that far. For it is already here, folded within us…

So we should not worry if in the coming days or years or few decades there is difficulty and darkness and chaos. Because this vision that we are seeing is already assured. No matter what anyone tries to do, the Divine plan and the destiny of earth and humanity will be fulfilled. This reality exists already. Forget about time for a moment. Forget about the amount of time. See that on a deep level of creation that this plan for humanity exists— for universal peace, abundance, the abolition of ignorance, the end of disease, and the growth of enlightenment in every person on the planet. Earth will itself be a beautiful space ship floating through the cosmos. On one level of linear time, all these wondrous worlds await us; but in reality it's *already here*. You can see it; you can feel it.

We are, in a sense, the children of the half-light. The light is there - but it's only half there, hidden in all the current darkness. But "God loves those who work together". We can join with people and spend time with people who share this vision and are working in some way to fulfill this good future.

We have to be aware of the chaos, but we should not only focus on that. It's easy to dwell on the negative. But there is so much that's beautiful that's all around us and there's so much that's happening that's positive. We can discipline ourselves to dwell on that which is good and beautiful and draw that to us and bring it into the world. It isn't easy, because we live in a world that's increasingly harsh and destructive. But this propels us all the more to connect firmly to truth and to a deeper vision.

We must have the courage to choose enlightenment, and take responsibility for our own evolution and the progress of humanity.

We live in the most interesting of times. We're the last generation that will fully have the experience of both the old world and the new era. We're too close to it to really see it, but we have a beautiful station that is pivotal. It is unlike any generation before or that will come after. We are the generation of transformation. It is at once overwhelming and beautiful. We should be joyous and amazed at the extraordinary time we are in and the unparalleled opportunities we have.

Efforts expended through the difficulty of this time, for this purpose- for the establishment of universal peace- will be honored and remembered for thousands of years. If we seize the opportunity, we are providing a service to humanity that no other generation could provide— and that's why we're here.

46

The Group Meditation:
Contacting ET Beings and a Meditation
and Prayer for Earth

Let us sit here together in silence, centered within our own selves. Let us close our eyes and take some deep cleansing breaths, from this sacred and ancient place. As we breathe in, see that we are centering, and our consciousness is expanding. As we exhale, become very relaxed, and release all negativity, tension and fears, and feel yourself settling into a deep peace. We breathe in light and life, and the expansion of mind, while fully expanding our lungs, and as we exhale, we release all things, all attachments, and become perfectly centered, and at peace.

As we sit here together in silence, we watch our breath, as it goes in and out, and we see that we are centered in a vast ocean of silent consciousness.

Gently, without straining, allow yourself to see the awake-ness that is watching the breath. Observe that you are awake, and that this awake-ness is silent.

Now, see that this awake mind, which is still and steady, is observing all the sounds, the thoughts, the feelings, all perceptions, and yet the mind itself is quiet.

Dive deeply into this vast ocean of quiet awareness. Going more deeply now, see that all the perceptions are receding, becoming more distant, and quiet, and you are being established more deeply, in this ocean of awake-ness within.

You see that it is easy to simply be awake and perceive awake-ness itself -- neither pushing away other perceptions, nor straining to know awake-ness. We effortlessly, simply are awake and are aware of that mind that is conscious and quiet within us.

Now, settle more deeply into this ocean of quiet awareness, where all perceptions are like distant ripples on the surface of the ocean. And you perceive that this vast awake mind extends infinitely in all directions. And you see that this awake-ness is omnipresent. It is not bound by space or time. And so it is infinite, and it is eternal. This is the true nature of the awake-ness whereby we perceive our own breath, our own self, sight, sounds, thoughts. We feel the joy and peace of knowing that this awake Being, this Mind is ever present within us.

Now, releasing ourselves from all attachment to perception or even self, we see the unbounded quality of this awake-ness as universal. And every person in this circle is awake, and while we are unique individuals, the light of awareness is a singularity, and that awake-ness is one, and we are one being in many bodies, one light illuminating every soul and conscious mind.

We see this same vast awake-ness permeating the earth beneath us and expanding into the sky above us. Omnipresent, it is awake in all places. And soaring on the wings of this vast and limitless awareness, we expand upwards into the sky, and we see that the entire earth is shining in the light of this awake-ness, and beyond us, space, and the planets of our solar system, all spinning, swimming, in an ocean of awake mind.

This simple awake mind within us is the same awake mind that permeates all things, which is omnipresent, omniscient, and eternal.

As we expand further into the vastness of space, we see the entire solar system, with the beautiful blue earth now an orb before us, and we see that she is conscious, and is her own individual being, and she is awake, with the same light of awareness whereby we are conscious, whereby we have awareness.

The sun, and all the planets, each have their own conscious identification and are all unique beings. And yet the awake-ness within them, within every atom, within every photon, permeating the space of our solar system is the same awake mind that is within us.

As we expand further, we go beyond our solar system, and we soar through the entire Milky Way galaxy, and expand through the vastness of 100,000 light years of space and beyond the outer edge of the Milky Way into inter-galactic space, and we behold the beautiful spiral galaxy of our Milky Way, and we see that it is awake, pure consciousness shining, phasing as stars and planets and an infinite number of awake beings.

Gazing then beyond the space of our Milky Way galaxy, we behold inter-galactic space, and we see stretching in all directions an infinite and endless cosmos with billions of galaxies, each with billions of star systems, and planets teeming with intelligent life.

Now effortlessly, we dive into this vast cosmic awareness, and find the infinite peace, an infinite, endless awareness permeating the entire creation, and we behold that this cosmic mind, this omnipresent awareness, is always indivisible and is the same awake-ness whereby we are conscious here and now and always.

Being thus awake, we now perceive that the universe, which is itself endless, has advanced extraterrestrial life forms, and all are awake even as we are conscious. And through this connection, we are one. We know that there is one conscious Being, shining, standing, within all life. And through that, we connect to them. As we gaze across the cosmos, through the galaxies, within the Milky Way, within our solar system, around the earth, we allow ourselves to see any extraterrestrial people with their beautiful celestial spacecraft.

And as we see them, we ask permission to gaze within, and as we see these beings, we invite them to join us here on earth as we join together as people celebrating the time of universal peace and the establishment of an enlightened civilization on earth.

As we see each of these beings, we see that they are connected to an inter-planetary council— highly evolved spiritual and ambassadorial in nature. We invite them to join us here as we show them our galaxy. And as we zoom in ever more closely to our solar system, we show them this beautiful planet Earth, the third planet from our star, the sun.

As we connect to their minds and to their guidance system, we show them our exact location. As we come zooming in more closely, we show them this field with our circle, and we invite them here, at this time and place, in a spirit of universal peace, acknowledging our oneness with them through the universal awake Being within us, this cosmic Mind, shared by all beings.

Now, as we see these beings, aware of us, and in our mind's eye, we see them, we ask that they join us at this time in a meditation and a prayer, for Earth and for its transition to the time of its destiny as a place of peace and enlightenment.

Let us take each other's hands as we do this. As we connect with each other, we see that there are extraterrestrial beings, celestial beings, the great Prophets, and the enlightened ones, all joining with us. And we send from person to person, around this circle, counterclockwise, a golden light in our conscious awareness, a beautiful astral light empowered with oneness, peace and love. And as this light goes from left to right, making a beautiful circle, it becomes a ring of light.

In our minds, we empower it with tremendous energy, and we send it upwards as a column of light rising from this spot, going into space as a beacon, carrying with it the love of Earth, the oneness we share, and the time of peace that we are establishing.

This beacon is calling to all beings, joining with us in peace. And we see it connecting to every world, every star, every heart, and every life. It spreads out and diffuses throughout the cosmos, this beautiful golden light.

And so, too, we see this light extending into the ground and across the earth beneath us. And this light of peace and oneness and love, suffuses the earth in this light, and every heart is illumined, and every mind awakened and every dark place is filled with light.

In this state of illumination, we ask the great Being, to give peace to the Earth, to turn every selfish heart into an open fountain of love and generosity. And wherever there is hatred and enmity, we see peace being established. And wherever there is greed, we see altruism and generosity. And wherever we see separation and sadness, we see the joy of oneness and love.

As we do this, we see the cosmos and all enlightened beings, material, celestial and divine joining with us, pouring forth this vision, and the Earth coming to its time of peace, and the chaos ending.

Now stretching before us, we see thousands of generations of humans living together in peace on the earth with wondrous new technologies and sciences that enable us to be in harmony with the Earth. And with abundance we banish all disease and poverty, and all injustice and all want.

On the foundation of this peace and prosperity, we see the hearts of all humanity turning to the pursuit of enlightenment. And in this state we are welcomed into the vast regions of the stars, and we become an inter-stellar species, and are welcomed into the family of planetary societies.

As we gaze down through the ages, we ask the great Being at this moment to set us forth in the direction of enlightenment. And in that instant, we see the time where every man, woman, and child abiding on earth, is in a state of cosmic awareness, of God consciousness. The divine sciences and enlightenment prevail.

We ask the great Spirit that we may be channels, vehicles, tools, for the establishment of this peace and the entry of humanity into enlightenment.

We see that we are joined by beings celestial, extraterrestrial, and divine, and that we are not alone and we have never been alone. And we ask that this Great Being enable us to all work together in the establishment of universal peace and a universal civilization.

This we leave as our cherished gift to our children, and our children's children. And we are certain that this beautiful vision is already manifest, that the Creator has already given to us the knowledge, the sciences, and the wisdom to create this world and to manifest this reality. And we consecrate our lives to the establishment of this divine civilization.

Namaste.